H the hidden key to appinesS

Drayton Nabers, Jr.

Published by Cornerstone Books

THE HIDDEN KEY TO HAPPINESS
ISBN 978-0-615-40708-1
Copyright © 2010 by The Nabers Foundation
Published by Cornerstone Books

www.hiddenkeytohappiness.com

Printed in the United States of America
2010—First Edition
10 9 8 7 6 5 4 3 2 1

WHAT OTHERS ARE SAYING ABOUT
THE HIDDEN KEY TO HAPPINESS

This is a very important book. Seeing the obedience of faith as the key to true happiness, the door to a close relation with God, and to spiritual growth is much needed. Applying the principles of this book will be life changing. Don't miss this one.

Dr. Frank Barker, Pastor Emeritus, Briarwood Presbyterian Church

Drayton Nabers has written an important corrective to the cheap grace that is being peddled by so many churches today. He by no means espouses the false doctrine of salvation by works. Instead he maintains that obedience to the Lord's commands is the appropriate response to God from people who are saved by grace through faith in the Lord Jesus Christ. Drawing upon Scripture, history and personal experience, Nabers shows that radically obedient Christians find biblical happiness while living lives that bring glory to God. I pray that this timely book finds a wide audience.

Rev. Dr. Lyle Dorsett, Billy Graham Professor of Evangelism, Beeson Divinity School

The Hidden Key to Happiness shines the light of biblical truth on the obedience of faith. The result provides both a pathway for following Jesus in practical day-to-day decisions and a guide for knowing joy and peace in our hearts. Using Scripture and a host of examples from the lives of the faithful, Nabers shows that obedience is a thing of beauty and a source of delight. I recommend this book highly for those who want a closer walk with Christ.

Chris Hodges, Senior Pastor, Church of the Highlands

Author Drayton Nabers masterfully reveals what he calls "the hidden key to happiness" in the Christian life - the inseparable union between obedience and faith. With sound scriptural support and personal experience, he presents practical wisdom on how to live a life of obedience, not by our own rule-keeping efforts, but through the dynamic, personal power of the Holy Spirit. Every follower of Christ will be inspired by this book.

John A. Loper, Jr., Senior Pastor, Garywood Assembly of God; Assistant Superintendent, Alabama District of the Assemblies of God

In this wonderful book, Drayton Nabers reveals how one of life's great paradoxes is that happiness is found in a place where no one seems to be looking. He makes a very compelling case that true happiness cannot be found outside the will of God, but is found only as we as Christians seek to align our will with His will - and he shows us how to do so in practical ways. This book is a must read. I highly recommend it!

Richard Simmons, Executive Director, Center for Executive Leadership

The mark of Christian maturity involves a change not only in life but in prayer, a moving from continual supplication to continual praise. With this in mind, Judge Nabers' *The Hidden Key to Happiness* offers more than a roadmap for full and joyous living. Drawing from Scripture as well as the experience of wise Christians in every place and time, these pages lead us to our ultimate goal and answer to life's questions, a relationship with Jesus.

Rev. Richmond Webster, Rector, Saint Luke's Episcopal Church, Birmingham, Alabama

Dedication

To our children, Deak, Mary and Sissy, gifts of God to Fairfax and me, who bring us much joy.

Contents

ACKNOWLEDGEMENTS

Writing *The Hidden Key to Happiness* was not easy. Biblical teaching about obedience is contrary to what we learn and experience about obedience as we grow up. The obedience of faith is a God inspired obedience that we do because we want to, not because we have to. It is a source of delight and great blessing. Getting this right – at least for me – has been no easy thing.

To complete this book, therefore, I needed a lot of help.

I am enormously indebted to many masters in the faith who have written clearly and with great insight on the basic themes of this book. They put me on the right path and gave me the confidence, courage and guidance to finish the task. Among them are Andrew Murray, George MacDonald, Charles Spurgeon, C.S. Lewis, Oswald Chambers, John Piper, Dietrich Bonhoeffer and Charles Colson. They, by the way, are wonderful company to keep, both for the depth of their faith and the clarity of their thought.

Eric Stanford provided outstanding assistance in helping me express and think through ideas. Anne McCain Brown and Robert Record played pivotal roles in carefully reviewing the manuscript and helping me shape the design and content of the text. Steve Briggs, Edmund Perry, Norman Jetmundsen and Nita Thompson read through the manuscript and made many helpful suggestions for improving it.

My daughter, Mary, with whom I jog every weekend, listened patiently and was a constant source of encouragement. And Fairfax, my wife, bore the brunt of the distractions of a husband's writing a book and was the source of many helpful ideas from start to finish.

My assistant, Mitzi Lafferty, typed the manuscript and a seemingly endless number of edits as we sought to clarify and polish my writing.

Sarah Pikal provided invaluable assistance in the design and layout of the book.

Of course, the final product belongs to me and its frailties are my responsibility alone. You can rest assured that where there is a weakness, one or several of those who sought to help me probably tried, unsuccessfully, to have me eliminate it.

The ultimate Counselor and Helper and, I pray, Author has been the Holy Spirit. If the content of the book – despite its human author – is not God's, this work is in vain. To God alone be the honor and glory.

INTRODUCTION

IN 1887 A young man, brand new to Christian life, came to the stage at a D. L. Moody crusade. Uncertain about much of what the great evangelist had preached, the young man said simply, "I'm not quite sure—but I'm going to trust and I'm going to obey." Though we know no more about this man, his simple words inspired an old hymn, "Trust and Obey," whose refrain goes like this:

Trust and obey, for there's no other way
To be happy in Jesus, but to trust and obey.[1]

Only a few minutes into his new life, this young man put in a nutshell the secret to a happy life—trust (faith) and obedience. There's no other way to be happy in Jesus but to trust and obey.

Faith and obedience operate as one, what we call the obedience of faith. Each needs the other. Faith without the works of obedience is dead. Obedience without faith leads to deadly legalism and pride that is not pleasing to God. While we as Christians have an easy time in acknowledging that faith is a key to a happy life, we don't so easily accept that obedience must join faith if we are to open the door. Obedience, therefore is not the only key but it is the *hidden* key to happiness.

In *The Divine Conspiracy*, Dallas Willard, a Baptist minister and formerly a philosophy professor at the University of Southern California, observes, "Kingdom obedience is kingdom abundance." The obedient life is abundant both in its rich inner rewards and in the energy and resourcefulness that flows from it. Professor Willard continues, "This truth about obedience seems a secret very well kept today."[2] It is indeed.

Before we move on, though, let me assure you of some things.

Guilt-free Zone

First, it is not my intention to condemn anyone or make anyone feel guilty about times when we have failed to obey God. At age sixty-nine, I have not the slightest motivation to write a book that would do anything other than encourage. If I thought that the obedience to which Christ calls us has any result other than greater peace, joy, and happiness than we could otherwise imagine, I would not write this book. This book is intended to bring hope, not condemnation.

Fellow Learner

While I'm at it, let me assure you of something else: I am not speaking as someone who claims high grades on the report card of obedience.

I realize that writing a book on obedience gives the appearance of moral smugness. If Warren Buffett wrote on investments or Joe Torre on baseball, the books would be successful because these men are exceptionally good at what they write about. Let me state clearly that I do not write from such a perspective.

There are golfers who can't score under a hundred and yet who nevertheless have studied the game and can speak about it knowledgeably. That is the way I have sought to be with obedience. I do not score very well, but I have given it a lot of thought from the standpoint of someone facing the same issues you do in work, marriage, parenting, and the like. I intend to share with you what I have learned from many people, especially from the biblical writers. It has fed my soul. I hope it does yours.

Rescue Mission

To repeat: I don't want to make anyone feel bad or to presume moral goodness. But I do want to do something much less threatening . . . and much harder. I want to change your likely perception of obedience, painting it not as boring but as beautiful, not as duty but as delight. And then I want to convince you that we *can* become more obedient children of God and that that's how we will come to know deep, soul-satisfying happiness.

Jesus said, "If you obey my commands, you will remain in my love, just as I have obeyed my Father's commands and remain in his love. I have told you this *so that my joy may be in you and that your joy may be complete*" (John 15:10–11, emphasis added).

We may find joy as followers of Jesus even if we pay little attention to the subject of obedience. *Some* joy, that is. But if we want "complete" joy, a fullness of joy sent straight from Christ, we need to become his disciples and obey him.

Oswald Chambers, whose devotional book, *My Utmost for His Highest,* has been a best seller for more than a century, wrote, "We must rescue the word obedience from the mire."[3] In a sense, that is the purpose of this book.

It is not my goal to make a harsh subject a little more palatable. Rather, it is to shine biblical light on the obedience of faith so that we see it for what it is—a thing of loveliness. The path of faithful obedience, though not the easiest, is always the most rewarding because it alone leads to the fullness of happiness. It is what we were made for.

As we examine the obedience of faith, we are going to find that it is much more than mere external conduct that bears fruit for God's glory, though it is certainly that, and if it were only that it would be worthy of our study. But obedience is also an essential part of our spiritual well-being. We will find that it creates channels for the flow of grace allowing grace to enhance every facet of our inward spiritual being. Without the obedience of faith our spiritual life withers. With it our spiritual life flourishes and we partake of the abundance of life that Jesus came to give us.

Food and Fellowship

Let me give you a couple of quotes from Christ just to get us started.

Jesus said this about what really fed his soul: "My food is to do the will of him who sent me and to finish his work" (John 4:34). There's a lesson in this for us. If we are to be nourished with spiritual food deep within our souls, it will be in doing our Father's will and accomplishing the work he gives us, just as it was for Jesus.

Jesus also told us who qualified for the fellowship of his family. "My mother and brothers are those who hear the word of God and put it into practice" (Luke 8:21). If we want the intimacy of a family relationship with Jesus, we must hear God's word and do it.

Spiritual nourishment and a family relationship with Jesus, then, depend on doing God's will—that is, obeying him.

All serious Christians seek to deepen and strengthen their relationship with Jesus Christ through such practices as reading and meditating on the Bible, praying, participating in small-group discussion, worshiping, and others. What we may not understand is that the obedience of faith is a necessary key to this relationship and to a multitude of blessings that flow from it. Bible study, prayer and other spiritual disciplines are essential and beautiful, but if we are practicing them without an obedience growing from faith, they will not open the door to fellowship with Christ and its blessings. For, as we shall see, it is only in the obedience of faith that this relationship comes to life.

Preview

Let's take a look at the course that lies ahead . . .
- In *Part 1*, we will look more fully at what happiness is and how seeking and finding it (in the right places) is what God wants us to do. We will see how the obedience taught in the Bible, Old Testament and New, produces an abundant life, full of all kinds of blessings and happiness.

- In *Part 2*, we will answer objections to an emphasis on obedience by looking at how, biblically, obedience is linked to faith. The obedience we will be studying is the obedience of faith, not an obedience that focuses on our personal effort.
- In *Part 3*, we will look at how by grace we mature in the obedience of faith. Walking in the power of the Holy Spirit, denying ourselves, making love our pole star, listening for God's guidance, having a renewed mind, a regenerate will, and transformed emotions, and developing a Christ-like character—are all important in making us the kind of people who will know the joy, peace, and happiness that God created us to have as we walk with him in obedience.
- Last, in *Part 4*, we will see what obedience looks like in daily life, discussing the obedience of faith in light of our calling to belong to Jesus Christ; our work; how we order our days; and leadership.

How to Use This Book

Though this book is by no means a comprehensive review of the obedience of faith, it touches a number of bases. So that the book might be easy to use, its chapters are essentially self-contained and, therefore, do not need to be read in sequence. If several chapters are of particular interest to you, you can flip to them in any order you desire.

Likewise, for small group discussion, your group can select those chapters most relevant to its interests and begin with them.

* * *

I can say that the hours I have spent exploring the obedience of faith and how it connects us to a living relationship with Christ and his immeasurable blessings have been deeply rewarding to me. This study has helped transform my understanding of my personal relationship with God – Father, Son and Holy Spirit. By his grace, it will continue to guide me in how I seek his will for my life and by faith live into it, and through this obedience I will have the key to enter more fully into his fellowship and the happiness he has prepared for me. I hope that this book can be transformative for you as well.

Now, let's turn to the insight of two very wise men.

PART 1

The Hidden Key Revealed

CHAPTER 1
The Hidden Key

IN *A PREFACE TO PARADISE LOST*, C. S. Lewis writes that "the great moral which reigns in [John Milton's] *Paradise Lost* is that obedience to the will of God makes men happy and disobedience makes them miserable."[4]

More than two thousand years earlier than Milton, Solomon, one of the wisest of all biblical figures, and the most prosperous, concluded Ecclesiastes with this insight:

> The last and final word is this:
> Fear God.
> Do what he tells you.
> And that's it. (Ecclesiastes 12:13,14 MSG)

Here are two servants of God, both of them very wise. They put obedience at the center of what human life is all about.

What's behind their wisdom?

A Few Preliminaries

As we begin our understanding, let's note a few preliminary thoughts which should be with us throughout our discussion.

First, we need to define obedience and the obedience of faith....

1

Obedience:

Obedience is aligning our wills with God's.

The emphasis in understanding obedience is on the will; hearing God and choosing to do what he has willed for us to do.

The Obedience of Faith:

The obedience of faith is the obedience that God's grace, through our faith, motivates and empowers.

The idea is that God's grace through faith equips us to seek and do his will.

Second, we must ever be mindful of the gospel truth that through the perfect obedience of Christ (not our own obedience) and his sacrificial death alone are we made right with God and adopted into his family.

Third, if we are to accept that the obedience of faith is a key to happiness, we need to be comfortable with the deep, deep goodness of God's will.

God's will is sovereign. It will be accomplished (Proverbs 19:21; Isaiah 46:10). It is immense in strength and scope. By it God created and sustains the universe and each of us (Genesis 1:1; Colossians 1:16-17; Hebrews 1:3). It is centered in love (1 John 4:16). By it Jesus died for us and we have salvation (Matthew 26:36-45; Romans 5:8). It governs the smallest details (Matthew 10:29). God works out *everything* in accordance with the purpose of his will (Ephesians 1:11). Its ways are far above our comprehension (Isaiah 55:8-9, Ephesians 1:9). His will is good (Deuteronomy 10:13). It is pleasing to and perfect for us (Romans 12:2). When we consent, God works his will in us for his pleasure (Philippians 2:13).

But let me pause here and check with you. Are you suspicious, setting up arguments in your mind against obedience being a key to happiness? You're hardly alone.

Most of us aren't deeply interested in the idea of obedience to God. Even in Christian circles we have tended to marginalize obedience in our study and conversation. Obedience can be treated as the proverbial stepchild at the family reunion—invited but left out of the conversation. In some Christian circles, he is not even invited. There are precious few books on the subject, despite its having a central place in the teaching of scripture. We Christians would acknowledge the importance of obeying God when asked, but for the most part we see obedience as a problem. It's something we downplay—even ignore. It does not resonate in our souls.

It's worth considering why this is so.

Allergic to Obedience

Why is obedience an off-putting subject, almost toxic, to so many of us? There are many reasons.

As Human Beings . . .

We naturally want to be autonomous. By "naturally," I'm referring to our human nature—a nature created good but now tainted with sin. And by "autonomous," I'm referring to the literal meaning of that word: "a law of our own."

We understand obedience in relation to rules others impose on us against our will and we want as few of them as possible.

Because we are sinners, we seek autonomy from God. We want to be as free as possible to define our own notions of good and evil. We do not lightly cede control of our will to the Lord. This was the primordial human urge that Satan exploited in the Garden of Eden and in varying degrees of strength, it remains alive in each of us today.

As Americans . . .

We distrust "the Establishment."

Our heroes are those who have resisted and taken on the established order, beginning with Jesus but also including such groundbreakers as the Protestant Reformer, Martin Luther, the founding fathers of our country who birthed a revolution, and the civil rights activist Martin Luther King Jr.

Southerners admire the concept of the rebel. In America we have and cherish a free government and free markets. We celebrate our freedom.

We tend to see law, though necessary for our safety, as anything but a source of happiness. Happiness, we think, lives in a world of freedom beyond law.

We reflect the attitudes of a nation where the exercise of all authority is subject to question and criticism. This is the way democracy works, and it is essential to searching for the truth, even moral truth, on issues of government and society. But if we take it too far, or take it into our relationship with God, we're in trouble.

As Christians . . .

We don't want to take away from faith and grace.

We know grace to be God's unmerited favor and therefore worry about the teaching that blessings from God are connected to our obedience. We rightly fear the legalism and Pharisaic pride that will always accompany obedience when it is separated from faith and understood as an attempt to conform to an external code. We recoil from preaching against sin that produces feelings of shame and self-condemnation.

Why, therefore, should we delve into a subject so fraught with difficulty and controversy and so seemingly out of step with many of our church traditions? Due to the theological traps around this subject, it is easy to pay it lip service but largely ignore it.

And as Christians…

Some of us have drifted toward a consumer orientation to Christianity where the emphasis is on what Christ can do for us, without a corresponding consideration of what we can do with him. Though the obedience of faith flows from God's grace in what he has done, is doing, and will do for us, we tend to want a message that assures us that God will solve our problems without a balancing focus on his call to go into the world and participate in his redemptive purposes.

And in Addition…

We tend to look at obedience divorced from faith and rightfully view such obedience suspiciously. The elder son in the parable of the prodigal son was obedient, but out of selfishness and not love for the father. We criticize an obedience that flows from selfish motives and not from a trusting heart.

For these reasons and probably more, we don't want someone in authority telling us what to do. We don't want to have to comply with moral rules others lay down. We want to create our own lives and work out our own salvation without anyone (perhaps even God) telling us what to do. When we face problems, we want easy solutions based on what God will do for us. We will agree that we are to do God's will, but we want that will to be wide and permissive, subject to our own interpretation, leaving us free to do our own thing without consequences as long as we hurt no one. Seeing them in conflict, we want gospel and not law, grace and not commandments. So we lose sight of the central importance of obedience to God.

Thank goodness there are many people who seek to be truly obedient to God in faith and are happy because of it. These people are free from the allergy to obedience, and their stories prove that we can live a different way.

One of these is my friend John Rucyahana.

The Bishop of Rwanda

Whenever I'm around John Rucyahana (pronounced *roo-chee-yuh-hah-nuh*), I see how he radiates peace and joy. One can immediately tell that he's fully in love with his Lord and fully content with his situation in life.

Is John wealthy? No.

Is he famous? He's gained something of a reputation, but he's not famous.

Is he powerful? Not as the world knows power.

Has he lived a life of comfort and ease? Definitely not.

Today John Rucyahana is the Anglican bishop in northern Rwanda, a nation in east-central Africa.[5] It is not because of his high position in the church that he is a happy man. Indeed, no church position, in itself, could be worth what he's gone through to get where he is. It's the relationship he's had with Christ over the years, and what God has brought into existence because of that relationship, that make him happy.

John was born in Rwanda but twice was forced out of his native land by rebel forces, once when he was a child and another time when he was a university student. He found sanctuary in the near-by nation of Uganda, where he was married to his lifelong bride, Harriett, and began ministry in a small, impoverished parish as an Anglican priest. Through a few contacts in the United States, he was able to start a ministry to Ugandan children who had been orphaned by the HIV scourge.

Following the horrible genocide in Rwanda, he was asked to return with his wife and nine children (four of them adopted) as bishop of believers living on a small slice of land in northwest Rwanda.

When I visited him in 2002, the "cathedral" church of his diocese had a dirt floor, wooden benches (think of those on a high school basketball court), and a tin roof. Of the two hundred people who attended, most walked (some for many miles) and a few rode bicycles. As I recall, there were two motor scooters.

Now there are more than 150,000 communicants in the diocese.[6] (That compares to about 30,000 in the Episcopal diocese of Alabama that stretches from Montgomery to the Tennessee border.) Furthermore, the bishop has built the finest primary and secondary school in the nation for some nine hundred children, many of them orphans. Approaching retirement, he now plans to build a trade school.

His ministry is driven by evangelism, but he knows that, beyond receiving Christ, a grown human being needs an education and a job. So his ministry has three focuses: evangelism, education, and work. He has found investors to build a hotel and conference center and created jobs for others in a construction supply business.

Why do I call John Rucyahana happy? Certainly the challenges of his life overwhelm any of mine and probably those of most Americans. But John, since his conversion in 1966, has always been driven by a sense of purpose—a purpose given him by God, to which he has been faithfully obedient – namely to minister to some of the poorest and most devastated people on earth. And he has sought the will of Jesus Christ in every step of his walk. I have never had a conversation with John in which he did not repeat over and over, "We must pray on it." John knows the joy of walking close to his Lord. As he has been faithful to his Christ and to his purpose, through grace God has rewarded John's faithfulness with a tightly knit family and a burgeoning ministry.

John is a happy man. He knows what it means to say, "Godliness with contentment is great gain" (1 Timothy 6:6).

Happiness: Available

Do you believe that obeying God, as John Rucyahana and others have, will lead to your happiness? Do you believe it enough to act on it? Stick with *The Hidden Key to Happiness,* and I believe you will be convinced.

We'll get to *how* to become a more obedient and happy person later. But before that, we have to deal with some important issues. You see, we have been talking about happiness and the obedience of faith as if we knew and agreed on what we're talking about. But do we? Maybe not. So it's time to understand happiness and faithful obedience better. We'll turn to happiness first.

Chapter 2 has some surprises in store for you.

CHAPTER 2
True Happiness

NITA THOMPSON IS Executive Director of Cornerstone School, a private Christian school in the inner city of Birmingham, Alabama.[7] Before taking her job with Cornerstone, she was one of the best elementary school principals in the Alabama public schools and had earned a doctorate from a local university.

She is a driven person—driven to teach disadvantaged kids what it means to love and serve Jesus Christ and to give them the finest education that can be had. She's not shy about telling people her goal. She wants Cornerstone to be a better school than those the rich kids attend in the suburbs.

Nita loves the Lord deeply. She lives her whole life with a consciousness of walking with Jesus Christ. As much as any person I have known, she knows what Paul meant when he wrote that we should "pray without ceasing" (1 Thessalonians 5:17, ESV). Her life is living prayer. She spends much of the weekend on her knees holding up Cornerstone and her kids in prayer. Perhaps because of this, she has a total confidence in the Lord to provide for those who have been entrusted to her. Her favorite comment is, "I can't wait to see what the Lord will do next."

She also is a woman who is full of smiles and enthusiasm about what she is doing. She knows the Lord has given her an assignment to serve the kids at Cornerstone, and she's accepted that assignment and is doing her best at it. Every day, she sees God blessing her work—and blessing *her* in the process.

Nita already has the hidden key to happiness in her grasp, though she may not have thought of it as such. She trusts and she obeys, so she is happy. It's simple, really.

But for those of us who want to have her kind of happiness, it is helpful to understand the sources of true happiness. If you're like me, you need to work your way past some mistaken notions about this basic human objective: happiness.

The Loss and Recovery of Happiness

Happiness is not a preferred word for many Christians. Some are uncomfortable with the idea of seeking happiness. To them it seems too selfish, too centered on *me, me, my, my.* Shouldn't we be thinking about others' happiness instead of our own? Others say happiness is a superficial concept, related to luck or chance.[8]

I have considered many words to describe the blessings of obedience—*joy, peace,* and *abundance of life* are some of them. I have decided that *happiness* is the best word our language has to describe this blessedness.

The concept of happiness is entirely biblical. Both the Hebrew and Greek words translated "blessed" in our bible could be translated "happy." As for the Greek, Billy Graham tells us, "The word *blessed* is actually a very difficult word to translate into modern English because in the original Greek language of the New Testament it has a far deeper meaning than the everyday content of our English word. . . . Perhaps the word *happy* comes as close as any single English word in conveying the idea of 'blessed' to us today."[9]

Why not joy? Joy is an essential part of the happiness we know when we walk with Christ. But happiness is broader than joy in that it contains an important ethical dimension relating to living into God's purposes for our lives. Happiness includes the satisfaction resulting from choosing the right path and walking in it in a manner pleasing to God.

Thus, happiness embraces both the joy of abiding in Christ and the satisfaction of doing God's will, trusting in his grace.

In fact, *happiness* used to be a strong, venerable word, one at the center of all serious ethical thought. Gregg Easterbrook gives us a brief overview of the esteem we once had for it:

> To be happy is not an exercise in self-indulgence, rather, one of the primary objectives of life. Aristotle called happiness "the highest good" and said that an enlightened society would be ordered with the goal of helping its citizens become happy. The framers of American democracy did not laud "the pursuit of happiness" because they considered this self-indulgence. Rather, they knew that happiness both ought to be a goal of life, and makes for better citizens. Dennis Prager has devoted an entertaining . . . book, *Happiness Is a Serious Problem*, to the notion that people have a duty to become happy, because happiness is the wellspring of altruism. Higher up the scale of literature, a century ago the poet Robert Browning wrote, "Make us happy and you make us good"; twenty-three centuries before that, Aristotle said, "Living well and doing well are the same as being happy." In Aristotelian usage, "doing well" meant exercising virtue.[10]

For centuries all Christian theologians were clear that happiness is a good thing, something God wants us to have and created us to want. Desiring it is hardwired into all of us, saint and sinner alike. Thus Saint Augustine wrote, "Everyone wants to be happy. Everyone will agree with me on this, almost before the words are out of my mouth."[11] Blaise Pascal agreed.[12] Jonathan Edwards also saw *happiness* as something good.[13]

Throughout the early centuries of the church, no one thought that desiring happiness was somehow wrong. The moral question was where should we find it?

Then somehow happiness got pushed aside in Christian thought, and the moral life became based on obligation and duty. Happiness was seen as a self-centered thing. We, as creatures, had a duty to obey our Creator. Happiness became irrelevant, something to be blocked out of Christian moral choices.[14]

So we have two poles. One says that true happiness is a good thing and the question is where it can be found. And the other says that we read the law and the commandments and do them because God is our Creator; it is our duty to obey the divine will; and happiness is beside the point.

We all know, or at least hope in our hearts, that the old-timers had it right. If we are honest, we agree with Augustine. We all seek happiness in every choice we make. God made us that way. Even if we enter a monastery and take an oath of silence, we do so because we think such is a path to happiness, though our focus may be on eternity as well as our time here on earth. The husband who runs around on his wife is likewise seeking happiness—but in the wrong place where he will never find it.

And there is a move afoot to return to the old way of looking at happiness.

John Piper is leading the way on the Protestant side. This Baptist pastor—who coined the phrase "Christian hedonism"—writes, "We should never try to deny or resist our longing to be happy, as though it were a bad impulse. Instead we should seek to intensify this longing and nourish it with whatever will provide the deepest and most enduring satisfaction."[15] For Piper, that satisfaction is in "glorifying God by enjoying him."

Theologian Servais Pinckaers has taken up the challenge on the Roman Catholic side. Similarly to Piper, Pinckaers points out that we can't impose our narrow modern attitude toward obedience on the way we think about biblical morality. Too many of us think of obedience in terms of obligations and legal imperatives. The moral teaching of the Gospels, Pinckaers points out by contrast, "is a response to the question of happiness and of salvation. It offers a description of the ways of wisdom that lead to holiness and perfection through living the virtues."[16] As an example, he points out that the Sermon on the Mount starts out with the Beatitudes—a series of descriptions of people who are happy through godly virtues.

There it is again: wanting happiness is good, and living God's way is how to get it.

It is worth jumping on the bandwagon and becoming comfortable with wanting happiness and recognizing obedience as indispensable to finding it. Happiness is a multi-faceted and noble concept and as we shall see, it is joined at the hip with obedience.

Four Concepts of Happiness

When we use the word *happiness*, there are several concepts that might be in our minds. I think that four are most relevant, and I call them by the following names:
- Pleasure
- Owner-manual happiness
- Purpose-filled-life happiness
- Abiding-in-Christ happiness

Each of these notions of happiness bears closer scrutiny. Our happiness depends upon it!

Pleasure

Perhaps one reason we're nervous about wanting happiness too strongly is that we are thinking of it in the wrong way.

It's easy to equate happiness with the enjoyment of sensual pleasures—eating, drinking, and being merry. But this kind of pleasure is only counterfeit happiness.

Aristotle rejected the notion that happiness consists in a life of sensual pleasure.[17] But in ancient Greece another group of philosophers, called the Epicureans, had a different view. They considered pleasure to be the highest goal of life. Some of them, including Epicurus himself, avoided overindulgence. But other Epicureans went to an extreme in striving for pleasure as the way to happiness.

We have many Epicureans among us today. Almost all our television ads are aimed at them.

Certainly Epicureanism, or its modern version, is not what we mean by happiness. A self-centered pursuit of pleasure does not bring true happiness.

There are some $50 trillion of assets in the United States. Not a penny of them can buy happiness, though they can buy much pleasure. Luxury cars, big houses, fine wine, powerful pick-ups, elegant cosmetics, the best degrees, the most prestigious clubs, well-shaped bodies—none of these can bring happiness. Happiness is not a collection of earthly pleasures. Piling more on does not increase happiness one whit.

Gregg Easterbrook, in his book *The Progress Paradox*, calls his fifth chapter "More of Everything Except Happiness." He argues that the feverish pursuit that most of us are engaged in to own more and do more does *not* bring us the happiness we think it will. And he brings out facts and statistics to prove it.

Similarly, Jon Gertner, in his *New York Times* article "The Futile Pursuit of Happiness," cites research showing that the things we think will bring us pleasure don't actually bring us pleasure in as great a degree or for as long as we had expected. He gives an example: "We might believe that a new BMW will make life perfect. But it will almost certainly be less exciting than we anticipated; nor will it excite us for as long as predicted."[18] I certainly know the feeling of "buyer's regret." I bet you do too.

Yet still we look for happiness in many wrong places, such as wealth, power, sex, acclaim, and approval. These are not only inadequate to provide real happiness; they can also leave us empty.

When we follow the desires of our sinful nature, we are never fulfilled. If the desire is for money, we never have enough. If it is for acclaim, it is never sufficient. And so on it goes.

But here's where it gets tricky. We need to draw a distinction. You see, we are not saying that pleasure has nothing to do with enjoyment in life.

Not all pleasure is bad. Much of it is good, even very good. God is not like the dour image many may have of him—he doesn't frown when we enjoy a dessert, laugh with friends, or take a vacation. Some pleasure is, in fact, divine. Worship, prayer, and Bible study all create much pleasure. There is nothing wrong with desiring pleasure in the right places. After all, "every good gift and every perfect gift is from above, coming down from the Father of heavenly lights" (James 1:17).

Righteous pleasure is good, but it, too, passes with time. The available sources of pleasure are not enough to add up to real happiness. We must look elsewhere.

Perhaps the second concept of happiness can get us closer to our goal.

Owner-Manual Happiness

In the movie *Groundhog Day*, Bill Murray's character somehow gets caught in a time loop that causes him to relive the same day—Groundhog Day, of course—over and over. No matter what he does, he still wakes up the next morning in the same place, at the same age, on Groundhog Day.

This repetition frees him from all constraints. He can gorge on food with no thought of being overweight—he will wake up in the morning with all the calories erased. He can disobey all laws, have raucous pleasure with women, and still be protected by the same eraser. And so, for a while, he chooses to engage in selfishness and debauchery. In other words, he gets what we all seek when we engage in the selfish pursuit of pleasure—he gets to do whatever he wants with no consequences.

But a strange thing happens: this course doesn't make him happy. He's more miserable than ever. It's only when he starts caring for other people that he begins to be happy.

The Bill Murray character makes a change that we all need to make—a change in the way we think about happiness. Happiness is not the pursuit of all kinds of pleasure; it is something much deeper and more real than that.

As the movie ends, Murray is a happy man. He reconciles neighbors who are fighting, becomes an accomplished artist, saves a child falling out of a tree (because he's lived the day many times before, he knows exactly what will happen), and wins the love of the girl of his dreams because his character has become a noble, appealing one.

There is no religious dimension to Murray's happiness. There is no conversion, no church. And this does not surprise me. I think we all have friends (at least I have some) who hardly ever go to church or synagogue but are "good" people with solid families and successful careers. They have been taught and have practiced the virtues that lead to a happy life—they are faithful in marriage, honest, considerate, generous in community work, even sacrificial, scrupulous in meeting and exceeding expectations, hardworking, and good natured. They have many friends. To be sure, they like the rest of us have warts. But the point is that some people who are not religious in any orthodox way have "happy" lives because by common grace they live in accordance with – we can say obey – immutable moral laws established by God and applicable to all.

Christians cannot be happy unless we live in the same way—by being obedient to the owner's manual for human life. This is the first step toward happiness for any human in any culture anywhere in the world.

Stephen R. Covey wrote a powerful book about the principles of owner-manual happiness: *The 7 Habits of Highly Effective People*. He called these "lighthouse principles" as he opened his book with this illustration:

> Two battleships assigned to the training squadron had been at sea on maneuvers in heavy weather for several days. I was serving on the lead battleship and was on watch on the bridge as night fell. The visibility was poor with patchy fog, so the captain remained on the bridge keeping an eye on all activities.
>
> Shortly after dark, the lookout on the wing of the bridge reported, "Light, bearing on the starboard bow."
>
> "Is it steady or moving astern?" the captain called out.
>
> Lookout replied, "Steady, Captain," which meant we were on a dangerous collision course with that ship.

The captain then called to the signalman, "Signal that ship: We are on a collision course, advise you change course 20 degrees."

Back came a signal, "Advisable for you to change course 20 degrees."

The captain said, "Send, I'm a captain, change course 20 degrees."

"I'm a seaman second class," came the reply. "You had better change course 20 degrees."

By that time, the captain was furious. He spat out, "Send, I'm a battleship. Change course 20 degrees."

Back came the flashing light, "I'm a lighthouse."

We changed course.[19]

Covey is absolutely right as he explains that our world is filled with "lighthouse" principles that govern human growth and happiness. These are natural laws that are woven into the fabric of every civilized society throughout history and comprise the roots of every family and institution that has endured and prospered.

Biblical people have always agreed, finding our owners manual in the Bible and specifically in the teachings of Jesus, the Ten Commandments, and the Golden Rule.

The book of Proverbs is a cornucopia of God-given principles for living a practical, successful, and happy life. Proverbs' teachings include the dangers of sloth, sex outside marriage, idle talk, and pride. They teach about the importance of being generous, seeking the advice of counselors, and much more. These rules are universally true for all people. All happy people, any happy family, and most businesses successful over time live by these precepts.

In the words of J. C. Ryle, 19th century Bishop of Liverpool, "God has so wisely ordered it, that our well-being and our well-doing are linked together."[20] That, in fact, is a law of the universe.

Though we often overlook it, it has always been true.

We get to experience happiness whenever we obey God's moral laws even if we don't acknowledge him as their Author. So let's not underestimate the present benefits of obedience to the owner's manual. They are inestimable.

But living by the owner's manual alone is not enough for true happiness. It provides precepts for how we live our lives. But the manual and life itself need to have a purpose, and we need to obediently live into that purpose.

Purpose-Filled Life-Happiness

Happiness has always carried with it a sense of being satisfied with what we do with our lives. Years ago I read a book by Charles Murray, the brilliant conservative thinker, called *The Pursuit of Happiness*—a book on happiness as it has been traditionally understood, beginning with the Greeks. His definition of the classical understanding of happiness is this: "Lasting and justified satisfaction with [the defining aspects of] one's life as a whole." [21]

Happiness in this sense has a long-term orientation. It relates to the perspective that looks back over life at any point in the journey, young or old, and concludes that we are in the process of obediently living into the purposes for which God created us and Christ called us. In this light, a vital root of happiness is the satisfaction of living well the purpose-filled life. Just like Nita Thompson, we are happy when we are living out our purpose by having a will aligned with God's will trusting in his grace to guide us along the way.

Jesus gave us a simple snapshot of this dimension of happiness when at the end of his life he prayed to his Father, "I have brought you glory on earth by completing the work you gave me to do" (John 17:4). Would that we all could offer such a prayer. When we come to realize that God has created us for a purpose and has a plan for our lives, we will be happy as we live into and complete it. Paul reflects this kind of satisfaction with his life when at the end of his ministry he writes Timothy, "I have fought the good fight, I have finished the race. I have kept the faith" (2 Timothy 4:72).

Happiness in this sense, then, is all about fulfilling God's plan for our lives through faith. It is about aligning our wills with his and bringing him glory by doing and finishing the work he gives us, trusting in him to equip us with his power to do it and his wisdom to show us how to get it done.

Dennis Prager, formerly a columnist for the *Los Angeles Times*, writes, "Happiness can be attained under virtually any circumstances provided you believe that your life has meaning and purpose."[22] The God-created universe has an eternal purpose and so do our individual lives. We are called to belong to the Lord of all creation. We are his "workmanship, created ... to do good works which God prepared in advance for us to do" in family, work, church and community (Ephesians 2:10). It is in doing these good works that we always have a sense of peace deep in our souls. (We will develop this subject more fully in chapters 23 and 24).

If we live by the owner's manual and fulfill well the purposes for which we were created, we will have the foundation for a happy life. But there is the crown of happiness still to be added – that which comes from a personal relationship with Christ. We can call this dimension of happiness, abiding-in-Christ happiness.

Abiding-in-Christ Happiness

If we have this relationship, we can be truly happy even if we don't have much in the way of earthly pleasures or success. When I travel to Rwanda, I find Christians, many of them widows from the genocide, living on a little piece of land, who walk miles to market, and supporting a family on less than two dollars a day. And yet they are deeply happy because they abide in Christ and live in the favor of God. The Bible uses words like "joy" and "blessedness" to describe happiness in this sense.

And how is our relationship with Christ nurtured? We have the answer by now: through obedience—the obedience of faith. Dietrich Bonhoeffer, the German minister and martyr executed by the

Nazis, writes that "the only true relation we can have with [Christ] is to follow him."[23]

The great evangelist Charles Spurgeon captured this truth:

> God comes down to walk with men who obey. If they walk with Him, He walks with them. The Lord can only have fellowship with His servants as they obey. Obedience is heaven in us, and it is the prelude to our being in heaven. Obedient faith is the way to eternal life; no, it is eternal life revealing itself.[24]

Certainly, eternal life revealing itself to us is the core of happiness. It is ours deep down inside *only* as we obey in faith.

Blaise Pascal spoke of an "infinite abyss" that no pleasure can ever fill and that can only be filled by God. Here is what Pascal said:

> There once was in man a *true happiness* of which now remain to him only the mark and empty trace, which he in vain tries to fill from all his surroundings, seeking from things absent the help he does not obtain in things present. But these are all inadequate, because the infinite abyss can only be filled by an infinite and immutable object, that is to say, only by God Himself.[25]

Above other gifts from God is the privilege of knowing his presence and sensing his pleasure in us. This is what it feels like when our God-shaped hole is filled properly with God himself and no substitute. And therein lies what Pascal calls "true happiness." C. S. Lewis agrees, "God cannot give us happiness and peace apart from Himself.... *There is no such thing.*"[26]

Andrew Murray, an astute student of biblical obedience in the early 20th century also agrees, and Murray tells us the only way this happiness can be found: "*With God and with Christ our restoration to obedience was the great aim of redemption. It is the only way to union with God in which our happiness consists.* Through it alone God can reveal His life and power within us."[27]

Murray has distilled the essential truth about obedience into a couple of sentences. Obedience is central to God's plan of redemption. Uniting our wills to God's provides the only path to fellowship with God and, through this fellowship, to true happiness. Through obedience of faith alone does God's life and love fill Pascal's "infinite abyss in our souls."

So Bonhoeffer, Spurgeon, Pascal, Lewis and Murray get us on the right path. They are, however, merely reflecting the teaching of our Lord.

Jesus said of the Father, "He has not left me alone, for I always do the things that are pleasing to him" (John 8:29, ESV). It was through obedience to his Father's will that Jesus remained in the fellowship of his Father.

At the Passover dinner the night before he was crucified, Jesus poured out his heart to his disciples. These were essentially his last words to them. He emphasized again and again that it is through obedience founded in love for him that we will . . .

- have fellowship with him and his Father (John 14:23—"If anyone loves me, he will obey my teaching. My Father will love him, and we will come to him and make our home with him.")
- receive the gift of the Holy Spirit (John 14:15-16—"If you love me, you will obey what I command. And I will ask the Father and he will give you another Counselor to be with you forever – the spirit of Truth.")
- have his friendship (John 15:14—"You are my friends if you do what I command.")
- abide in his love (John 15:10—"If you obey my commands, you will remain in my love.")

John, in his first epistle, develops this theme: "Those who obey his commands live in him and he in them" (1 John 3:24).

Do we want deep, intimate fellowship with Jesus and the joy and peace that flow from it? Do we want access to his life and power? If so, then we must trust and obey him.

We all love this refrain from the old hymn:
>Just a closer walk with thee,
>>Grant it Jesus, is my plea.
>Daily walking close to thee,
>>Let it be, dear Lord, let it be.

"Daily walking close to thee." How? we ask. We have this fellowship when our wills are aligned with Jesus', through faith. A closer walk and the resulting happiness deep in our souls are nurtured in the obedience of faith. There is no other way.

Summing it Up

The Westminster Shorter Catechism—a historic Q&A on basic beliefs of Christianity—states that "man's chief end is to glorify God, and to enjoy him forever." As a summary of what true happiness means, we could hardly do better than the idea of enjoying God forever. And that enjoyment begins now, in this life. It is not just for the hereafter.

"Enjoying God" speaks to a quality of relationship with him. But note that in the catechism enjoying God is paired with glorifying him. How do we glorify God? Through the fruit of good works flowing from the obedience of faith.

Enjoying God forever—that is the summation of the blessings that grow from obedience and the source of a happiness we can know now, today, if we will trust and obey.

I hope that you have become more comfortable with *happiness* as the word to describe the blessings that flow from the obedience of faith. Indeed, true happiness is a many-splendored thing, including the blessings of living a morally good life, doing and completing God's purposes for our lives and abiding in the love and fellowship of Jesus Christ. We have looked at the essence of the happiness that flows from the obedience of faith. But there are many more blessings of grace that obedience adds to our happiness, and to these we turn in our next two chapters.

CHAPTER 3
The Blessings of Obedience, Part 1

MISSIONARY, KAREN WATSON was, killed in Iraq on March 15, 2004. Below are portions of a letter she wrote just one year earlier.

Dear Pastor Phil and Pastor Roger:

You should only be opening this letter in the event of my death.

When God calls there are no regrets. I tried to share my heart with you as much as possible, my heart for the nations. I wasn't called to a place. I was called to him. To obey was my objective, to suffer was expected, his glory my reward, his glory my reward...

The Missionary Heart:

Care more than some think is wise.

Risk more than some think is safe.

Dream more than some think is practical.

Expect more than some think is possible.

I was called not to comfort or success but to obedience... There is no joy outside of knowing Jesus and serving him. I love you two and my church family.

In his care,
Salaam,
Karen[28]

Obedience does not necessarily preclude suffering, but Karen Watson speaks gospel truth when she says, "There is no joy outside of knowing Jesus and serving him." Obedience provides a channel for God's grace to bestow a bundle of blessings that begin in this life and build over time.

Grace and Its Blessings

Before we look at the blessings obedience adds to our happiness, let's touch on a question you may be asking: Isn't grace unmerited and if so, how can its blessings be conditioned on our obedience? Good question!

All of the blessings we will discuss flow from God's grace and they are all unmerited. None of us can earn them. They are undeserved gifts. But the Bible is clear that they flow along certain paths relating to our walking in God's will and in this sense they are conditional. When we turn our back on God's moral law and walk in our own way, the flow of grace is hindered. When we trust and obey, the floodgates open up.

So grace is always unmerited, but it can be conditional. If you want to think more about this, I have collected some of the thought of respected biblical scholars on the relation of grace and obedience in Appendix A. Now to the blessings of obedience.

The Holy Spirit

As we will see more fully in Chapter 12, it is through the ministry of the Holy Spirit that we are motivated and empowered to obey. By grace we receive the Holy Spirit through faith and more of the Holy Spirit through obedience (Galatians 3:14; John 14:15–17; Acts 5:32). It is in the union of faith and obedience that the Holy Spirit comes alive in our life even as he strengthens faith and obedience. From the Holy Spirit, manifold blessings flow, including all of his fruit: love, joy, peace, patience, gentleness, kindness, faithfulness, goodness, and self-control (Galatians 5:22-23).

Life

Christ came to give us abundant life, a quality of life that matures in this world through the obedience of faith and continues in the world to come.

This life is incomparably greater than biological life. George MacDonald, a Scottish poet, author and minister in the 19th Century and C. S. Lewis' Lewis' mentor[29], explains the vast difference this way: "The life the Lord came to give us is a life exceeding that of the highest mere human being, by far more than the life of that man exceeds the life of the least animal. More and more of that divine life awaits each who will receive it."[30]

Throughout Scripture, this life is tied directly to obedience. This theme is introduced in Genesis, where we learn that Adam was cast from paradise for his disobedience and barred from ever reentering the Garden of Eden, "lest he reach out his hand and take also of the tree of life and eat, and live forever" (Genesis 3:22, ESV). The fullness of life that was to come from eating of the fruit of the tree of life returned with Jesus Christ. As John tells us in the first paragraph of his Gospel, "In him was life, and that life was the light of men" (1:4, ESV).

The relation of life to obedience was made clear by Moses in his Deuteronomic sermon. "Take to heart all the words I have solemnly declared to you this day. . . . They are not just idle words for you—they are your life" (Deuteronomy 32:46–47).

Jesus also keyed on the relationship of obedience to life. In the Sermon on the Mount, he taught, "Enter through the narrow gate. For wide is the gate and broad is the road that leads to destruction, and many enter through it. But small is the gate and narrow the road that leads to life, and only a few find it" (Matthew 7:13–14).

On another occasion, a rich young man asked Jesus, "What good thing must I do to get eternal life?"

Our Lord replied, "If you want to enter life, obey the commandments" (Matthew 19:16–17).

I do not mean to suggest that the life we receive at the new birth is in any way earned by obedience or any work we may do. That life is a gift of sheer grace that we receive through our faith in Jesus Christ. But maturing through grace into the fullness of the new life we are given here on earth *is* directly tied to the obedience the Holy Spirit engenders in our lives.

Depth of Insight About God

Oswald Chambers writes, "One reads tomes on the work of the Holy Spirit when five minutes of drastic obedience would make things clear as sunlight. . . . The tiniest fragment of obedience and heaven opens up. We can read something 365 times and it means nothing. Then all of a sudden we understand because we obey."[31] This points up another blessing of obedience: depth of insight into God and his truth.

Jesus taught, "If you hold to [obey] my teaching, you are really my disciples. Then you will know the truth, and the truth will set you free" (John 8:31-32).

What is the condition on which Jesus bases our knowing the truth? It is obeying him. Dietrich Bonhoeffer states it simply, "[I]t is only through obedience that you come to learn the truth."[32]

We are introducing here a basic principle that we will discuss more fully in Part 2. Believing in the truth (faith) and living it out (obedience) are inseparably joined.

In John 14:21, Jesus speaks of the one who "has my commandments and obeys them" and then promises, "I will . . . manifest myself to him" (ESV). Personal knowledge of Jesus comes through obedience.

We may think we can know Jesus by reading the Bible, listening to sermons, and attending a Bible study, and indeed all of these are vitally important. When two or three of us are gathered together in his name, he is there in the midst of us. But Jesus becomes manifest to us in a vivid way when we keep his commandments. In 1 John, the beloved disciple reinforces this truth in telling us, "We know we have come to know him if we obey his commandments" (1 John 2:3).

In biblical usage, the word "know" refers to an intimate, personal, and interactive relationship. So if we want to know Jesus intimately, if we want a personal and interactive relationship with him, we need to obey his commandments.

George MacDonald sums it up this way:

> Men would understand; they do not care to obey. They try to understand where it is impossible they should understand except by obeying. They would search into the word of the Lord instead of doing their part in it. . . . It is on them that do his will that the day dawns. To them the day star arises in their hearts. Obedience is the soul of knowledge.[33]

This is a great phrase to remember. "Obedience is the soul of knowledge." Find the poorest peasant who trusts and obeys, and her knowledge of biblical truth will exceed that of a great university scholar who does not know the obedience of faith.

Answered Prayers

In 1 John 3:22 we read that we "receive from [God] anything we ask, because we obey his commands and do what pleases him."

We all want answered prayer. We can have it if our wills are aligned with God's and we live a life pleasing to him.

There are several keys to effectual prayer. We need to pray in the name of Jesus, recognizing that God hears because we are clothed with his righteousness, not our own. We need to pray with faith. But we also need to pray with a clean conscience, free from disobedience. Our sins separate us from God, so he will not hear (Isaiah 59:2). In his first letter, Peter quotes from Psalms:

> The eyes of the Lord are on the righteous
> and his ears are attentive to their prayer,
> but the face of the Lord is against those who do evil.
> (1 Peter 3:12; see Psalm 34:15–16)

James teaches us that "the prayer of a righteous man is powerful and effective" (5:16). Righteousness, which includes a life of faithful obedience, causes us to pray those prayers that God loves to say yes to.

Love

At the Passover meal Jesus said, "As the Father has loved me, so have I loved you. Abide in my love. If you keep my commandments, you will abide in my love, just as I have kept my Father's commandments and abide in his love" (John 15:9–10, ESV). The most sublime, the highest degree of happiness we can know is the love of God through a personal relationship with him. How to know his love and to live in it is a primary teaching of all Scripture. Here, Jesus makes clear that to live in this love we must keep his commandments.

Paul makes the same point in Romans 8, where he teaches that our relation to our heavenly Father is that of a child to his father. The Holy Spirit testifies with our spirit that we are God's children and thereby can call him "Abba, Father," or Daddy. Paul introduces this teaching, saying, "If by the Spirit you put to death the deeds of the body, you will live. For all who are led by the Spirit of God are sons of God" (Romans 8:13–14, ESV). The relationship of a trusting child to a loving Father is for those who are led by the Spirit of God and have put to death the deeds of the body.

We know this to be true from our experiences with our own children. I have several close friends (and you probably do too) who have a rebellious child. Some are into drugs; others may have relationships that are far from the will of God. The love of the parent is in no way diminished by the wayward activity of the child, but the child cannot "abide" in this love. The child, rather, is cut off from it. The child may come home and ask for money or a car or other benefits, and the parent's heart may ache to respond to the needs of the child, but the parent knows that to do so would only enable the destructive disobedience. Until the child repents and ceases his rebellion, there can be no "Daddy" relationship with the father, nor will the child be able to know or receive the deep, deep love of the father.

We, thankfully, can know intimacy with the Father in heaven as we turn to him in faith and obedience.

Joy

Jesus teaches at John 15:11, "I have told you this [to obey my commands so as to remain in my love] so that my joy may be in you and that your joy may be complete." The world would try to convince us that joy is elsewhere. But Jesus makes clear that joy lies in the love that we know flowing from our obedient response to biblical truth.

In the faithful community in Le Chambon-sur-Lignon, France, which we will discuss in Chapter 10, there was a woman who asked to be called Jispa. This woman had no money and hardly any food, but she risked her life to save Jewish children fleeing from the Nazis. The name Jispa is an acronym made up of French words that say "the joy of serving in peace and love."

Where did Jispa find joy? In rescuing Jewish children. That is, in obedience to her Lord's command to love them.

I had an assistant for many years who is a Jispa. Marjorie Mann has found joy in serving her Lord and others in peace and love. Marjorie never married, never had a driver's license. She worked at our company, Protective Life, for over forty years. She was a leader, conducting a large building program and capital funds drive for a camp at her beloved Methodist church. She never had any enemy but has hundreds of devoted friends. In God's grace she has always been very happy. And now, at 88 years old, she continues to be happy in her retirement home, with frequent notes to her friends bringing cheer to all.

Peace

We have seen that love and joy bloom only in the garden of obedience. So does peace. That's why the psalmist declared,

Great peace have those who love your law;

nothing can make them stumble. (Psalm 119:165, ESV)

When Paul urges the Philippians not to be anxious about anything, he concludes, "Whatever you have learned . . . from me—put it into practice. And the God of peace will be with you" (Philippians 4:6, 9).

Paul is echoing Christ's teaching on obedience. In Matthew 7:24–27, Jesus teaches:

> Everyone who hears these words of mine and puts them into practice is like a wise man who built his house on the rock. The rain came down, the streams rose, and the winds blew and beat against that house; yet it did not fall, because it had its foundation on the rock. But everyone who hears these words of mine and does not put them into practice is like a foolish man who built his house on sand. The rain came down, the streams rose, and the winds blew and beat against that house, and it fell with a great crash.

Here, Jesus is concluding his Sermon on the Mount. And he does it on the subject of obedience. The one who puts Jesus' teachings into practice is the one who has the peace and security of living in a house with a sure foundation.

The great poet Dante captured this truth when he described Paradise with these words:

> For in His will is our peace. It is the sea
> To which all things existing flow, both those
> His will creates and those that nature makes.[34]

"For in His will is our peace. It is the sea to which all things existing flow." Do we doubt these words? We need only ask any mature Christian to have them confirmed.

We've more blessings to discuss, but those already outlined are enough for one sitting. Chapter 4 may be a controversial one.

CHAPTER 4
The Blessings of Obedience, Part 2

As we resume our discussion of the manifold blessings of obedience, we can begin with one very much on the mind of Americans. We love success and prosperity—and our God by his grace desires that we have it, as we walk in the obedience of faith.

Success and Prosperity

One of the most frequently recurring themes in all of Scripture is the nexus between obedience and blessing, or virtue and reward, here on earth. This is what the owner's manual is all about. But above the principles of the owner's manual is the teaching that God exercises his power in a special way to bless his children who faithfully obey him.

The connection between obedience and blessing is vividly introduced in Chapter 28 of Deuteronomy: "If you fully obey the LORD your God and carefully follow all his commands. . . . All these blessings will come upon you" (v. 1). And there follow promises of blessings in the city, the country, childbearing, farming, work and harvest, security against the enemy, and everything one does ("when you come in . . . and go out" [v. 6]). In summary, Moses teaches the children of Israel, "The LORD will open the heavens, the storehouse of his bounty, to send rain on your land in season and to bless all the work of your hands. . . . If you pay attention to the commands of the LORD your God . . . and carefully follow them" (vv. 12–13).

The Lord instructed Joshua, the newly appointed leader and general of Israel and its army, to take the children of Israel into the land of Canaan. "Be careful to obey all the law my servant Moses gave you," the Lord said; "do not turn from it to the right or to the left, that you may be successful wherever you go." He went on to counsel Joshua to meditate on the law "day and night" and "be careful to do everything written in it." And the Lord repeated, "Then you will be prosperous and successful, . . . for the LORD your God will be with you wherever you go" (Joshua 1:7–9).

Psalm 1, which in many ways is a prologue to all of the wisdom given us in the Psalter, opens by describing as happy the one whose "delight is in the law of the LORD" and who meditates on this law "day and night" (vv. 2):

> He is like a tree planted by streams of water,
> which yields its fruit in season
> and whose leaf does not wither.
> Whatever he does prospers. (v. 3)

Psalm 1 goes on to teach us that "the LORD watches over the way of the righteous" (v. 6). The Psalms and the Proverbs are resplendent with this theme.

This is not to say that every leader will be blessed with financial prosperity by obeying the moral law of God. God has plans and purposes that are inscrutable and he may build Christ-like character in those he calls through the agony of defeat. Nevertheless, with obedience comes fellowship with the Lord and the only foundation of success that will bring happiness.

The Least of Us—and Our Bank Account

There are two categories of good works that are accentuated above all the others in the faithful obedience from which blessings flow.

The first is how we treat the least of our brothers and sisters. This theme likewise is introduced in Deuteronomy where Moses teaches the Israelites to "give generously" to the poor "without a grudging heart; then because of this the LORD your God will bless you in all your work and in everything you put your hand to" (15:10). Similarly, in Proverbs we are taught,

> He who gives to the poor will lack nothing,
> but he who closes his eyes to them receives many curses (28:27).

The second category of good works especially commended for blessing relates to how we use our money. The theme that if we give generously we will receive generously is taught throughout Scripture.

- "Give, and it will be given to you. A good measure, pressed down, shaken together and running over, will be poured into your lap. For with the measure you use, it will be measured to you" (Luke 6:38).
- "Whoever sows generously will also reap generously" (2 Corinthians 9:6).

Perhaps this theme is most broadly stated in Malachi 3:10, where God challenges the Israelites to "bring the whole tithe into the storehouse." If they were to do so, the Lord tells them, "See if I will not throw open the floodgates of heaven and pour out so much blessing that you will not have room enough for it."

As we think about obedience and the happiness that grows from it, how we treat the poor and what we do with our money are the two gauges on the instrument panel with which we should be most concerned. The compassionate and generous are always the happiest. The coldhearted and greedy are always the most miserable. If you doubt these sweeping generalizations, make a list of the happiest and most miserable people you know, and see whether the compassionate and generosity indexes are not clear guides to your conclusions.

My former assistant, Marjorie Mann, whom we introduced in the last chapter, moved to a retirement apartment when she was 78 years old. Previously she had lived in a house she owned in a blue-collar neighborhood. It was free of debt and the only source of any savings Marjorie had, save a few shares in Protective Life (where she had worked) and her pension. She gave the house "free and clear" to Sam, her next-door neighbor, "because he took care of me all these years." Marjorie simply trusted and obeyed. She has no sense of right or entitlement, just a simple trust in Jesus.

Prior to moving and deeding the house to Sam, Marjorie had opened her home for more than two years to a woman whom she had found homeless.

I have never known anyone happier than Marjorie.

Now let's turn to the greatest blessing that flows from the obedience of faith—one you may not have expected to see on the list.

Salvation

It comes as a shock to most evangelical Protestants (as it did to me) to learn that our salvation and obedience are connected. But such is clearly taught in Scripture. In Hebrews we read that Christ learned obedience through suffering and "became the source of eternal salvation to all who obey him" (Hebrews 5:9).

It is common to think of salvation as something that takes place at a point in time. We say, "I was saved at a Billy Graham Crusade" or "I got saved when I was twelve." In theological terms, what we are referring to in such statements is *justification*, which is where salvation begins. (See Romans 3:21-31.) When we receive Christ in faith, once and for all, we become justified to God—our sins are forgiven and we are deemed righteous solely on account of Jesus' perfect obedience and sacrifice for our sins.

But *salvation* continues in a progressive way as we grow in grace and as by grace through faith the power of sin is conquered over time. In this process, to use Paul's terminology, we "work out our salvation" throughout our lives as God "works in us" (see Philippians 2:12-13). Theologians call this ongoing salvation, *sanctification*. Salvation embraces both justification *and* sanctification, and faithful obedience is the essence of sanctification.[35]

I know I am getting into theology here. So let's turn to three scholars in the faith.

- First, John Piper, a Baptist pastor and one of the world's leading theologians today: "Salvation is the big biblical term that describes all God's saving work for us and in us, past, present and future . . . . Salvation is not one state in the Christian life. It *is* the Christian life. . . . The obedience which pleases God is the obedience of faith, and the obedience of faith is an essential part of salvation. We are chosen to be saved *through sanctification*, which is the same as the obedience of faith."[36]

- Second, Charles Spurgeon, one of the most respected and powerful preachers who ever lived: "We look at obedience of the heart to the will of God as salvation. We regard sanctification, or obedience, as the great purpose for which our Savior died. . . Obedience is the principal objective of the work of grace in the hearts of those who are chosen and called."[37]

- Third, Andrew Murray, the Dutch Reformed pastor whom we quoted earlier: "With God and with Christ our restoration to obedience was the great aim of redemption."[38]

These learned students of biblical teaching are all telling us that the obedience of faith or sanctification is the principal objective of the grace that called us and the aim of redemption that is saving us. We are chosen to be saved not just from the guilt of sin but also from the power of sin as we walk by grace in the obedience of faith.

You might ask, is not obedience the *result* of salvation, not its *cause*? In fact, it is both. Salvation, both justification and sanctification, has but one source—God's grace. Obedience certainly *results* from the freedom from sin's bondage we have in Christ by grace. Without redemption from the power of sin, we cannot obey.

But as we have seen, through faithful obedience we receive

many blessings of grace: a greater measure of the Holy Spirit, the fullness of life, depth of insight, answered prayer, and others. These blessings are not earned by obedience. They are the work of God's free grace, and, in turn, contribute to our redemption from the reign of sin in our lives which is salvation. For example, having more of the Holy Spirit's power fortifies us against sin. Answered prayer protects us from temptation.

The obedience of faith becomes a deep river in which blessings of grace flow, enabling us to overcome the power of sin and giving us happiness. Obedience is, therefore, both the result of, and a source of, salvation. The two work together in a beautiful cycle.

To sum it up, by Christ, the "source of eternal salvation to all who obey him" (Hebrews 5:9), we were saved once and for all from the guilt of sin. And then, throughout our lives, we are being saved from its power as through faith we obey more fervently and in this obedience by grace are enabled to overcome sin. Thus, we can conclude that salvation is organically related to the obedience of faith.

Now, we are ready to consider the final and eternal blessings that flow from obedience.

Blessings Here and Hereafter

As we study the blessings of obedience, it is easy to concentrate on the blessings of this life—our fellowship and friendship with Jesus, receiving the full measure of God's love, the insight and wisdom that obedience gives us. But these blessings will be with us at most a few decades. Other blessings awaiting the obedient will last for eternity.[39]

Here's where the pie-in-the-sky perspective is true. And there's nothing wrong with looking forward to experiencing God's full measure of happiness for us.

How did Jesus endure the cross? "For the joy that was set before him" (Hebrews 12:2). What was Jesus' reward in heaven? "God exalted him to the highest place and gave him the name that is above every name" because he became obedient to death (Philippians

2:8-9; see Isaiah 52:13; 53:12).

How did Paul endure the stoning, the flogging, the shipwreck? Because there was laid up for him in heaven "the crown of righteousness" (2 Timothy 4:8).

What was the invitation of the master to the good and faithful servant? "Come and share your master's happiness [representing heaven]!" (Matthew 25:21).

With the happiness of obedience, there's always more to come.

Jesus was careful to make sure that we would be aware of the "more" that is to come. Luke 14 recounts the story of Jesus' going to the house of a prominent Pharisee for a Sabbath meal. When he noticed how the guests assembled themselves, carefully picking the places of honor, Jesus turned to his host and told him that, when he gave a luncheon or dinner, he should not invite his friends or his relatives or his rich neighbors, for they would be able to repay him enough in the present age. Rather, he said to his host, he should "invite the poor, the crippled, the lame, the blind, and you will be blessed, because they cannot repay you. For you will be repaid at the resurrection of the just" (Luke 14:13–14, ESV).

The parables of the minas and talents speak of stewardship of the earthly resources we have received by God's grace (Matthew 25:14–30; Luke 19:11–27). It is to the faithful and diligent in the use of those gifts that the rewards in eternity are promised.

Bruce Wilkinson in his *A Life God Rewards* lists kinds of faithful obedience for which we will receive rewards in heaven.[40] Those include submitting to our employer as a faithful steward (Matthew 24:45-47), denying ourselves (Matthew 16:24-27), serving those in need (Mark 9:41), suffering for the sake of Jesus' name (Luke 6:22-23), making sacrifices (Luke 6:35), and sharing our time, talent, and treasure in the work of the kingdom (Matthew 6:3-4; 1 Timothy 6:18-19).

The Happiness Paradox

Earlier we learned that wanting happiness is okay. And it is.

We've seen that obeying God is the way to get real happiness. And it is. We've reviewed many of the blessings that can be ours through obedience. And aren't they wonderful? But now we have to face a curve ball. We need to see there's a higher reason for obeying God than wanting happiness.

It's been said that we can never become humble by seeking that virtue directly. If we do, we'll become proud—and we're worse than when we started! That's the humility paradox.

The happiness paradox is similar.

When it comes to true happiness—the highest form of happiness, which comes from a right relationship with God—that is not something we can or should seek directly. Instead we should just focus on faithfully obeying God, and the happiness will come to us.

The truth is that we find happiness only when self is out of the picture. (We will spend a whole chapter on this essential truth; see Chapter 14.) This is because the self has an insatiable appetite. It always wants more—more sex, more money, more power, more acclaim, more seductive looks, more cars, and so on. And when we get more, it is never enough for the self. Those who are truly happy, therefore, do not think about themselves or their own needs but about others and God.

We might put it this way: If we reach out to grab the bird of happiness, it will fly away. But if we go about our business (live the way God wants), the bird of happiness will come to rest on our shoulder.

This is true because real happiness is not an achievement; it's given to us by free grace. It's not something we earn; it's a gift of God.

It goes back to the character of our relationship with God. What matters is not trying to comply with laws for what we get out of that compliance. As we grow in Christian maturity, we are obedient, not out of greed for what God will give us, but out of our love for God and our gratitude for what he has done for us.

And one other thing. Now that we've reviewed all the blessings we have in obedience, if you want to use a word other than happiness to describe this bundle of blessings, it's okay with me. Let's not get hung up on semantics. The important thing is that we understand that these blessings are all connected to a life that trusts and obeys our Lord.

Obedience for God's Sake

After promising to unlock the door to happiness, extolling the blessings of happiness, and describing the manifold qualities of that happiness, we're going to do something that might sound crazy—we need to forget about happiness! We will set it aside for now, and focus instead on trusting God and obedience. We need to see obedience to God as a worthy objective in its own right.

The rest of this book focuses much more on obedience than it does on happiness. The hidden key, after all, is the obedience of faith. Happiness is the treasure we find only when we open the door with the key.

We'll be getting to more of the practical aspects of obedience in Parts 3 and 4. But before that, let's deal with preliminary questions we might still have. Is an emphasis on obedience a path to legalism? Need it be a source of pride? Absolutely not. Does obedience create friction with a deep, trusting faith? Not at all. Obedience is not *against* faith. The kind of obedience we are talking about is the obedience *of* faith.

Part 2

The Obedience of Faith

CHAPTER 5
Obedience All Around

TAKE A MOMENT and consider the physical book you are reading. How did it come to be? The molecules in it are perfectly obeying natural laws; so did the trees that produced the pulp. The men and woman who felled the trees and transported them, who worked in the paper mill, who manufactured the ink, glue, thread, and other ingredients all followed directions and a myriad of laws. You are able to read the book because of an unimaginably great amount of obedience in nature and commerce that has occurred to produce the book, not to mention the chair, light, house (or are you on a plane?), etc., that combine to allow you to enjoy the book (I hope).

When we give obedience a little thought, we recognize:

- Nature rests in perfect obedience. The blooms and fragrances of flowers come from biological systems operating in obedience to the laws of nature established by God. The upthrust of mountains, the tidal action of oceans, and the swirling of storms all obey natural laws. Indeed everything in nature from tiny subatomic particles to vast galaxies obeys the established laws.

- Human commerce and progress require obedience. Buildings, roads, and bridges are constructed in strict obedience to blueprints. Automobiles are manufactured in obedience to design specifications. When we own a complex piece of machinery, we must obey the operator's manual or it will soon break down.

- Personal success depends on obedience. People clamor to work for and follow the directions of the great men and women in their field, whether it be finance or law, engineering or architecture, the academic world or the church.
- Life itself displays obedience. From moment to moment, our heart, lungs, and other organs obey the instructions encoded in our DNA. Meanwhile, our arms, legs, mouths, and eyes obediently follow the direction of our wills.

So here's an extraordinary truth to ponder. Nature, society, and even our own bodies—indeed well nigh the whole of the universe—operate in obedience to God's codes and laws. (And were such obedience to be relaxed even for a second, we would all perish.) But there is one prominent exception to this pervasive obedience. *The will of sinful humanity does not trust and obey God!*

We love obedience when it happens all around us. We know it to be vital to our lives. Yet we insist on autonomy when it comes to obeying the Lord and his commands. As Blaise Pascal would say, what a "strange disorder"![1]

A Warning

Since the so-called Enlightenment of the 18th century, there have been many who have sought to be free of obedience to God and his moral order. Freedom, they say, is to live as they want, creating their own notions of good and evil.

Those who choose not to trust God and obey him, however, should beware. They will not be free and autonomous beings. If they don't obey God, they will come to obey someone or something else. As Bob Dylan sings, we've "gotta serve somebody."

In our sinful nature lurk desires that cause us to pay homage to all kinds of false gods that threaten to corrupt and destroy us. For instance, lust entices us to obey the false gods of beauty and sex. Pride causes us to obey the gods of power and adulation. Greed seduces us to obey the god of wealth.

As we turn from the one true God, we will obey counterfeit

gods. They will make us anxious, maybe miserable, and ultimately—as the Bible teaches us—their end is death (Romans 6:16).

Can we find anyone who does not worship and obey some god? The Bible teaches that there are none (Romans 6:11–22). Even the weak, bored souls without purpose whom we find in crack houses, bars, and casinos, and who seem to care little about anything, are worshiping and obeying "the god of their bellies" (see Philippians 3:19).

All of us live in "Paradise Lost." And Jesus came to redeem us. But we must be mindful that even though we may have turned to Jesus and vowed to trust and obey him, the seduction of false gods remains with us. We have been redeemed from the guilt of serving them, and by God's grace we are ever being redeemed from their power. Lust, greed, envy, pride, and other sinful desires, however, are always there to draw us from trusting and obeying our Lord and to destroy our happiness.

Obedience Under the New Covenant

What does the Bible tell us about obedience?

It's not hard to convince people that the Old Testament teaches the necessity of obedience. After all, that's where we find the books of the Law, the Ten Commandments and the prophets teaching the fear of God.

But the New Testament? Doesn't that part of the Bible basically tell us that grace trumps law? We will discuss this more fully in Chapter 9, but suffice it to say here that obedience is central to New Testament teaching.

First, the key to Christ's teaching ministry was the kingdom of God. The kingdom of God is not a concrete territory and government. It is the reign and rule of God in the human realm wherever we freely invite and welcome it. The Sermon on the Mount, the parables and indeed the whole of Jesus' teaching and example tell us what God's reign and rule look like.

In addition, Christ repeatedly emphasized the importance of our obedience:

- Among the first recorded words out of Christ's mouth were "follow me" (Mark 1:17).
- To doubters in the enduring legitimacy of God's law, he said, "Until heaven and earth disappear, not the smallest letter, not the least stroke of a pen, not an iota, not a dot, will by any means disappear from the Law until everything is accomplished" (Matthew 5:18).
- In the Lord's Prayer, the will of God has a prominent place: "your will be done, on earth as it is in heaven" (Matthew 6:10).
- Warning unwitting hypocrites, Jesus declared, "Not everyone who says to me, 'Lord, Lord,' will enter the kingdom of heaven, but only he who does the will of my Father who is in heaven" (Matthew 7:21).
- Answering the rich young ruler's question about how to inherit eternal life, he said, "If you want enter life, obey the commandments" (Matthew 19:17).
- When parting from his followers, Jesus exhorted them, "If you love me, you will obey what I command" (John 14:15).
- His Great Commission included, not just making new disciples and baptizing them, but also "teaching them to obey all that I have commanded you" (Matthew 28:20).

There's no way around it: Jesus expects us to obey God's will.

Other New Testament writers say the same. For example, Peter addressed a letter "To God's elect . . . who have been chosen . . . for obedience to Jesus Christ" (1 Peter 1:1–2). The writer of the letter to the Hebrews said that Jesus "became the source of eternal salvation to all who obey him" (Hebrews 5:9). And James, of course, said, "Be doers of the word, and not hearers only" (James 1:22).

Jesus' apostles were, therefore, in agreement with him. In their teaching, obedience is not an option. It's not an add-on. It's fundamental.

But teaching is one thing; example is another.

If you're like me, the most important lessons we've learned have come more from example than from words of wisdom. So, as disciples of Jesus, what should we be learning about obedience from Jesus' own life? During the days he walked the earth, was he centrally or only peripherally concerned about obedience?

Answer: he lived and breathed obedience . . . and sometimes struggled with it, as you and I do.

An Obedient Son

In the Garden of Gethsemane, the disciples were sleepy after a long day and a good meal. Jesus, however, knowing the suffering that awaited him the next day, was the furthest thing from sleepy. He was in agony. Everything in his humanity wanted to run away from the sacrifice his Father was calling him to.

In this event as in no other we see the veil pulled back on Jesus' emotions. Telling the disciples that he was "very sorrowful, even to death," he fell facedown to pray. Three times he asked his Father to take away the cup of suffering. But each time he concluded his request with words of submission: "Not as I *will*, but as you *will*" (Matthew 26:36–45, ESV, emphasis added).

At this most defining point of temptation, did Christ hold steady? He did. When the book of Philippians says that Jesus was "obedient to the point of death, even death on a cross," this is what it means (2:8, ESV).

But in reality Jesus was just continuing the pattern of obedience that had marked his life all along. Consider these words of Jesus.

- "My food is to do the will of him who sent me and to finish his work" (John 4:34).
- "I seek not my own will but the will of him who sent me" (5:30).
- "I have come down from heaven, not to do my will but to do the will of him who sent me" (6:38).

- "I do nothing on my own, but speak just what the Father taught me" (8:28).
- "The words I say to you are not just my own. Rather, it is the Father, living in me, who is doing his works" (14:10).[2]

We have discussed obedience in terms of our relationship with God. Jesus' obedience to God was what most defined his relationship to his Father. There was no separation between the wills of the Father and Jesus while Jesus did his work here on earth. The Father was with Jesus every moment, every step of the way, speaking to him, empowering him, guiding him in what he should say and do. His Father was at work in everything Jesus did.

As I meditate on the teachings and example of Jesus, I begin to take in the beauty of Jesus' relationship with his Father, expressed in Jesus' devotion to hear his Father clearly, to understand his will precisely, and to do it perfectly. That was Jesus' food—that is what gave him delight and happiness, that is what made his day. In his last recorded prayer, Jesus reflected with his Father, "I have brought you glory on earth by completing the work you gave me to do" (John 17:4). External circumstances were of little consequence. What mattered was hearing God, doing his work and finishing it.

And so, what about us?

Jesus' beloved disciple, John, declared, "Whoever claims to live in him must walk as Jesus walked" (1 John 2:6). Jesus' driving passion was obedience to God; so must be ours. It's what our faith in him should make us eager to do.

Of course, the obedience of the Son to the Father was not limited to a few years here on earth. It exists in eternity as the pattern for us as creatures to imitate. C. S. Lewis writes:

> Now the proper good of a creature is to surrender itself to its Creator—to enact intellectually, volitionally, and emotionally, that relationship which is given in the mere fact of its being a creature. When it does so, it is *good and happy*. Lest we should think this is a hardship, this kind

of good begins on a level far above the creatures, for God Himself, as Son, from all eternity renders back to God as Father by filial *obedience* the being which the Father, by paternal love eternally generates in the Son. This is the pattern which man was made to imitate—which Paradisal man did imitate—and whenever the *will* conferred by the Creator is thus perfectly offered back in delighted and delighting *obedience* by the creature, there, most undoubtedly, is Heaven, and there the Holy Ghost proceeds. (Emphasis added)[3]

What is C. S. Lewis telling us? As creatures, we were made to be obedient to the Creator, and when we are obedient, we are *"good and happy."* Christ as the Son renders filial obedience to his Father perfectly and eternally, and when we follow his example, we can glimpse what heaven is all about.

One final point. Obedience is so central to the divine order of creation that Christ's perfect obedience was required for our redemption (Romans 5:19). George MacDonald, always provocative, writes, "With all the sovereignty in the world, Christ could not save us but by obedience."[4] This profound truth alone should be sufficient to galvanize our attention to the subject of obedience and cause us to plead to God for his grace to empower and guide us in obedience.

For, as we all know, obedience is a struggle, even for the greats of our faith.

A Sinner Finds Happiness

It's an old story. A young man tries to find the good life in the ways that seem best to him. Sexually self-indulgent, he has the first in a string of lovers when he's just a teenager, going on to father a child out of wedlock. Spiritually curious, he adopts one of the trendy alternative religions that's available. Ambitious, he earns a name for himself as a university professor and while barely in his thirties lands a post at the pinnacle of the academic world. Yet when everything in his life seems to be going as well as it could, he's miserable and questioning what he should be doing with his life.

In this case, it's a *really* old story. Aurelius Augustinus—better known to us as Saint Augustine—lived in the fourth and fifth centuries A.D.

At first resistant to the Christian faith, Augustine became more open to it over time. The tearful prayers of his mother, Monica, and the preaching of the local bishop, Ambrose, saw to that. Faith in Jesus made sense to him, but he hesitated before committing himself.

Augustine had begun to have doubts about the teachings of his chosen religion—a now mostly forgotten cult known as Manichaeism. So that wasn't keeping him back from Christian faith.

He also was attracted to the idea of spending his time studying Christian truth, in part because he was ready to give up his job as professor of rhetoric at the imperial Roman court. (One day, while riding in a carriage to deliver a speech before the emperor, he lamented that a drunken beggar he passed on the street had an easier life than he did! Earthly pleasures have never satisfied.) His career wasn't holding him up either.

But giving up his women *was* a problem for him. So much pleasure was there. Obeying God's rules of sexual morality seemed impossible to Augustine and God left him free to continue his life of sexual pleasure. Augustine agonized and delayed before being willing to obey God and finally accept God's gift of grace through a simple trust in Jesus.

In many ways life didn't get easier for Augustine after turning to Jesus. He broke an engagement to marry a socially well-placed young woman. His mother and son died. He took a vow of chastity. He got roped into church duties he didn't want. He had endless labors and more than a little controversy to work through.

But still, there was no comparison with his former life. He would never want to go back to his prior existence. Why? Because now he knew that he was right with God and his will was to do God's will. To put it simply, he was obedient, he had a deep fellowship with God, and he was happy.

Perhaps now we are on the same page in acknowledging that creation's obedience to physical laws is essential to life, that obedience to earthly authority is essential to the quality of our lives, and that faithful obedience to God is at the center of biblical teaching and the divine order. But what exactly does that kind of obedience look like? We'll get into that next.

CHAPTER 6
The Obedience in the Obedience of Faith

IN OUR EARTHLY courts of law, the question used in determining innocence or guilt is usually straightforward: Did a person abide by the prescribed law or break it? What do the facts say about that?

But in an environment of law *and* grace, the matter is not so straightforward. God's will is not laid out in its entirety in books. Actions are not all that matter to the court of heavenly inquiry; motive and attitude matter too. The obedience of faith is not mere obedience to a code. Obedience of faith is spiritual, personal, and from the heart.

We need to ask what life looks like for the Christian when faith and obedience are wedded. There are several points that will help us get a sense of balance before we go further. They all illustrate what happens when grace (through faith) is added to obedience. Here's a preview of what we're going to discover about the nature of faithful obedience:

- It's more than just obeying the Bible's commands; it's also following God's individual direction for our lives.
- It's more than just what we do; it's also doing it out of love.
- It's more than just doing what seems like the right thing to us; it's also doing what God tells us is the right thing.
- It's more than just obeying because we have to; it's also obeying because we want to.

Two Sources of God's Will

We all have a tendency early on to ask, "What exactly is it we are supposed to obey?"

It's a good question! And the answer is that we are basically talking about two kinds of obedience.

To begin with, we're talking about . . .

1. Biblical Commands

By the reckoning of the ancient rabbis, the Old Testament law contains 613 separate commands. Christian theologians over the centuries have attempted to assign these laws to categories, such as moral laws, civil laws, and ceremonial laws, and have typically declared that the moral laws are still in effect for Christians while the others were to serve a purpose for the Jewish nation that has already been accomplished. The Ten Commandments have a special standing as enduring benchmarks of God's will for his people.

The New Testament precepts often reiterate commands from the Old Testament or are otherwise in line with God's will from the era before Christ's (God's moral character never changes). But the New Testament's ethical teaching tends to have a different flavor—precepts, principles, and parables as well as commands.

Taking them all together, these Old and New Testament commands include things we are *not to do* (examples: don't murder, don't be greedy, avoid sexual immorality) and things we are *to do* (examples: provide for the poor, bless those who persecute us, submit to the governing authorities). This means that, just as there are sins of omission and sins of commission, so there is also the obedience of omission and the obedience of commission.

It's not my purpose to try to give a comprehensive picture of biblical commands. Instead, it's my hope to instill in all of us a hunger for pleasing God through trusting obedience. So let me just say here that if we know that God has given a command in the Scriptures, we shouldn't argue with it, we shouldn't seek to find excep-

Bob Jepson

Challenge Grant

$125,000. —
Enrollment Mgt.

+

$125,000 Same
toward Condos

tions, we shouldn't hesitate; we should just do it. It's for our good, and for the greater good, and it will lead us toward increased long-term happiness. God's will expressed in commands is "good, pleasing and perfect" (Romans 12:2).

But of course there is more to obeying God than following commandments. There is . . .

2. Individual Leading

God, principally through his Holy Spirit and Word, gives each of us personal guidance for a unique path he has for each of us. Being led by the Holy Spirit is a hallmark of all who are children of God (Romans 8:14). It looks different for each one of us, but the Holy Spirit is there to guide us in the path of our work-lives, warn us about a dangerous relationship, nudge us toward a type of ministry, soften our hearts toward a needy person, prompt us to forgive someone who has wronged us, or give us any number of other leadings.

It's this type of obedience that shows most clearly how obedience does not have to be a passive, dour submission to a set of imperatives. Obedience can be bold, revolutionary, anti-authoritative. It can take us on an adventure with God as it did Abraham and Moses, Martin Luther and Martin Luther King Jr., William Wilberforce and Chuck Colson!

As Bruce Wilkinson has said, "True faithfulness . . . is extraordinary entrepreneurial excellence.[5]"

Jesus' perfect obedience to his Father's will is our model. And in this obedience he obeyed the commands of his Father. But the obedience that Jesus emphasized most is to God's plan for his life on earth, doing his Father's will, and completing the work the Father gave him to do (John 6:38; 15:10; 17:4). When Paul writes of Jesus' being obedient to death, Paul is speaking of Jesus' being faithful to God's plan for his life, "even [to] death on the cross" (Philippians 2:8).

Likewise for us. The commands of God written in Scripture

and in our hearts are to be kept, but the overarching purpose of our lives is living into God's calling and finishing all the work he has planned for us to do in the redemption of his creation. One can live scrupulously by the law and miss altogether the reason God gave him life.

Of course, these kinds of personal directives are not always as clear to us as are commands in the Bible. And of course, they do not come with the infallibility that attaches to biblical commands—we can be wrong about them. But God does lead us in personal ways because he has a personalized plan for our lives. (We will discuss this more thoroughly in Chapter 24 on calling.) Our part is to obey.

Two Approaches to Obedience

Just as there are two sources of God's will, so there are also two approaches to obedience. The first approach has to do with . . .

1. What We Do

When we give our first thoughts to obedience, we think about what we do. And of course, the *what* of obedience is of vital importance. We've learned that the *what* of obedience includes both biblical commands and God's individual direction for us.

But while the *what* is important, the *how* is also critical. We do well to remember the old saying "God loveth the adverbs," referring to those *–ly* words that describe how something is done.

And that brings us directly to the second approach to obeying God, which is . . .

2. How We Do It

The obedience of faith is from the heart. God could have created human robots that look and act as we do. He could have even given them flesh and blood. He could have programmed them to obey his laws as perfectly as do the stars and planets. But he did not. He created us for loving relationships with himself and others, and *how* we relate to others is a critical part of *what* we do in relation to them.

Paul provides the Bible's simplest and most vivid teaching on the importance of *how* we produce fruit.

> If I speak in the tongues of men and of angels, but have not love, I am a noisy gong or a clanging cymbal. And if I have prophetic powers, and understand all mysteries and all knowledge, and if I have all faith, so as to remove mountains, but have not love, I am nothing. If I give away all I have, and if I deliver up my body to be burned, but have not love, I gain nothing. (1 Corinthians 13:1–3, ESV)

In other words, if love (*how* we do it) is not a part of *what* we do, then the *what* is a waste of time and energy.

The Bible puts more emphasis on the quality of our obedience than on the deed itself. The fruit of the Holy Spirit is expressed in terms of quality, not quantity. Our obedience is to be done not only lovingly but also patiently, gently, joyfully, and so on. The Pharisees did the things of the law in meticulous detail, but that gave no pleasure to our Lord. They obeyed in a self-centered way, not in love.

If we are to please God in our obedience, if we are to enjoy the happiness that comes from the fellowship of faithful obedience, our hearts need to be filled with the Holy Spirit so that the fruit of our deeds honors him. Grantland Rice, the great sportswriter who also could capture biblical truth in poetry, summed it up well:

When the Great Scorer
Comes to mark against your name,
It matters not that you won or lost
But how you played the game.[6]

Two Ways to Obey

There are two ways we can approach our relationship with God in general and our obedience in particular. We can call the first one . . .

1. Our Way

When we obey God "our way," we rely on our own best judgment and personal abilities and ask God to bless their output.

For example, let's look at a simple example of creating a new business enterprise. One approach ("our way")—by sincere, well-meaning Christians—would be to assemble a great team, put minds together, find the capital, create a strategy, abide by biblical principles and human laws, and present the enterprise to God for his blessing.

That might be fine as far as it goes, but God's will is essentially ignored except for a prayer to bless our efforts. But it might not be really what God wants. More than "our way," we have to focus on . . .

2. God's Way

In its simplest terms, "God's way" is *the* way. By maintaining a fellowship with God in which we commit everything to him, we can walk in *the* way, following his plan. And his plan often looks different from what we might create on our own.

Let's think about this second approach, again with regard to a new business. Following God's way, we would at the outset and through prayer and discussion seek his will as to whether to commence the project. Then we would commit the entire process to God and trust him to guide and equip us, so that, as best our hearts and minds could discern, the company's team and strategy would be built in accordance with his will. The whole project and process from start to finish, day by day, hour by hour, would be entrusted to God and for his glory.

When we take this latter course, a fellowship in prayer and dialogue and a partnership in work are formed with Christ that gives us joy, peace, and a sense of assurance. In the process, we have happiness.

The counsel of Proverbs—"Commit to the Lord whatever you do, and your plans will succeed" (Proverbs 16:3)—can and should apply equally to church and business work, "whatever" we do. And in every such commitment and partnership, and in the success flowing from it, there is much happiness.

But I think you will agree with me that we are all continuously slipping from God's way to our way. I certainly do. We can get so involved in our work that we become too busy to pray or we think the project is too routine. Or—to tell the truth—we can become lazy when things are working smoothly.

Of course, when things begin to go awry, when our uncommitted plans are failing, we again turn to God.

We should thank God for such problems. The Bible teaches that we learn obedience through suffering, for suffering turns us to God to seek his way and his blessing (Hebrews 5:9).

How many made investments, took out home-equity loans or borrowed on a credit card without committing the decision to Christ in 2004–2006 and then turned to him in 2008–2009 and prayed, "O Lord, give me wisdom and help me out of this mess"? For those who belong to Christ, suffering always brings us back to him, re-establishes fellowship and partnership, and moves us from our way to his and into the happiness that grows from this obedience.

Two Motives for Obedience

We've seen two objects of obedience: biblical commands and Holy Spirit leading. Two approaches to obedience—what we do and how we do it. And two ways of obeying—our way and God's way.

Finally, there are two motives for obedience. Why should we obey God? Let's start with . . .

1. The lower motivation—duty

We do a lot of things just because we have to. The company we work for requires us to move from a community we love. Or our boss directs us to work on the weekend. Or the government makes us pay taxes. This kind of direction does not add pleasure to our lives. But what can we do? The message is, obey—or else! We hear it, we do it.

Is this why we should obey God—because we have to?

In Chapter 3 we met a dominant philosophical party in the ancient world, the Epicureans, who advocated a hedonistic indulgence of one's desires. Epicureanism, we learned, is *not* what brings happiness.

But there was another major philosophical party back then: the Stoics. In many ways the opposites of the Epicureans, the Stoics encouraged the determined, unemotional fulfilling of one's duties. Whereas the Epicureans were all about pleasure, the Stoics were all about honor. They were heavy into owner-manual obedience. That, they believed, was the route to happiness.

There's something admirable about the Stoics' emphasis on duty, or obligation. But for us as Christians, that is only a part, and not the better part, of our motivation in obeying God.

It's true that God has all authority and every right to demand our compliance. Speaking to the ancient Israelites, he outlined curses for disobedience and blessings for obedience. Even Paul warned of wrath for disobedience to God (See Romans 1:18-32). So we should be willing to obey if for no other reason than that God tells us to. If (for example) someone avoids committing adultery for fear of the wrath of God, that is more noble (at least in human terms) than committing the sin.

But we're left dissatisfied by this motivation for obedience. Certainly it is not, in itself, a source of much happiness. We need something more to open our hearts to doing God's will, and that is . . .

2. The higher motivation—love

In the second motive of obedience, we obey, not because we have to, but because we want to. Through faith we believe that God has made us and loves us. He has redeemed us and come to dwell in us. He has given us all manner of earthly and spiritual benefits and will be in and beside us in all we do in accordance with his will. And so, because of our love and gratitude toward God, we delight to comply with his laws and plan for our lives.

While obligation may be the motivation of some obedience where faith is lacking, the essential motivation in obedience comes from gratitude for who God is and what he has done and will do for us in his love, which we accept only by faith. Motivated by love for God and the gratitude that is a part of it, we obey, and this always leads to the fullness of happiness. The Holy Spirit transforms our minds and our desires so that we want to do God's will. Over time, the burden of a commitment to obligation is replaced with the freedom and joy of gratitude.

Love-based obedience is the key to happiness. It is not conformity to a written code. It is not grim determination to obey from a sense of obligation. It is essentially a spontaneous reaction to do whatever pleases our Lord Jesus Christ because we know how much he loved us when he created us, how he became a man to teach us and show us, how he died to redeem us, how he gave us the Holy Spirit to empower us, and how he lives at the throne of grace forever interceding for our benefit.

The obedience of faith is summed up in Jesus' parting counsel to his disciples, "If you love me, you will keep my commandments" (John 14:15, ESV).

When our daughter, Sissy, was a senior in high school, she was giving my wife and me fits by paying little attention to our rules and guidance. We laugh now at the "contracts" I had her sign. Finally my wife, Fairfax, said to me, "It's only four months before she goes to college and will be out of our control anyway. Why don't we quit trying to force her to obey our rules? Let's allow her to experience freedom now and see how she deals with it."

I was uncertain about this. But I went along with it . . . and a funny thing happened. Sissy started behaving better during her last months in our home. She went on to have a successful college experience, and today she is as responsible a young woman as you could find.

My daughter's experience shows that we respond better when we take it on ourselves to do what is right because we want to, not because we feel we have to.

In this life, disciples of Jesus have mixed motives for obedience, but all of us are somewhere along the road from obligation to gratitude. In heaven, I'm sure, the motive is pure love and gratitude.

From Duty to Love: A Personal Journey

I'm the sort of person who loves working. I have too often made work an idol. This bent of my personality influences my life of faith, too. Being casual about what I believe, or how I act as a believer, is just not in me. (My wife once called me a "hair shirt Christian," comparing me to ancient monks who put on shirts lined with prickly hair to make life less enjoyable.) So no doubt I possess more than the usual inclination to obey rules. In ancient Greece I would have been a Stoic. Nevertheless, as I look back over my three decades of following Christ, I can see a shift that's taken place in my approach toward obedience.

Early on, I would obey God's commands out of a sense of duty. My thought was that, since God is Almighty and I am his creature, I must do what he tells me. So I strove to permeate my work life with honor toward God, to keep my language pure, to be generous to the poor, to serve in the church, and to live by the other biblical commands. Not that I did it (or now do it) well, but nevertheless I felt it was my responsibility to live up to God's code.

Over time, though, while the *what* of my obedience is not radically different from when I was a new Christian, my *motivation* for the obedience has changed and therefore my joy in the obedient life has changed as well (and so has, hopefully, the joy I bring to others). Obeying God really has become more and more a delight to me. I want to do it. I look forward to it. Through it I have a deeper, more intimate fellowship with Christ.

What has happened in me is the result of God's grace. It is not my doing at all. All growth in obedience is by grace through faith. It takes place as our hearts are filled more fully in the Holy Spirit and our old selfish nature is put to death. And in my case, by the way, the old selfish nature has been a tough dragon to slay.

I hope it's becoming clearer now that that the obedience of faith is at the heart of biblical teaching. Thinking about the obedience of faith is the soul food this book has to offer. And the next helping shows how faith and obedience are wed. In the following two chapters, we'll learn how grace and love help us to understand the combination of faith and obedience.

What God has joined together, let no man put asunder.

CHAPTER 7
The Marriage of Faith and Obedience, Part 1

WHAT IF OBEDIENCE was elevated to the same rank as faith? What if obedience was not a threat to faith but its marriage partner? What if, in fact, obedience and faith were mutually dependent and, when combined, produced a powerful synergy that is the key to a happy life?

In fact, they are.

In this connection let's think of what the apostle Paul said in Colossians 2:6:

"As you received Christ Jesus the Lord . . ." *That's faith.*
". . . so walk in him." *That's obedience.*

There it is, all in one short, flowing sentence. Faith and obedience—they belong together. In fact they are wed one to the other, as we will see in this chapter and the next.

Let me assure you that I am not standing on my own as I make this point.

Voices for Obedience and Faith

The intimate connection between faith and obedience and its good works is mainstream teaching from great minds throughout the centuries of the Christian era and across the Christian theological spectrum. Skim over the following selections if you don't believe me.

Martin Luther:
It is impossible to separate works from faith, quite as impossible as to separate heat and light from fire.[7]

George MacDonald:
Do you find it hard to trust [Christ]? Hard it will remain while the things he tells you to do, things you can do, you will not try! True faith, true belief, is not possible where there is not a daily doing of the things he says.[8]

Andrew Murray:
Obedience and faith are but two aspects of one act—surrender to God and his will. As faith strengthens for obedience, it is in turn strengthened by it.[9]

Charles Spurgeon:
It has been supposed by many badly instructed people that the doctrine of justification by faith is opposed to the teaching of good works, or obedience. There is no truth in the supposition. We who believe in justification by faith teach the obedience of faith.[10]

K. H. Von Bogatzky
Whenever there is a true faith, it must fix on Jesus Christ alone for salvation; that is its principal act. This same faith unites to Christ; and where there is union, there must be love; and where there is love, there must be obedience; and where there is obedience, there will be a reward of grace; and when the reward is acknowledged to be of grace, and not of merit, God will have all the glory in time and eternity.[11]

Dietrich Bonhoeffer:
[T]he following two propositions hold good and are equally true; only he who believes is obedient, and only he who is obedient believes....

66

[There is an] essential [unity between obedience and faith]. Faith is real where there is obedience, never without it, and faith only becomes faith in the act of obedience.[12]

Karl Barth:
Faith differs from any mere thinking and believing and knowing, or indeed from any other trusting, in the fact it is an obeying. . . . The humility of faith is the humility of obedience.[13]

D. Martyn Lloyd-Jones:
What is the purpose of doctrine? Obedience. Any so-called faith that does not put its emphasis on obedience is not worthy of the name.[14]

Watchman Nee:
The purpose of life becomes single: to do the will of God . . . to obey Him becomes the sole objective of life.[15]

John Paul II:
It is urgent to rediscover and to set forth once more the authentic reality of the Christian faith, which is not simply a set of propositions to be accepted with intellectual assent. Rather, faith is a lived knowledge of Christ, a living remembrance of his commandments, and a truth to be lived out.[16]

Charles Colson:
Obedience is the key to real faith.[17]

John Piper:
The obedience God loves is the obedience of faith. Faith and obedience are necessarily connected as root and branch.[18]

The Apostle of Obedience

All of the voices sampled above are actually echoes. They are echoing the apostle Paul when he first spoke of "the obedience of faith," firmly uniting the two concepts that we modern Christians have too often tended to separate.

What's interesting here is that Paul has a reputation for his emphasis on grace and faith as opposed to works or obedience. After all, the apostle famously said, "By grace you have been saved through faith. And this is not your own doing; it is the gift of God, not a result of works, so that no one may boast" (Ephesians 2:8–9, ESV). Paul also taught that our "righteousness . . . is by faith from first to last" and that "no one will be declared righteous . . . by observing the law" (Romans 1:17; 3:20).

So, given these strong words about grace and faith, what place does obedience have in Paul's thinking? The answer is that it is front, center, and deep. For Paul, the obedience of faith is at the heart of the gospel!

I'll prove it to you.

Take out your Bible and flip to the first page of Paul's great letter to the Romans. Look at the opening verses, where he addresses his readers. If you are using the same version I have, it reads like this:

Book of Romans Opening

> Paul, a servant of Christ Jesus, . . . through whom we have received grace and apostleship to bring about *the obedience of faith* for the sake of his name among all the nations. . . . (Romans 1:1, 4, ESV, emphasis added)

Did you see it? Right there at the start of Romans: the obedience of faith.

We need to pause and think about this. What was the purpose of Paul's calling to be an apostle? Certainly it was to take the gospel to the Gentiles (Acts 26:17–18). Certainly it was to teach them to believe on the Lord Jesus Christ and to be saved through his atonement by faith. But the *overarching* purpose that Paul highlights in the introduction to his magisterial letter was to bring about the obedience of faith among all nations.

Now flip to the end of the letter. How does Paul *finish* Romans?

Book of Romans Ending

> Now to him who is able to strengthen you according to my gospel . . . that . . . has now been . . . made known to all nations, according to the command of the eternal God, to bring about *the obedience of faith*—to the only wise God be glory forevermore through Jesus Christ! Amen. (Romans 16:25–27, ESV, emphasis added)

There it is again. The gospel and the preaching of Jesus Christ have as their goal to bring about the obedience of faith. This was the last word Paul had for his readers in Rome.

In his commentary on Romans, the preeminent Reformed theologian, Charles Hodge states that the obedience of faith is "the obedience of which faith is the controlling principle. The design of apostleship was to bring all nations to believe in Christ the Son of God that they should be entirely devoted to his service."[19] We believe, we obey. Obedience proceeds from and completes faith.

Discerning the will of God and conforming our lives to God's will through faith and in the power of God's grace was central to Paul's teaching.

- Paul's great Colossians prayer includes these words: "That God may fill you with the knowledge of his will through all spiritual wisdom and understanding. . . in order that you may live a life worthy of the Lord, and may please him in every way, bearing fruit in every good work. . . ." (Colossians 1:9–10).
- He admonished the Romans that they "be transformed by the renewing of your mind. . . to test and approve what God's will is" and through faith obey that will (12:2).
- He emphasized that enabling the good works of our obedience of faith was the fundamental purpose behind the cross: "Jesus Christ . . . gave himself for us . . . to purify for himself a people for his own possession who are zealous for

good works" (Titus 2:13–14, ESV).

What is the ultimate purpose of the gospel for Paul? It is not merely that we be "saved" in the sense that we are justified through faith. Justification is comparable to admitting students to a university. It is a vitally essential first step. The ultimate purpose of the gospel, however, is to bring forth a faith through which we are motivated and empowered to be obedient to the will and purpose of God for our lives, thus living a life that glorifies him.

We need to give up our either/or thinking about faith and obedience. It's not either/or. It's both-and. To quote John Piper again, "Faith and obedience are joined as root and branch."

Because of the intimate connection of obedience to faith, as we have said, any basic understanding of obedience begins with the idea of *aligning our wills with God's will by faith through grace.* This reminds us that obedience is not conforming to a code but rather agreeing with the lover of our souls. It also reminds us that we can't be obedient through our own exertion. Only as God works his grace in us through our faith in the Son can we hope to obey him.

The role of faith in the obedience of faith is to connect our obedience (or we can say our walk) to the grace of God. Faith is a connector; grace is the power source. Our obedience flows from the power of grace.

Faith—Connection to Grace

God called George Mueller and appointed him to a ministry to orphans in Bristol, England, in 1836. These were the days before governments provided any care for impoverished and abandoned children. When Mueller responded to God's call, he resolved to trust God entirely for the financial resources for the ministry—and he did. He never asked anyone for a penny to support the work. By prayer and in faith, he trusted God to provide—and God did. Ultimately the ministry built on trust grew to feed and house more than five hundred orphans, to run a Christian school, and even to support a large part of Hudson Taylor's foreign mission in China.

The financial resources for this work all flowed from the faithful prayers of a pauper on his knees. I do not know of a single believer who from current income contributes more to kingdom work than George Mueller received, on his knees, trusting God to provide the needs of the orphans and the Chinese mission.

Mueller's profound faith connected his work to God's grace, and by grace, his work thrived.

In Romans, Paul teaches that, "since we have been justified through faith, we . . . have gained access by faith into this grace in which we now stand" (Romans 5:1–2). How do we have access to grace? "By faith."

We are born again through faith, and thereafter the entire Christian life is a walk of faith. The strength for this walk comes as faith connects the humble heart to the grace of God.

Martin Luther based his theology on a new understanding of faith that revolutionized the Christian world. In explaining faith in his famous preface to his commentary on the book of Romans, Luther said that faith is a "living, daring confidence in the grace of God" that "makes [us] glad and bold and happy" as we walk with Christ in the way he has prepared for us.[20]

What was Luther saying? Faith is living and dynamic, daring and creative. It is the source of life and vitality in believers. Faith makes us confident, bold, and happy in obedience. It was this kind of unshakable trust in God's grace that empowered Mueller's obedience in the 19th Century and John Rucyahana's and Nita Thompson's today. It was this kind of trust that is shown in the heroes of the faith we extol—Abraham, Moses, Joshua, David, the prophets, Paul, and most of all Jesus himself. They trusted in God's grace and were empowered to do great things for him.

Grace Through Faith

The word "grace" is used in two ways in the Bible. First, it is the unmerited favor of God for forgiveness. By grace through faith in Christ, we are pardoned from our sins. Second, grace also refers to the love of God expressed both in his power that enables us to live into his purposes for our lives and also in his all-sufficient provision to meet our needs as we do so. We can call this grace for living. It was written all over Mueller's life. Peter teaches that we are to "use whatever gifts [we have] received to serve others, faithfully administering God's *grace* in its various forms" (1 Peter 4:10, emphasis added). How do we "serve others"? We administer God's grace through faith. And Paul writes to the Corinthians that "all *grace* [may] abound to you, so that having all sufficiency in all things at all times, you may abound in every good work" (2 Corinthians 9:8, ESV, emphasis added). How do we "abound in every good work"? By abounding in grace by faith.

Likewise faith has the same two dimensions. There is justifying faith, which looks back to what Jesus has done for us once and for all. And there is the faith that drove George Mueller's work, a living faith in God's grace for daily power and provision through which we are strengthened to do all that God has planned for us to do.

This living faith that connects us to God's grace for living is illustrated repeatedly in Scripture.

Throughout his ministry, Christ performed miracle after miracle, but he attributed the power for the miracles to the faith of those he healed (see, for example, Matthew 8:10; 9:2; Mark 5:34). When he went into his hometown, Nazareth, he was unable to perform many miracles because of the people's lack of faith (Matthew 13:53–58). God's grace in Christ's miracles was administered through the trust of those healed in that grace.

The connection of faith and grace is illustrated at the time of Christ's death, when the Lord was aware that Satan had asked to destroy Peter, "sifting him like wheat." Christ had the power to protect Peter from Satan, but direct intervention was not his way. Instead, he told Peter, "I have prayed for you that your faith may not fail" (Luke 22:31–32, ESV). The power of God's grace was available to Peter to resist the onslaught of the devil, but this grace was not to flow from God to Peter unmediated by faith. It was faith that was to connect Peter to the grace of God and thereby to be Peter's shield.

Though faith is a personal thing, we can understand its functional dimension as being like a gasoline hose that allows fuel to flow into the engine. Living faith is a conduit between man and God. It is neither the power (God's grace) nor the engine (man's character) that puts the power to its intended use. Faith depends on both. A gasoline hose is useless without the source (gasoline) and something that works (an engine).

This principle is at the heart of James's teaching that "faith by itself, if it is not accompanied by action, is dead" (James 2:17). And on the other hand, without faith, our obedience is legalism—it leads to deadly pride.

The metaphor of the gasoline hose is helpful as far as it goes. God is the power source; grace is the power; faith is the hose that transmits it, and we are empowered. But God's grace does more than provide power. When the power is put to use through the obedience of faith, it builds and transforms our characters. To complete the metaphor, God's grace is like a gasoline that can transform a junk heap into a Lexus while at the same time propelling it down the road. For the process to work through the obedience of faith we must keep the car on God's road. When we detour to take our own road, the process breaks down.

Faith and Fiber

For three years, actor Stephen Lang performed the one-actor play *Beyond Glory*, which brings to life the courage of eight recipients of the Congressional Medal of Honor, the highest honor that can be given a U.S. soldier for valor. For instance, one of the soldiers Lang portrayed was Admiral James Stockdale, who spent seven years as a prisoner of war at Hoa Lo Prison, the "Hanoi Hilton."

On the day the play finally closed, Lang was asked, "What do you think *Beyond Glory* is about?"

His answer: "For the longest time I couldn't give it a name. I finally concluded that what bonds these men is faith and fiber."[21]

That sums it up pretty well. Faith needs fiber. Faith needs obedience as the root needs the branch. Obedience needs faith as the branch needs the root.

Some may object that I have lapsed into "works righteousness." But the point I am making is not that we earn our acceptance with God by obedience. Rather, it is that the faith that saves without works, unrelated to merit, through grace alone, will inevitably by grace produce both the desire and the strength to obey. We will not come to perfectly obey, but we will move in the direction of faithful obedience more and more over the course of a lifetime.

So faith connects grace to a life of obedience.

Belief, Trust, and Obedience—Spiraling Together in Faith

Looking at faith as a cord that connects God's power to our lives, it is as if the cord has three strands spiraled together. The first two strands are "belief" and "trust." The word "faith" is our translation of the Greek word *pistis*, which can mean either "belief" or "trust." There is in faith both a belief element and a trust element. Faith is most fundamentally trust in the testimony of God contained in Scripture. The measure of faith is how deeply we trust his Word. We believe Christ to be our Savior; we trust in him as Savior. We believe that God so loved the world that he gave his Son that all who believe in him might have everlasting life, and we trust that this is the case. But that in which we believe and trust directs what we do.

To believe in something is to act as if it is true, trusting in it. As Bonhoeffer says, "Faith is real when there is obedience, never without it." If we believe that Warren Buffett is an extremely wise investor and trust that the principles he adheres to in investing are valid, then based on that belief and trust, we will follow them. If we don't follow them, we neither believe nor trust them.

Thus the two dimensions of faith, belief and trust, always exist in connection with a third, obedience. And in fact the three—belief, trust, and obedience—not only are connected; they also mutually reinforce and strengthen one another.

Let us take a simple example from golf.

One of the great golfers of the 20th century was Ben Hogan. He won seventy-one championships and dominated the PGA in the mid-20th century. Following his successful career as a pro, he wrote a short book entitled *Five Lessons: The Modern Fundamentals of Golf.*[22] This book has since become a classic and is read widely by aspiring golfers.

Why do golfers read the book? We read it because we believe Hogan to have been a great golfer and the book to be a classic, and thus we have an initial degree of trust in the validity of what it says. We read the book and learn the five lessons. Likely they make sense and we believe them. So we have trust in the book and an initial belief in the principles set forth in the book.

All of that, however, is useless unless we put the principles into practice. Therefore, the golfer goes to the practice tee and seeks to apply what the book taught. It may seem awkward at first, but if the golfer perseveres, and as he puts the fundamentals into practice, he may begin to see their validity. Therefore, he has a deeper trust in the book and believes what it teaches more fully.

After practice, the golfer plays a round and the principles work to bring his score down a stroke or two. He goes back to the book to be assured that he properly understands the principles, practices them more, and applies them in his game. His score may come down a stroke or two more.

What we have here is a mutually reinforcing and strengthening combination of trust, belief, and obedience. Take the obedience factor out, and the trust and belief will die.

We need to see that obedience is much more than what we do. It is a catalytic agent at work deep in our souls. Obedience is seen in its external deeds. But by grace obedience is also active internally to strengthen faith in our souls.

Obedience in Football

When Nick Saban became head coach of the University of Alabama football team in 2007, it was soon apparent that serious change had come to the program. Saban expected *much* of his players. Practices were tough and highly regimented. The players were instructed to run, not walk, from one drill to the next. Outside of practices, the young men were expected to engage in rigorous weight training. They had to go to class and study.

That first year Saban was at Alabama, some players accustomed to less discipline under the prior regime tried to just slide by. They went through the motions of following Coach Saban's regimen, but as much as possible, they avoided real compliance with his give-it-everything-you've-got approach. It wasn't simply a case of laziness; they did not believe in the Saban system.

The result? The team fell victim to disunity and its record for the season was a disappointing 7-6.

The second year of the Saban era at Alabama provided a different story. Now the dissidents were gone, some talented freshmen had entered, and all the players had come to realize that the Saban way would produce success. When the coach spoke, they listened and did what he said to do.

They won games—in fact, the first twelve games of the season. A bond developed between the team and Saban. He saw them as a special group and they praised him and his system. The Crimson Tide players experienced the joy and fulfillment that come from winning.

What happened between the first and second years? The players had come to trust Saban, believe what he said was true, and follow his instruction. It was not imposed discipline that produced the obedience. After all, the players were free to leave the system, and some did. Rather, trust and confidence (we can call it faith) produced the obedience.

And now we know "the rest of the story." In the third year, the team was undefeated and won the national championship.

Football is not life (although in Alabama we claim that it is), yet the same principles in operation on Coach Saban's team are in operation for us. When we as Christians resist the call to obedience to God, it is simply because we do not trust him nor believe that what he says is true and for our happiness.

We've accomplished a lot in this chapter in understanding how tightly faith and obedience are intertwined and mutually dependent. But we have more to think about in fully understanding the marriage of faith and obedience, and that will take another chapter. The most important part is yet to come.

CHAPTER 8
The Marriage of Faith and Obedience, Part 2

IMAGINE THAT YOU live in the Sudan and are the parent of a single child, a three-year-old girl who is very sick. A medical missionary visiting your village determines that your daughter will die shortly from a liver disorder. The only way she can be cured is through an operation by a team of physicians at Johns Hopkins Hospital.

It sounds like an impossible hope. Johns Hopkins is ten thousand miles from your home. You have no way to get there and no money to pay for the operation even if you could.

You spend a sleepless night grieving over the fate of your daughter.

The next day the missionary doctor tells you that he has contacted the surgery team in Baltimore and they have agreed to perform the operation for the girl at no cost. The doctor will personally fly you and her to Baltimore and then fly both of you back home—still at no cost to you.

The doctor is as good as his word. He takes you both to the United States, the surgery is successful, and the girl returns in perfect health.

If this had really happened to you, what would you not do for that doctor? You would do anything for him, wouldn't you?

And think for a minute: What has prompted such a willingness to please him? Isn't it his love expressed in what he has done for your daughter?

Similarly, yet on *an infinitely higher level*, this is our situation with Christ. Out of his great love for us, he has done so much for us that we want—or at least we *ought* to want—to do anything he would ask of us.

In Chapter 6 we considered the higher motivation for obedience, namely love (as opposed to the lower motivation of duty). Now I would like to dwell for a little while on what makes God worthy of our love and how important it is that we bear such love for him. His love inspires our love—and therefore our willing, eager, happy obedience. There is nothing more delightful to contemplate in the whole subject of the obedience of faith than what our gracious God has done for us!

Compelled by Love

Before we knew Christ, we were "dead in [our] transgressions and sins" and were "objects of wrath" (Ephesians 2:1, 3). A hopeless situation? From our side, yes. From God's, no. Because "God demonstrates his own love for us in this: While we were still sinners, Christ died for us" (Romans 5:8). This is the foundation of the atonement that applies to us personally when we believe in Christ.

And what then? Is our proper response not summed up in the words of the old hymn, "When I Survey the Wondrous Cross"?

> Were the whole realm of nature mine,
> That were a present far too small;
> Love so amazing, so divine,
> Demands my soul, my life, my all.[23]

When through faith we can take in that Christ, who was fully God, gave up all to come to earth to die for our sins so that we, through faith, might have eternal life, what would we not do for him? So, as Paul states time and again, it is in light of Christ who died for us that our obedience flows.

- "Christ's love compels us. . . . He died for all, that those who live should no longer live for themselves but for him

who died for them and was raised again" (2 Corinthians 5:14–15).
- "The life I live in the body, I live by faith in the Son of God, who loved me and gave himself for me" (Galatians 2:20).

We are "compelled" to serve Christ, "eager to do what is good" (Titus 2:14) out of gratitude for his love for us—because Christ died for us. In faith, obedience no longer is a begrudging response to obey the dictates of a written code. Rather, we are eager to do whatever assignment Christ gives us, motivated by a desire to please him flowing by what he has done for us.

Andrew Murray sums it up simply, "Obedience is the loving response to the divine love resting on us."[24]

Inspired by the Blood of the Lamb: The Moravians

There may be no more powerful illustration of the faithful obedience that emanates from Christ's love for us than that of the Moravian brothers and sisters. This courageous community of Christians originated as a group of persecuted Protestant refugees who found sanctuary in what is now eastern Germany in the early 18th century.

Their leader carried the fancy name of Ludwig von Zinzendorf. When he was a young man, he saw a painting of Christ on the cross wearing a crown of thorns entitled *Ecce Homo* ("Behold the Man"). Under the painting was the question "What will you do for me?" Inspired by the message of this painting, Zinzendorf resolved to devote his life and all his possessions to doing Christ's work—we might say, to obeying Christ.

He owned a lot of land and opened it up for the Protestant refugees to settle on. They named the small community Herrnhut, meaning "The Lord's Watch," taken from Isaiah 62:6-7.

The whole community became centered on Christ's Passion and, specifically, the blood of the Lamb. One Sunday in 1727, after a sermon by Zinzendorf, there was a mighty outpouring of the

Holy Spirit, and from that time the community was inflamed with missionary zeal and a spirit of prayer for Christ's kingdom worldwide. That prayer was to continue twenty-four hours a day, every day, for one hundred years.

From this small community, hundreds of Moravians went to the far reaches of civilization, including Western Europe, Iceland, Greenland, the West Indies, and the Americas, fulfilling the Great Commission. They did not plant churches. They worked as laborers among the natives—in the fields, in carpenter shops—as they preached and lived the gospel. Lives were transformed. So were communities.

Notably, it was a Moravian, Peter Bohler, who by God's grace in London had a profound, life-changing influence on John and Charles Wesley. From that influence flowed the Methodist movement, which transformed England.

All because of the great love of these people inspired and motivated by the blood of the Lamb.

And there is still another way God's grace and our faith work together to empower obedience—one that looks forward.

The Confidence to Obey[25]

We are motivated to obey when we look backward to the Cross. We have the courage and confidence to obey when we consider God's all-sufficient love and care to provide for us now and in the future. Remember Luther's comment? Faith is a "daring confidence" in God's grace that makes us "bold and happy." Faith and grace combine for "daring," "bold" confidence because we know, in Paul's words, "If God is for us, who can be against us?" (Romans 8:31).

The most prevalent and powerful theme in the Bible is that God loves us in a way that is indescribably long, deep, wide, and high, that God is omnipotent and omniscient, that his love is forever, and that he will provide for us.

We know this love and trust in this power only by faith. When we grasp it, obedience is a piece of cake, to put it in trite language. The problem, of course, as Jesus noted time and again, is that our faith is so weak, and so therefore is our obedience.

What does the Bible tell us about this love? As we have already seen, it was demonstrated in that, while we were yet sinners, totally undeserving of it, Christ died for us. But there's more . . .

- It will endure forever. The refrain of Psalm 136 states this 26 times.
- It is constant and personal—Christ is interceding for us at God's right hand at this moment (Romans 8:34).
- It works all things for good for us (Romans 8:28).
- It will graciously give us all things (Romans 8:32).
- Nothing we can anticipate or even imagine will separate us from it. And Christ, in his love for us, has already prepared a place for us in heaven where we will be glorified (Romans 8:38-9; John 14:2).
- It is all sufficient (Romans 8:32; 2 Corinthians 9:6-8; Philippians 4:19).

The Old Testament portrays such love and provision over and over. For example, the book of Deuteronomy—Moses' restatement of God's law—is filled with reminders of God's provision for the children of Israel in the past and his promises of protection and prosperity in the future. God prefaced the Ten Commandments with a reminder that he had delivered the Israelites from slavery in Egypt. God then promised them "a land with large flourishing cities," "houses filled with all kinds of good things," and abundance if they would walk in obedience with him (Deuteronomy 6:10–12).

The New Testament follows the Old in the portrayal of such love. God feeds the birds of the air; he arrays the lilies of the fields in splendor. Since that is so, Jesus implores us, we ought to trust that the God who loves us will provide "much more" for us (Matthew 6:25–34).

But if God is so wonderful to us, meeting our daily needs and promising to take care of us in the future, then why are we so inconsistent in doing what he asks? The answer, of course, goes back to faith. We don't really believe in his love and sufficiency and therefore we do not trust in it—at least not enough.

Disarming Temptation

The power of all temptation to disobey is our belief that the tempted path will make us happier than the obedient path. We sin from our lust for money, power, acclaim, and sex because we think more of these things will make us happier. When we succumb to the temptation, it is because we do not trust that the faithfulness and grace of God, rooted in his love, will make us happier. Or in other words, when we shrink back from doing God's will because of our fear of the risks of walking in it, it is because of our weak trust in God's gracious provision.

Some biblical examples help us understand.

On the one hand . . .

Why did our ancestors eat the forbidden fruit? Lack of confidence in God's sufficiency for their happiness.

Why did the Israelites forge the golden calf while Moses was on the mountain? Lack of confidence in God's provision.

Why did David commit adultery with Bathsheba and murder Uriah? Lack of trust in God's sufficiency.

Why did the rich man walk away from Jesus sorrowful? Lack of trust in God's love.

Why did Peter deny Christ? Lack of trust in God's grace.

On the other hand . . .

Why did Abraham obey "when called to a place he would later receive as an inheritance, . . . even though he did not know where he was going" (Hebrews 11:8)? A daring confidence in God's grace.

Why did Moses choose "to be mistreated along with the people of God rather than enjoy the pleasures of sin for a short time" (v.

25)? Courageous faith in God's sufficiency.

What gave Daniel the bold confidence to enter the den of lions? Faith in God's power to protect him (Daniel, 6).

What gave Esther the courage to risk death in going before King Xerxes to save her people, the Jews (Esther 4-6)? Faith in God's power to protect her.

It really comes down to this: all obedience, every virtue, every good work, and every daring, bold venture for the kingdom grows in the garden of trust in God's grace to provide for our needs and happiness, whatever sacrifices are required or pain is endured along the way. And every form of sin—pride, greed, envy, sloth, lust, gluttony, and anger—grows in the garden of unbelief in God's all-sufficient love for us.

We disarm temptation when we trust in God's grace, freeing us to walk the path of obedience of faith—the only path that pleases God or is worthy of him.

The Obedience That Pleases God

As Hebrews puts it, "Without faith it is impossible to please God" (Hebrews 11:6). And Paul writes, "Whatever does not proceed from faith is sin" (Romans 14:23, ESV). These teachings were inscrutable to me until I came to better understand the dynamic dimension of faith that connects the humble heart to the grace of God. It is not obedience through our strength or effort that pleases God; it is the obedience from a humble heart empowered by God's grace flowing through faith that is pleasing to him. A "faith" that is only intellectual assent accompanied by good works that flow from our own strength is not pleasing to God, sincere as it may be. Thus Paul teaches that the righteousness that pleases God is "a righteousness that is by faith," whereas a righteousness that is pursued by works is no righteousness at all (Romans 9:30-32).

Rooted in Love

I love Paul's prayers. I've prayed them regularly for years. (Most of them are collected in Appendix B.) And as beautiful and pungent as they all are, and as relevant to our lives, I believe the one that should be at the top of the list, prayed every morning for ourselves, for all we love, and for every discipleship ministry on our radar, is that at Ephesians 3:14–21.

> I kneel before the Father, from whom his whole family in heaven and on earth derives its name. I pray that out of his glorious riches he may strengthen you with power through his Spirit in your inner being, so that Christ may dwell in your hearts through faith. And I pray that you, being rooted and established in love, may have power, together with all the saints, to grasp how wide and long and high and deep is the love of Christ, and to know this love that surpasses knowledge—that you may be filled to the measure of all the fullness of God.
>
> Now to him who is able to do immeasurably more than all we ask or imagine, according to his power that is at work within us, to him be glory in the church and in Christ Jesus throughout all generations, for ever and ever! Amen.

There are two points, among many, that we should note in this prayer.

The first is that Christ dwells in our hearts through faith. The transmission of grace through faith is a personal thing. Though God's providential grace may orchestrate events around us, God's grace for living is mainly given to us from his abode within our hearts which he enters through faith. We receive Christ by faith and he dwells in our hearts by faith through his Holy Spirit.

The second point is that by God's grace we are empowered to know the love of Jesus Christ. And when we do, God through his grace is able to do immeasurably more than all that we ask or imagine through his power at work within us.

As Christ indwells us and we come to truly grasp how great the love of Christ is, our petty fears and inhibitions planted in the soil of unbelief wilt, and in their place our freedom and willingness to let Christ be all he can be in our lives spring to life, planted in the garden of faith in God's grace. What a precious day that will be! We will know God's love, and as we trust in it, his power will be unleashed in us to walk in obedience and do all the things he has planned beforehand for us to do.

There will be obedience, but not the obedience that carries such a heavy, off-putting connotation in our minds. There will be a new kind of obedience. We can call it the obedience of faith rooted in God's all-powerful, everlasting love. And when we understand it in this way, we can say to Oswald Chambers that in our lives we have "rescued the word obedience from the mire."

But let's do even more than that. Let's lift obedience all the way to heaven.

Obedience in Heaven

We saw earlier in Chapter 5 how C. S. Lewis said that "filial obedience" is being offered eternally to God the Father by God the Son and that where there is "delighted and delighting obedience by the creature, there most undoubtedly is Heaven." Is there obedience in heaven?

Certainly there is—a perfect obedience in perfect freedom, perfect delight, and perfect faith. In heaven we will still be creatures, though with eternal life. Our Lord will still be the one and only Lord. And God's will *will* be done. We acknowledge that reality daily in our prayers. "Thy will be done as it is in heaven."

Jesus makes it clear that doing the will of our Father is an essential characteristic of all who enter the Kingdom of heaven. "Not everyone who says to me Lord, Lord will enter the Kingdom of heaven but *only* he who does the will of my Father who is in heaven."

(Matthew 7:21, emphasis added).

Paul tells us that faith is a gift abiding for all eternity (I Corinthians 13:13). Is not this the faith that connects us to the grace that motivates and empowers obedience? Revelation reveals that the heavenly chorus stands in eternal adoration and thanksgiving before the Lamb of God. Is not this the adoration and gratitude that motivates obedience? Jesus tells us that those who have been good stewards of a few things on earth will be put "in charge" of "many things" and "cities" in heaven (Matthew 25:21; Luke 19:19). How can one be "in charge" without the authority to generate order, though certainly a heavenly order?

The point is that obedience is in the eternal order of things and in heaven the wills of all the heavenly hosts will, just like the Son's, be in perfect alignment with God's. We learn and grow in the obedience of faith on earth in preparation for a heavenly obedience that will be perfect delight.

"Obey on earth, and then you will have learned to obey in heaven," says Charles Spurgeon. There is no more important objective in all of life than to develop characters forged in the obedience of faith, molded in the image of Christ, which generate a natural, delighted willingness to do God's will. It prepares us for heaven.

Spurgeon continues, "Obedience is the rehearsal of eternal bliss. Practice now, by obedience, the song you will sing forever in glory."[26] How diligently we practice golf, rehearse speeches or prepare for what is critical in our work. Spurgeon tells us our most important rehearsal is for our life in eternity. When we think about it, certainly we would agree.

Are we *now* ready to promote obedience to a higher rank in the eternal order of things? Are we positioned to see it, aligned with faith, as Paul, did at the center of his apostleship and gospel? Can we agree with Jesus that doing God's will and finishing his work are our spiritual food? Are we beginning to see that an intimate relationship with Jesus Christ is dependent on our trusting *and* obeying him as Lord by his grace?

I hope so.

We have one more subject to cover before we discuss how we

mature in the obedience of faith, and that is the relation of law and grace—a subject that can create enough confusion to be a stumbling block. This will require a little theology, but take heart! I am not enough of a theologian to make it complicated.

CHAPTER 9
Law and Grace

IN *THE RAGAMUFFIN GOSPEL*, Brennan Manning retells a story about Fiorello LaGuardia, colorful mayor of New York City during the Great Depression and World War II.

> One bitterly cold night in January of 1935, the mayor turned up at a night court that served the poorest ward of the city. LaGuardia dismissed the judge for the evening and took over the bench himself.
>
> Within a few minutes, a tattered old woman was brought before him, charged with stealing a loaf of bread. She told LaGuardia that her daughter's husband had deserted her, her daughter was sick, and her two grandchildren were starving.
>
> But the shopkeeper, from whom the bread was stolen, refused to drop the charges. "It's a real bad neighborhood, Your Honor," the man told the mayor. "She's got to be punished to teach other people around here a lesson."
>
> LaGuardia sighed. He turned to the woman and said, "I've got to punish you. The law makes no exceptions—ten dollars or ten days in jail." But even as he pronounced sentence, the mayor was already reaching into his pocket. He extracted a bill and tossed it into his famous sombrero, saying: "Here is the ten-dollar fine, which I now remit; and

furthermore I am going to fine everyone in this courtroom fifty cents for living in a town where a person has to steal bread so that her grandchildren can eat. Mr. Bailiff, collect the fines and give them to the defendant."

So the following day the New York City newspapers reported that $47.50 was turned over to a bewildered old lady who had stolen a loaf of bread to feed her starving grandchildren, fifty cents of that amount being contributed by the red-faced grocery store owner, while some seventy petty criminals, people with traffic violations, and New York City policemen, each of whom had just paid fifty cents for the privilege of doing so, gave the mayor a standing ovation.[27]

Manning's purpose in retelling this story, of course, is to give a picture of God's grace in action. God doesn't relax his law or justice for us sinners, but he does arrange for the payment of our debt by his Son, if we will only believe and trust in him.

We have seen that faith and obedience are joined as two blades of a scissors. We have paid particular attention to that aspect of grace that empowers obedience. Let's now turn to the relation of law and grace, a relationship we need to understand to get more comfortable with how the obedience of faith works.

We have a tendency to contrast the old and new covenants and to see law as opposed to grace, concluding that the New Testament teaching on grace is a sharp departure from the Old Testament on law. Then we associate obedience with law and have a tendency to push both aside. In fact, however, the Old and New Testaments are not in conflict on the subject of law and grace. The Old Testament serves as a solid foundation on which the New Testament builds.[28]

One key Bible passage from the Old Testament gets us on the right track.

God's Grace in the Shema

The core of what we need to know about law and obedience is outlined in the ancient book of Deuteronomy.

> Hear, O Israel: The LORD our God, the LORD is one. You shall love the LORD your God with all your heart and with all your soul and with all your might. And these words that I command you today shall be on your heart. You shall teach them diligently to your children, and shall talk of them when you sit in your house, and when you walk by the way, and when you lie down, and when you rise. You shall bind them as a sign on your hand, and they shall be as frontlets between your eyes. You shall write them on the doorposts of your house and on your gates. (6:4–9, ESV)

Our Jewish brothers and sisters call this text the Shema (pronounced *shuh-'mah*), meaning, "Hear." And to many Jews it is the most precious text in their Scripture, forming the basis of a prayer as familiar to many Jews as the Lord's Prayer is to Christians.

Why do I highlight it? Because it is at the very foundation of the old covenant and contains in a few lines profound teaching on biblical obedience. New Testament Scripture will subtract nothing from it but rather build on it. Here are the Shema's basic elements:

Who God is

The Shema begins with the most simple description of who God is. He is Lord. He is one, the one and only. The word "LORD" (Yahweh) is repeated three times in the opening words. He reigns; we serve and obey him alone.

Yahweh is God's familiar name by which he relates personally to his covenant people. As he was to the Jews, he is also "ours." He has chosen us specially. We belong to him. We have a personal relationship with him.

Further, he is "one." There are no other gods. All sovereignty is in him. He is all wise, all powerful, all loving. All other imagined deities, idols of wood or precious metals, and idols of the heart (such as money) are out. To serve any other god is idolatry.

There is a lot more about God that Scripture will add, but in terms of obedience, this is the essential foundation. This is where all thought about the obedience of faith begins.

How We Respond to God

After establishing the Lord as the one and only God, the Shema immediately adds a second, equally essential element. We love God. We love God with utter fullness, with everything we have. He is first in fact; he is first in our love. And he loves us very much.

Our love of God is primary to our obedience to him. We can even say that if there is no love, there is no obedience. There may be obedience to a written word, but no obedience from the heart. And our love of God is to be all consuming, undertaken with all of our faculties all the time.

How do we love God with all of our heart? In addition to giving God wholehearted love, the Bible teaches that we are to trust and to obey God with all our hearts (Deuteronomy 30:2; Proverbs 3:5). These responses must be inextricably intertwined because each requires the whole heart. When we love God wholeheartedly, we are totally devoted to him, so we trust and obey him with all of our hearts. Wherever our ultimate love may be—whether it is God or an idol—there our trust and obedience will be as well. This is exactly what Jesus teaches us about money (Matthew 6:24).

What the Source of Obedience is

The Shema then moves to the third element. God's laws are to be on our hearts. Obedience is an internal thing (from the heart), not external (on the basis of laws written in stone directing commands to a determined will). Deuteronomy, which is Moses' summary of the law, is suffused with references to the role of the heart, our inner being, in heeding the will of God expressed in his law. (The word "heart" appears in Deuteronomy forty-five times!) From the beginning, it has always been God's design that we obey from a loving heart.

When the law is "on our hearts," it is transformed from an external rule into an internal desire motivated by love for God so we walk with God in accordance with his will. Because we love him, we want to be with him, to have fellowship with him as the lover with the beloved. This fellowship comes only when we obey him out of our love for him, from the heart. Our obedience is not by calculation and measurement to an external standard but by inspiration growing from our relationship with a God whom we love with everything within us.

What We Teach and What We Practice

Last, the Shema tells us to impress God's commands on our children and be sure that the law becomes second nature to us. The whole object of biblical teaching on obedience, Old and New Testament, is that it be natural. God's Word is to be all around us all of the time, all of this in order that the law might become part of our characters from an early age. We obey God spontaneously, naturally, delightfully, from the heart.

There it is in four easy steps. We learn who God is—really, what his authority (singular and absolute) is—and that he is ours and we are his. When we do so, we will love him deeply, with all of our hearts. Out of this love, we will obey him from the heart and, in our love for his law, become so familiar with it, keeping it on our mind and in our consciences, that from our earliest years until the day we die obedience becomes second nature to us.

Law in the New Testament

The Shema provides a foundation in the old covenant for obedience to God's laws. But we ask, "Doesn't grace replace law in the new covenant?" After all, Paul taught that we are "not under law, but under grace" (Romans 6:14). He also wrote that we have "died to the law" and have "been released from the law" (7:4, 6).

But we cannot stop there. Paul also taught us that the law is "holy, righteous and good" and that "it is those who obey the law who will be declared righteous" (Romans 7:12; 2:13). "Keeping God's commands is what counts," he added (1 Corinthians 7:19).

How are we to understand this teaching that on the surface seems confusing? It is easy to throw up our hands and move to an easier subject. But stick with me for just a few more pages.

With the Shema, we've seen in capsule form the Old Testament teaching on law. To it, the New Testament adds a dimension of grace, but not in such a way that grace replaces law but rather in such a way that grace refines and beautifies it.

Grace is to law as the refining process is to gold. It removes the dross. Grace takes law written on stone and writes it on the heart.

But grace needs law. Law provides order and shape. No community on earth can exist without law. What is the role of the law in the New Testament?

The Permanency of the Law

First, we need to understand that when Scripture introduces the coming of a new covenant in the prophecies of both Jeremiah and Ezekiel, it is clear that the "law" will remain (Jeremiah 31:33; Ezekiel 36:27). These prophecies emphasize that the law will be in our hearts, and Ezekiel adds that God's Holy Spirit will become the enabling presence in our hearts for us to keep the law.

The new covenant builds on the old. It doesn't replace the old.

Dimensions of the Law

Second, we need to understand that there are two dimensions to law.

- Most fundamentally, law is an expression of will. When murder is made a crime, that is an expression of the legislature's will. When Dad says to come in at 10 o'clock, no exceptions, that is a "family law" which expresses his will.
- Likewise, God's law is an expression of his will. As the Lutherans said in their Formula of Concord, it is an expression of the "permanent will of God." It is this part of the law that remains "holy, righteous and good" (Romans 7:12).
- Another dimension of the law is that, when it is broken, it condemns. When we break the law against murder, we go to jail. When we break Dad's curfew, there are sanctions. And according to the Bible, when we break God's law, we are subject to death (Romans 6:23).

Though law as a permanent expression of God's will survives in the new covenant, the punishment function of the law does not. As Paul puts it after agonizing over his inability to keep the law, "there is now no condemnation for those who are in Christ Jesus" (Romans 8:1).

It is by God's grace that the condemnation of the law has been set aside though Jesus Christ. But the law as an expression of God's will—his good, pleasing, and perfect will—remains. So grace and law are both very much a part of the new covenant.

Love for the Law

But there is another way we must understand the relationship of grace and law. It is grace that puts the law on our hearts—God's objective for his covenant people as revealed in the Shema—and causes us to love it and to desire to live it.

The Bible uniformly extols law and its purity. David describes it as "perfect, reviving the soul," as "trustworthy, making wise the simple," and as "radiant, giving light to the eyes." The law is "more precious than gold...sweeter than honey" (Psalm 19:7-8, 10). The psalmist in Psalm 119 agrees with David. "Oh, how I love your law!" he exclaims. "How I long for your precepts!" (vv. 97, 40).

This love for God's law as an expression of God's will, and appreciating it as a thing of beauty so that we long for it, is just as much part of the heart of a Christian as a Jew.

And as we shall see in Chapter 12, where we study the relationship of the Holy Spirit to the obedience of faith, the grace of the Holy Spirit promised in Ezekiel creates not only a delight and love of the law but also a desire and the strength to keep it.

The Spirit of the Law

There is another way that grace refines law: it removes the letter of the law. After all, as we're told, the "letter kills" (2 Corinthians 3:6). As long as the law is external, something to be applied to life, then rules and regulations multiply. Such was the case in Jesus' day when the Pharisees had volumes of legal interpretations.

Jesus had contempt for such an approach. He showed how it limited the expression of love. His ethic was principle-based, as seen in this statement: "The Sabbath was made for man, not man for the Sabbath" (Mark 2:27; see Matthew 5:35–48).

For Jesus, all law was to be interpreted toward the fulfillment of the two great love commandments, which are limitless in their scope, beauty, and worthiness. We are to love God and our neighbor (Matthew 22:37–40). If love could be expressed through the miracle of healing on the Sabbath, the principle of love trumped the minutely detailed Pharisaical rules for Sabbath rest.

Likewise, Paul taught in terms of lofty overarching principles, not a written code. Examples?
- "Bear one another's burdens, and so fulfill the law of Christ" (Galatians 6:2, esv).
- "Serve one another in love." (Galatians 5;13).
- "Husbands, love your wives, as Christ loved the church and gave himself up for her" (Ephesians 5:25, esv).

Against such lofty standards, would we not prefer some external, man-made interpretations making it both clearer and easier for us? Instead, we have the grace of the Holy Spirit—to write the law on our hearts, to reveal the beauty of its truth to us, to empower us to obey from within—and the grace of our Lord to forgive us as we fall short and confess.

Grace and Truth Combined With the Law

John illuminates the relationships among law, grace, and truth in the prologue to his Gospel when he tells us, "The law was given through Moses; grace and truth came through Jesus Christ" (John 1:17). John is not telling us that grace and truth replace the law; he does not connect the two thoughts with a "but." He is telling us that our obedience, including obedience to God's law, will flow from the grace and truth Jesus adds to our lives.

It is easy to grasp how obedience flows from God's grace, really the grace of the Holy Spirit. We will study this in more depth in Chapter 12.

But what does it mean when John tells us that our obedience will grow from "truth"? As we know, John pays more attention to the concept of truth than do the other Gospel writers. He tells us that Jesus is the "truth" (John 14:6) and that the Holy Spirit is the Spirit of "truth," who will lead us into all "truth" (16:13). In John 8:32, Jesus tells us that the "truth" will set us free. It is in John's Gospel that Jesus tells Pilate that he came into the world to bear witness to the "truth" (18:37).

Truth does not mean simply a proposition that accords with reality, like a human hand has five fingers. As John (and Jesus and Paul) use the term, truth is a force. It has power. In this power, it sets us free.

When John adds truth to grace in talking about what Jesus adds to the law of Moses, he is talking about the power of truth.

What we believe has power over what we do. If you were to believe that you could drive to the bank and pick up $1 million in cash if you did so within the next hour, what do you think you would do? You would be hopping in the car in a minute! When we see the truth—live in the light of truth—so that we see clearly the reality of God's love and his all-sufficient provision, it will radically change what we do, just as it did for the prodigal son (Luke 15:11-32).

So John is telling us that the law came by Moses and that grace and truth enlighten our understanding of its beauty and empower our keeping it. Law needs grace, which empowers obedience and generates the desire to obey. And it needs truth, which illuminates God's unending, steadfast love, past, present, and future, and nurtures all obedience.

If God intended obedience to be a source of happiness, then we should not be surprised to find that his power is there to equip us to obey and that his love and providential care are there to motivate us and give us confidence to obey. And as we have seen, they are, through our faith.

So law and grace are not incompatible. Rather they embrace one another in the new covenant. And when Jesus teaches that not "one jot or one tittle" of the law shall pass away until all is accomplished, he is speaking of the law as a perfect expression of the will of God (Matthew 5:18, KJV)—law that, by the grace of his Holy Spirit, we will learn to love and be empowered more and more to follow.

The Garden Path

Years ago I was taught that the fruit of the Holy Spirit ripens only in the garden of obedience. There is much truth in this simple insight. It is only in the soil of trusting obedience, indeed, that all spiritual blessings grow. Thus in Part 3 we will wander down an inviting path through the garden of obedience, observe its beauty and savor the fragrance of the blooms.

As we begin that discovery, I have an extraordinary community and its leader to tell you about. They will teach us a lot about the obedience of faith. Let's visit France.

PART 3

The Garden of the Obedience of Faith

CHAPTER 10
The Village That Saved Five Thousand Lives

IF I WERE to choose a single example outside the Bible to illustrate how the obedience of faith works in our world, I would turn to a Frenchman, André Trocmé, and the community he pastored in Le Chambon, France, during the Second World War. In the four years following the fall of France, the Christians of Le Chambon, at risk of their lives, provided refuge to thousands of Jewish children and adults fleeing the Nazis.

Remember how I have said that obeying God is far more than merely avoiding sin? It's also following God's leading to do what he wants us to do. That is, it's constructive. It's positive. It can be bold.

And it's not always easy.

Picture the scene for the Chambonnais. It's the 1940s and the Nazis have overrun much of Europe. Jews all over the continent are being rounded up, barricaded in ghettos, and crowded into boxcars headed for places with names like Auschwitz, Dachau, Buchenwald. Even for the Gentiles under Nazi rule, noncooperation with German orders can mean swift death.

Yet in one rural community in the mountains of Nazi-occupied France, Jews from all over Europe slip in by ones and twos and families. They're quietly placed in homes, farms, and public buildings. They're fed and housed and, when possible, provided with documents and given transportation to the free world. If German soldiers come to town, the refugees are hustled off to the forest. And when the German soldiers go, the villagers head to work in their fields and sing hymns—the signal that it's safe for the Jewish visitors to come back.

Some Chambonnais are arrested. Some are executed. But the others keep on protecting the Jews who show up at their doorstep. In total, as many as 5,000 lives are saved.

The heroic work of the Chambonnais has been preserved for us by the writing of Philip Hallie in his book, *Lest Innocent Blood Be Shed,* and a pamphlet called *Surprised by Goodness.*[1] It is from these works that I draw most of the material that follows about this remarkable community. And to understand their example for us and learn from it, we first must understand the spiritual leader through whom God forged the soul of the community.

The Making of Pastor Trocmé

Born in 1901, André Trocmé was the son of a French Huguenot father and a German mother. His mother died in an automobile accident when he was ten years old. Later, during the First World War, Trocmé's father lost his business in France, and thereafter the Trocmés lived very modestly.

André was religious from an early age. His father was a devout Christian in the Stoic tradition. His was a religion of duty toward a distant God.

When André was a teenager, however, he joined the Union of Saint-Quentin, a group made up of young people who were children of French laborers, all of whom lived in poverty after the ravages of World War I. This group met in a bare room above a church. In contrast to Trocmé's father's religion, the Union of Saint-Quentin was informal and prayer centered.

One afternoon during World War I, one of the occupying German soldiers—a man named Kindler—visited the Saint-Quentin group. This soldier, who carried no weapon, explained that he had become a Christian and a conscientious objector and had been given noncombatant duties by his superiors. He gave his testimony to the boys and led them in a song we know as the refrain of "Revive Us Again."

> Hallelujah Hallelujah,
> Hallelujah Amen.
> Hallelujah Hallelujah,
> Hallelujah Amen!

Trocmé's biographer, Hallie (who, interestingly, was Jewish and a professor at Wesleyan University in Connecticut), describes the scene this way:

> In a moment they were all singing it together at the tops of their voices, like eager, happy children.
>
> Then they all knelt down together on the bare floor and prayed (Kindler in German). This was the first time in André Trocmé's life that he told his most intimate thoughts to God in a loud, clear voice. The German's love and courage had kindled in him a love and a courage that had been waiting for a spark to ignite them.[2]

Powerfully influenced by the Union of Saint-Quentin, Trocmé went on to study theology in Paris and won a scholarship to Union Theological Seminary in New York City. He was lonely and alienated at Union, finding the seminary's prevailing "social gospel" too liberal in its focus on secular solutions to spiritual problems. He longed for the personal faith Kindler had explained and the youngsters in the Union of Saint-Quentin had come to know.

Meanwhile, Trocmé was making his living as the French tutor for two boys named Winthrop and David, the sons of business giant John D. Rockefeller Jr. While working in the home of Rockefeller, he appreciated the faith of the man who would often sing old Baptist hymns at the dining room table, such as "He Leadeth Me," with tears in his eyes. But Trocmé had little respect for the business life of Rockefeller, which he found to be driven by greed and avarice, always for "more gasoline and higher prices."

Disillusioned with the liberal theology at Union Seminary and Rockefeller's preoccupation with wealth, Trocmé decided to cut short his study in the United States. His scholarship and a generous offer from the Rockefellers were not enough to induce him to stay.

Before he left the United States, however, he proposed to a young Italian woman named Magda, whom he had met in New York. In asking her to marry him, he made clear the kind of future he had in mind: "I shall be a Protestant pastor, and I want to live a life of poverty. I am a conscientious objector, and that could mean prison as well as all sorts of difficulties."[3] That's not the way we would do it in our day! Nevertheless, the pair returned to France to be married, and she went on to become his faithful partner in ministry for the rest of his life.

A Spiritual Awakening

Back in his homeland, Trocmé became a pastor in the Reformed Church of France. His first parish was at Sin-le-Noble, near the Belgium border. Here his ministry was to the poor miners of that region.

Trocmé encouraged the creation of small groups that met in the homes of his parishioners. One of these small groups was called the Men's Circle, made up entirely of impoverished Frenchmen, not a few of whom were suffering from alcoholism. It was in the Men's Circle that an event took place that was to have a profound effect on Trocmé for the rest of his life. As Hallie describes it:

> One evening, sitting in a worker's kitchen with the Men's Circle, Trocmé was discussing a book that was very influential at the time, a book that tried to prove that Jesus was a myth invented by Saint Paul. He found himself mustering the arguments and facts he had learned at the University of Paris, but while he was doing so, and, in the process, successfully refuting the book, he also found himself asking the question: "If Jesus really walked upon this earth, why do we keep treating him as if he were a disembodied, impossibly idealistic ethical theory? If he was a real man, then the Sermon on the Mount was made for people on this earth; and if he existed, God has

shown us in flesh and blood what goodness is for flesh-and-blood people."

All of this he said calmly to the ten men who were present. He had not planned to say these things, nor had he planned to take any particular action after their talk, but suddenly they found themselves on their knees together. Each made a confession to God of his own weaknesses, as the young people in Saint-Quentin had done, and they all stood up. They found themselves looking at each other with new eyes, without defensiveness, shyness, or pride. They all felt the [S]pirit of God in them, and decided to go right home to bring that extraordinary new awareness to their wives and children.

This was the beginning of what came to be called the "awakening of Sin-le-Noble." In its full intensity it lasted for more than three months, and in the course of it, all the divisions and disputes in the parish disappeared. People became as clear to each other as Jesus was to them. For Trocmé it was "a spiritual springtime. All those things that had formerly been vague, colorless, seen from the outside . . . became suddenly for me living, interesting, inspiring. Each man became inestimably precious in my eyes."

But the "awakening" was not only ecstatic; it involved action. It was not unlike the musical or poetic inspiration that makes some people *productive* geniuses. Such inspiration is not like a mystical trance; it raises people above their ordinary levels of energy, so that, celebrating, they rush out to meet and to change the world around them. Such an inspiration motivated the Hussites in fifteenth-century Czechoslovakia, and the Quakers in seventeenth-century Pennsylvania. They had what Trocmé called a *moral de combat* (an ethic of combat), an active way of living in the world.[4]

There have been times when God, in his grace, has poured out his Holy Spirit on whole groups of people. The first such time was at Pentecost. We recounted another in Herrnhut (see Chapter 8). We call these events, which can last days or months or years, "awakenings." Trocmé was privileged to be a part of two awakenings, one with the Saint-Quentin group and a second at Sin-le-Noble.

By fortifying Trocmé with the power of the Holy Spirit in a special way, Christ was preparing Trocmé to take an "ethic of combat" into war against the Nazis to save the children of the Jews, God's chosen ones.

City of Refuge

After six years in Sin-le-Noble, Trocmé moved on to his next parish: Le Chambon-sur-Lignon, a French village in the western Cévennes Mountains. Le Chambon was a community of about 3,000 people, two-thirds of whom were peasants who owned no land. The rest of the population was of modest means. Virtually all were Protestants in the Huguenot tradition.

After France fell to the Nazis in 1940, Trocmé decided to establish Le Chambon as a "city of refuge," so designated after the cities established in Deuteronomy 19:1–12 to provide sanctuary for exiles.[5] Le Chambon had a strategic location for protecting Jews because it was too small and remote to be a high priority for the Nazis or the subservient Vichy government, which had jurisdiction over Le Chambon. More importantly, it had a population who was willing to do what many more of their countrymen should have done.

The first refugee arrived in the winter of 1941 when Le Chambon was banked with snow, with temperatures well below freezing. This woman presented herself at the presbytery, trembling from the cold, and when she asked to come in out of the snow, Magda said simply, "Naturally, come in, come in." No questions asked.

Trocmé's "staff" consisted of a half-time assistant minister and his wife. There was no written plan nor any directory as to where the refugees were housed. But in the next three years, approximately 5,000 children and adults, mostly women, would be welcomed into the homes of the parishioners of the Le Chambon Reformed Church and other facilities Trocmé was able to procure.

It is hard to take in the sacrifice involved in carrying out this work. First, the penalty for providing sanctuary to the Jews was death. Second, Le Chambon was unimaginably poor. In normal times its primary trade (other than farming) was tourism, as its scenery was beautiful and its climate was temperate in the summer months. But, of course, during the war there were no tourists.

The Trocmés at least had the presbytery home, and they consistently had six or seven children living with them. During this period, their own children had a *daily* ration of one thick triangular slice of bread, two lumps of sugar, and beans that were not only tasteless but also incapable of being softened by cooking, so that they made a ping on the plate after having been boiled for hours.

When Hallie interviewed two of the Trocmé children long afterward and asked them whether they had been displeased by the refugees taking food out of their mouths, both of them answered, "Never." They said that in the thirty-five years that had passed it had never crossed their minds to think about this until Hallie raised the question.

It was essential that the Jews be given papers to protect them from immediate arrest in the frequent roundups made by the Vichy police. When Magda approached the mayor for help in protecting that first refugee, the mayor told her to get her visitor out of town within 24 hours. Later, officials from the Church ordered Trocmé to stop his activity of providing refuge to the Jews.

The Trocmés had to disobey both the civil and ecclesiastical authority. They appealed to a higher authority: Jesus Christ. This was where their ultimate obedience lay. And being faithful to Christ put them on a collision course with the people in power.

In 1943 Trocmé was arrested with his assistant pastor as well as the principal of the school, and the three were put in a nearby prison camp for political enemies of the Nazis. Most of their fellow prisoners were French Communists who had been carrying out an underground war with the Nazis.

The three Protestants of Le Chambon began to transform life in the prison camp. The angry and lifeless Communists took note of the joy and happiness that the three men seemed to share. The prison camp administrators allowed the three to conduct worship services, and soon the worship room overflowed as hymns were sung and Trocmé gave his sermons on loving one another.

There was insufficient evidence to hold Trocmé and his assistants, and so they were granted release on the condition that they sign a statement promising to respect the Vichy leader, Marshal Pétain, and to obey his orders. Trocmé refused because an order of Pétain might require the identification or release of the Jews, and that Trocmé would never agree to. As a result, he was thrown back into the prison, though he was miraculously released the next day without having to sign the oath. Several days thereafter, all of the remaining inmates were deported to concentration camps in Poland, and almost all of them died at hard labor or in the gas chambers.

Trocmé and his followers returned to protecting the Jews. Until the end of the war, Le Chambon was known as being truly a city of refuge in the Cévennes mountains of Southern France. Some Chambonnais died for their activities, including the pastor's own cousin Daniel Trocmé, who was executed in a Nazi concentration camp. But Trocmé himself survived the war years, and his memory is still revered today in a community that can justly take pride in its history of loving others when the cost of loving was as high as it could be.

How are we to understand such an extraordinary example of group obedience to the call of God? What can account for it?

Let's examine a couple of more specific questions.

- How did Trocmé lead God's people to such valiant obedience to their Lord?
- What was behind the Chambonnais' obedience of faith?

Trocmé's Leadership

How did Trocmé lead his people to such valiant obedience to their Lord? First by sermons.

Preaching Power

Trocmé was a great pulpit preacher who made practical points with strong emotional appeal. His sermons were biblically based, with a heavy emphasis on the source of the believer's power to follow God.

> He often talked about the "power of the [S]pirit," which he described as being a surprising power, a force that no one can predict or control. He offered no systems or methods—this would be to violate the surprising force of the [S]pirit—but he had one principle that he never forsook: the obligation to help the weak, though it meant disobedience to the strong. Apart from that repeated principle, he embodied the surprising force he spoke about so often.[6]

Learning Together

The second method for spreading the faith that sustained the courage of the Chambonnais was small-group meetings.

Trocmé had learned the power of small groups as a teenager in Saint-Quentin and had used small groups in Sin-le-Noble. At Le Chambon, every two weeks, he would assign thirteen leaders of the parish a biblical passage and discuss it with them. His leadership style was not to dictate but to help "stimulate their own interpretations and let them flower."[7] The thirteen would then discuss the passage with thirteen small groups throughout the parish in the next two weeks. It was through these meetings that the nonviolent resistance in Le Chambon developed its biblical basis and practical application.

These sessions were centered biblically and rooted in prayer and moved the hearts of those who provided refuge. They provided the basis for overcoming evil with good through the nonviolent "ethic of combat." Trocmé described the small-group sessions this way:

> "It was there, not elsewhere, that we receive from God solutions to complex problems, problems we had to solve in order to shelter and to hide the Jews. . . . Nonviolence was not a theory superimposed upon reality; it was an itinerary that we explored day after day in communal prayer and in obedience to the commands of the Spirit."[8]

Trocmé was a classic minister of the "new covenant—not of the letter but of the Spirit; for the letter kills, but the Spirit gives life" (2 Corinthians 3:6). The leadership was Bible-based, from the pulpit and in small groups. It was Christ-centered. Love for Christ inflamed it; his example inspired it. And it was Spirit-filled, dependent on the wisdom and power of the Holy Spirit, bathed in prayer and obedient to his leading.

Sources of Obedience

It's easy enough to understand the methods Trocmé used to point his people in the direction of obedience: preaching and small groups. But why did they respond as they did? How did a whole community come to share their poverty and protect strangers at the risk of their own lives—and keep it up for the duration of the German occupation?

What was behind the Chambonnais' obedience of faith?

Four sources stand out.

Understanding Hearts

First, the Chambonnais could understand the kind of unwarranted persecution that their Jewish visitors were being subjected to. That's because their own ancestors had endured centuries of persecution.

In the 1940s, less than one percent of France was Protestant. Most French Protestants were descendants of the Huguenots, who traced their roots back to Calvin's Geneva. The Huguenots had been viciously persecuted in the religious wars that ensued after the Protestant Reformation. For three centuries (with a few brief periods of tolerance), loyal Protestant, French Huguenots were stripped of their property, their liberty, and even their lives. The Saint Bartholomew's Day Massacre of 1572, leaving as many as 30,000 dead, was one of many bloody persecutions the Huguenots suffered. Closer to home, one of Trocmé's predecessors in Le Chambon had been burned alive for preaching the gospel, and early worship had been outdoors because Protestant churches were burned.

By the 20th century, the Huguenots lived in peace, primarily on the western side of the Cévennes Mountains—the area where Le Chambon was located. But they had not forgotten the history of their own people. Indeed, in his sermons, Trocmé emphasized the courage of his congregation's ancestors through the years of persecution. And thus the Chambonnais were primed to recognize and sympathize with the kind of mistreatment Europe's Jews were facing in their day. In protecting the refugees, the Chambonnais were resisting the Vichy government and the Nazis in a grand tradition.

The Example of the World's Greatest Victim

The second source of the Chambonnais' obedience was faith in the teaching and example of Jesus Christ. Trocmé thought that every human life was precious, and he based this belief primarily on the atonement. Hallie quotes from an article written by Trocmé in 1955:

> Basic truth has been taught to us by Jesus Christ. What is that? The person of any one man is so important in the

eyes of God, so central to the whole of His creation, that the unique, perfect being, Jesus (a) sacrificed his earthly life for that one man in the street, and (b) sacrificed his perfection [by taking the blame for sins] in order to save that single man. Salvation has been accomplished without any regard to the moral value of the saved man.[9]

Trocmé believed that whatever the physical appearance, the wealth, the success, and the moral strengths and weaknesses of a human being, there is something immensely valuable, beyond all price, that is worth protecting at all cost in every human being. If God was willing to give his own Son for that person, Trocmé was willing to give his life.

The faith of their leader drove the work of the Chambonnais. And he believed the words of Jesus Christ, recognizing them as constituting basic truth. This faith was a source of the village's obedience, connected as root to the branch.

And Trocmé's obedience was driven by his desire for fellowship with Christ:

> The example and the words of Jesus inspired awe in André Trocmé, and he did what he did because he wanted to be *with* Jesus, in the sense of imitating Jesus' example and obeying his words. His obedience to Jesus was not like the obedience of a soldier to a military leader; it was more like the obedience of a lover to his beloved. He wanted to be close to Jesus, a loving disciple who put his feet in Jesus' footprints with stubborn devotion.[10]

Implicit Faith in the Word

Another source for the obedience of the people of Le Chambon was that they were a Bible-based people. Hallie found that for many of the people of Le Chambon, the Bible was a book of truths and commandments that was to be taken at face value. "The word of God had to be taken that way or not at all. The felt allegiance of the Chambonnais to God's words convinced them in their heart of hearts that they were doing God's work by protecting the apple of God's eye, the Jews."

One of the young Jewish mothers who arrived at the village early on knocked on the door and asked a village woman for some food for her children. This was the first refugee this particular French woman had seen, and so she asked the young lady, "Are you Jewish?"

The refugee was terrified but told the truth.

The Chambonnais lady, rather than slamming the door in her face, called to the rest of her family to come to the door immediately. "We have in our home today a representative of the chosen people!"

Habits of Virtue

Finally, we can understand the obedience of the Chambonnais on the basis of their character.

The character of these Chambonnais who provided refuge to others was that of Christ. They were self-denied servants, and this character expressed itself in what Hallie called a "habit of compassion." Hallie understood character the old-fashioned way—as a collection of virtues, sources of strength engraved in us by upbringing and practice. There was engraved in the Chambonnais a "habit of helping" that "was the living core of the rescue operation of Le Chambon."[11] It derived from the carved inscription above the church door, "Love one another"; from the sermons of Trocmé; and from the Chambonnais' abiding in Scripture.

Speaking of Trocmé's faithful wife, Magda, who was the chief administrator of the operation, Hallie explained it this way:

> For centuries people have understood that habit can be second nature as much a part of our feelings and behavior as the physical traits that we were born with. People have also known that habit can be made of invisible, intangible iron. It can be hard to break. The iron of the habit of help-

ing was embedded in the soul of Magda Trocmé, as it was embedded in . . . others in Le Chambon. [Always ready to serve] is the iron axiom of villagers in Le Chambon. From this habitual readiness, helping the refugees sprang "naturally," like sparks from struck iron.

For Magda and for many of the other villagers, helping was automatic. They weren't conscious of it, let alone proud of it. Are we conscious—or proud—of our breathing when we are in good health? Helping and receiving help were like breathing out and breathing in to Magda Grilli Trocmé. She expected the women of the village to help her as matter-of-factly as she expected herself to open a door and invite a refugee into the middle of her busy, dangerous life.[12]

But how are the "heart virtues," such as compassion and generosity, taught and instilled in us? The answer—one we all know—is that they are instilled in us by example: "Deeds speak the language of the great virtues far better than words do. Shrewd Ben Franklin could write books about penny wisdom; Magda Trocmé and the other people of Le Chambon simply practiced the great virtues without ever trying to explain them."[13]

And, as we also know from the Shema and experience, this example begins in the home.

Though the Chambonnais made it look easy, acquiring the lucid, mysterious virtues of compassion and generosity is far from easy. To raise children the way Magda Trocmé . . . and others raised theirs in Le Chambon is not as easy as memorizing Benjamin Franklin's maxims would be for an American child. You do not have to do much to teach children how to be self-serving; it is part of their inherited biological apparatus. To raise children the way the Chambonnais did you must *be* what you are trying to teach. Words, however picturesque and passionate, are not enough. In the intimacy of a kitchen or a bedroom, the public face you prepare in order to meet the faces that you meet slips down a bit. At home you must teach by example, and the example you set must be flawless.[14]

The Chapters Ahead

The story of Le Chambon warms the hearts of us all. Professor Hallie, a hardnosed man who grew up on Chicago's west side and fought in the infantry in World War II, teared up when he first read of the love and courage of the Chambonnais.

But we tell the story for another reason. The obedience of faith is supported by a number of factors working together, and we find them all at Le Chambon.

Think of it this way.

When we see gifted athletes in action, they seem to perform effortlessly. But behind the performance, many things are and have been at work. There has been much learning and extensive skill, strength, and stamina training. Coaching and a coordinated body are at work.

So it is with obedience. We look at Le Chambon as spectators far removed in time and distance, and we admire the results. But the obedience that bore such abundant fruit was the result of a number of factors combining in the Chambonnais and their bold leader. We have observed some specific to the Chambonnais heritage. There are others common to us all.

Obedience of faith involves deep faith; regenerate wills, renewed minds, and purified emotions; submission to Jesus Christ, who exercises his leadership through the Holy Spirit; a guiding principle, namely love; a listening heart; and strong characters.

In the rest of Part 3, we will look at many of the factors involved in a life of faithful obedience. By the grace of God, they are available to us all. To be sure, as athletes, we must "put . . . them into practice" (Matthew 7:24), which will take diligence and effort. But as we do, we will forge characters more and more in the image of

Christ that by the power of the Holy Spirit will enable us more and more naturally and effortlessly to bear fruit for God's glory. Then, when the mission is accomplished, we can say to our Lord, "I have brought you glory . . . by completing the work you gave me to do" (John 17:4).

CHAPTER 11
Thy Will Be Done: The Key to Obedience

IF YOU'VE SEEN the 1958 film The Inn of the Sixth Happiness, then you know of Gladys Aylward (played by Ingrid Bergman in the movie). Aylward was an English servant who became a missionary in a remote region of northern China. The China mission agency in England refused to sponsor her due to her background and lack of experience. Consequently, in 1932, she set out on her own, believing she was called by God. Remember Martin Luther's comment on faith? It makes us bold. (page 84).

In China, she worked at an inn for traveling mule drivers. After the death of the inn manager, Gladys received an official government letter telling her that funding for the inn would be cut off because of her lack of experience.

In the movie version, her response is this: "I came here when they said I couldn't. And I'll stay here though they say I can't."

A captain, Lin Nan, tries to convince her to go. "It isn't your country. It isn't your problem," he says. "You're white. You shouldn't be in China at all."

Gladys replies, "I came here to be of value."

The captain says, "How? By trying to make people believe what you believe? By saving souls who don't want to be saved? We will agree to anything for an extra bowl of rice and laugh at you once the rice is eaten?

"The dangers that confront you—those are real. Leave now, while you still can. Go back to England where you belong."

"If I feel that God wants me in China," Gladys says, "then that's where I belong."

Gladys stayed and, through her God, converted the village's governor to Christianity. And when the Japanese army attacked China, she heroically led more than a hundred orphan children to safety.

Here is a woman whose will was aligned with God's, and it is with the will we begin our study of the obedience to which God calls us.

What Is the Will?

Remember our definition of obedience? Aligning our wills with God's. Obedience is centered in the will. The will is nothing less than the executive center of our lives. It is the faculty by which we choose, act and obey.

Christians through the centuries have struggled to express the critical importance of the will in a disciple's life. George MacDonald, for example, says that the will is the "deepest, strongest, divinest thing in man."[15] Oswald Chambers says that the will is "the whole man active" and "the profoundest thing in man." It is, he says, "the essential element in God's creation of man."[16]

The Will and Action

Our souls have three functional parts: the will, the mind and emotions. The goal in Christian living is for each of these faculties to be submitted to and coordinated by the Holy Spirit.

The mind informs the will in making choices, and the emotions may drive the will to action, but it is the will that ultimately chooses and does. With our will, we may choose to love, pray, give alms, be just, and worship God. Likewise, with our will, we may choose to cheat, oppress the poor, commit adultery, hoard wealth, and vent anger.

Imagine that you know a widow who has lost her job and needs financial help to feed her children. If she asks you for help, what will you do?

Your mind might tell you that helping the widow is the right thing to do. Your emotions, driven by selfishness, might tell you to say no. So, which will win?

It depends . . . on your will. Your will can either, out of love, decide to help the widow or, out of stinginess, decide to do nothing.

We were not given the life of God through the new birth solely to adore God in our prayer chambers and churches, nor merely to think kindly of our neighbor, but rather to do the things that glorify God and express love to our neighbor in action. We do such things because we "will" to do them. The Christian life begins with faith, but as we have seen, faith is a "living" thing that acts. And it acts through the will.

So it is quite natural that almost always when the Bible speaks of God's will, it joins it with doing.

- "Your *will* be *done*" (Matthew 6:10).
- "Only he who *does* the *will* of my Father who is in heaven" will enter the kingdom of heaven (7:21).
- "My food . . . is to *do* the *will* of him who sent me and finish his work" (John 4:34).

It is with the will that we decide to receive Jesus as our Lord and Savior and with the will that we choose to trust and obey him however he speaks. The will is closely allied with the heart.

The Will and the Heart

Christians rightly concentrate on our heart in the sense of our inner being, for we know that it is from our inner being that our actions flow. Who we are determines what we do. But doing what God has created us to do, living and acting in his will, for his glory, is the reason we are on earth.

When "heart" is used in Scripture, it refers fundamentally to the will as well as emotion. The *International Standard Bible Encyclopedia* explains, "The heart's role as the center of emotions is important. Its role as the center of will and purpose is more important. Will and purpose originate in the heart."[17]

To love God with all of our heart is not simply having a warm and deep sentiment about God. Rather, it is choosing to grow close to God in faith by willing to do what he wills for us to do.

The alignment of our wills with God's through faith so that the attitude of our heart and the conduct of our lives is solely "Your will be done" is the hidden key to all life and happiness. All else in "religion" exists to support this relationship. Prayer, worship, fasting, communion, small groups, sermons, CDs—these and more all exist to the end that for God's glory our will and God's will may be one, brought into perfect unity just as are the Father's and the Son's wills for eternity.

Purity of Heart

Sören Kierkegaard wrote a book entitled *Purity of Heart Is to Will One Thing*.[18]At first, to me, this title seemed strange, since I (like so many others) thought that the heart relates more to our emotions and affections than to our will. Shouldn't it be *Purity of Heart Is to Desire One Thing*? No. Kierkegaard had it right.

What Kierkegaard was saying is that our hearts are pure when Christ reigns in them so as "to will and to act" toward one purpose only, and that is to do the will of God (Philippians 2:13). It is the "pure in heart" who "see" God with a "single" eye (Matthew 5:8; 6:22, KJV). It is those who have a "single" heart, or a single-minded will, who are brought into the deepest fellowship with Christ.

I used to work for an insurance company. When I was given a promotion, I received various notes and letters of congratulations from friends. But two I have never forgotten because I wrote the Bible verses that each highlighted in the front of my Bible.

The eyes of the LORD range throughout the earth to strengthen those whose hearts are fully committed to him (2 Chronicles 16:9).

> Teach me your way, O LORD,
>   and I will walk in your truth;

give me an undivided heart,
> that I may fear your name. (Psalm 86:11)

Hearts fully committed to the Lord. An undivided heart. These phrases express what Kierkegaard was saying. Our hearts (meaning our wills) need to be completely devoted to the Lord's kingship, unaffected by the desires of our natures.

Peter Drucker, the father of business management studies, once said that nothing worthwhile is ever accomplished without a "monomaniac with a mission." Translated, that means it takes a strong and determined will to accomplish any important mission, whether it be God's specific mission for our lives or the mission of an organization.

As we use the example of Le Chambon and André Trocmé to understand the obedience of faith, we can see how it was the determined will—a face set like flint (see Luke 9:51)—that led the Chambonnais on their intrepid mission. Trocmé's heart was pure in that it was "fully committed" to Jesus Christ and "undivided" in its determination to "finish" the Lord's work whatever the cost.

It is such a will, to quote MacDonald again, that is the "deepest, strongest, divinest thing in man."

Wills in Harmony

In human relationships, personalities may differ, even be quite opposite, and yet fellowship can thrive. We agree that opposites (meaning opposite personalities) can attract. We can differ politically, economically, or socially and still enjoy the bond of wholesome friendship. But when wills clash, fellowship is broken.

Consider a marriage. A husband and wife might get along wonderfully when they want to do the same thing. But when they have different wills (say, he wants to spend money on a new sports car but she wants to save for the children's education, or he wants to buy an expensive boat but she wants to give the money to church), the air becomes filled with tension and they have to reach a resolution before they feel comfortable together again.

It is the same in our relationship with God. Fellowship cannot survive a clash of wills between God and us. And obviously, it is the creature who must align his will with the Creator's, not the other way around.

Our relationship with Christ is that of Lord and servant. We are subjects in his Kingdom. True, he is our friend and our relationship is one of mutual love. Nevertheless, our friend is the King of the universe, and we can never forget this. He is in authority over us more so than any earthly executive. When he makes his will known to us by his written word or his Spirit, we either do it or create disorder in our relationship, just as ignoring or disobeying the instruction of our boss or coach would create problems in that relationship.

On the other hand, when a relationship such as that between parent and child is founded in mutual love, that relationship deepens and flourishes when the two wills are aligned and function in harmony. That is simply how all authority works.

And this is equally so in the spiritual realm. As we have seen, Jesus and his Father are in complete unity (see John 17:21). Their wills are perfectly aligned, as Jesus does "nothing on [his] own. . . . [He] always [does] what pleases [the Father]" (John 8:28–29). We need to seek the same perfect alignment by submitting our wills wholly to God.

MacDonald—so full of insight on this subject—states it this way:

> Only, in the relation of the two wills, God's and his own, can a man come into vital contact with the All-in-all. . . . When a man can and does entirely say, *Not my will, but thine be done*—when he so wills the will of God as to do it—then he is one with God, as a true son of a true father. (emphasis added) [19]

"Vital contact" with God relates to our wills. We come into true sonship with the Father when we so "will . . . the will of God as to do it."

Andrew Murray makes the same point more fully.

> The living centre round which all the perfections of God cluster, the living energy through which they all do their work, is the will of God. The will of God is the life of the universe; it is what it is because God wills it; his will is the living energy which maintains it in existence.[20]

Murray is saying all the goodness, holiness, love, and faithfulness of God are founded and expressed in God's will. God's will sustains the universe. There is no way we can over-magnify the importance of God's will.

Murray goes on:

> The creature can have no more of God than he has of God's will working in him. *He that would meet and find God must seek Him in His will; union with God's will is union with Himself.* Therefore it was that the Lord Jesus, when He came to this world, always spoke of His having come to do one thing—the will of His Father. . . . It was this disposition, His obedience, that made Him worthy and fit to sit with God on the throne of heaven. *Union with the will of God is union with God Himself, and must—it cannot be otherwise—bring glory to God. And this is as true of us as of Him.*[21]

Murray is now at the crux of why the obedience of faith is so important, why it should be elevated to the highest rank of all Christian understanding and practice. All our fellowship with God is through obedience, the alignment of our wills with God. That's how it was and is with Jesus and how it is with us.

Of course, we resist this truth at first because we either cling to our desire for independence or know that in our sinful weakness we live too much by our own wills and not God's.

We can only thank God that his will is always to forgive the repentant sinner. His love for us is unending, and thus when we repent, are sorry for our disobedience, and receiving his grace, are committed to living in accordance with God's will, fellowship is always restored. This is the story of the prodigal son.

How do we align our wills with God's? The word Christians use most in this connection is "surrender." That is a good word in the sense that when a person surrenders, he relinquishes control of his will to another. But we should not think that in a functional sense our wills become subdued as in the life of a prisoner. When we surrender our wills to Christ, they retain their vitality and strength. (In fact, in the Holy Spirit, they are imbued with greater power.) They are simply under new management. It's like a company that has strong potential but failing results getting a new CEO who brings out its full potential.

Paul was a strong-willed, zealous Pharisee before his conversion. Following it, his will had a new CEO: Jesus Christ. His will was just as strong and zealous, even more so, but he now had a new mission given him by a new Lord.

A rogue angel (her words), whom I worked with in prison ministry, Mary Kay Beard, was executive director of Prison Fellowship in Alabama for many years. But that was only after she transferred control of her will to a new Master. Mary Kay grew up in rural poverty in the Midwest among seven siblings and with a physically abusive, alcoholic father and a devoutly Christian mother. Her mother was too sweet and passive to protect Mary Kay from her father, and Mary Kay became a tough child who trained herself to overcome all fear and make it on her own. Never having received the love of a father, while still a teenager, she sought it in a man named Paul. It was only after she married him that she found out he was a gangster. Their life together involved Mary Kay in burglaries, safecracking, and armed robbery across several states, and it even included Mary Kay's involvement in helping Paul escape from prison. Through it all, she earned a place on the FBI's Ten Most Wanted list.

Inevitably, she was arrested. It happened while she was in Alabama, and she was sentenced to twenty-one years in the Tutwiler

Prison near Montgomery. She joined a Bible study group there and one afternoon read in Ezekiel, "I will give you a new heart and put a new spirit in you; I will remove from you your heart of stone and give you a heart of flesh. And I will put my Spirit in you and move you to follow my decrees and be careful to keep my laws" (Ezekiel 36:26-27). She surrendered her heart to Christ, and he gave her a new one.

This is how it is described in her biography, *Rogue Angel:*

> Now she understood: Salvation had nothing to do with her promises to be good or how good she was able to be through the force of her will. It was not about anything *she* did at all; it was about what *God* did. She did not have to do anything except show up, present herself, say yes and receive. God would empower her to do what He wanted her to do. . .
>
> Relief and gratitude washed over her like a burst of clean rain. I don't even have to want to, on my own; he makes me willing and able. She slid off the bunk and knelt on the concrete, not noticing the cold hardness.
>
> "Father, if You mean that verse for me, if You will give me a new heart and make me the kind of person You want me to be, I'll give my life to You. Wherever You want me to go, whatever You want me to do, that's what I will do."[22]

Mary Kay gave her heart to God. The same will was there after the commitment as was before. But it was God's to direct through Mary Kay's faith. "Whatever You want me to do, that's what I *will* do." And that's what she did, by God's grace, building one of the strongest Prison Fellowship ministries in the country and founding Prison Fellowship's Angel Tree program, which extends Christ's love through Christmas gifts to tens of thousand children of inmates throughout the world.

The Cosmic Battle over Your Will

The will is the throne of our souls and the key to obedience of faith. The critical question is who controls the will.

Many of the most exciting movies we watch and books we read feature great battles between the forces of good and evil. Think of Luke Skywalker and his fellow rebels fighting Darth Vader and the imperial storm troopers in *Star Wars*. Or think of the Fellowship of the Ring and their allies fighting the orcs under Sauron in the Lord of the Rings trilogy.

Can you believe that a cosmic battle is being fought over you? It's true. Specifically, the battle is being fought for your will. The question is who will control your will, and the combatants are Christ and Satan.

At this point you may be saying, "Come on. There's no battle being fought by others over my will. *I* control my will."

In terms of human responsibility, that is a necessary response, for we are all responsible for our actions. But the ultimate truth is that either Christ or Satan governs our wills. It is important for us to realize that there is no middle ground.

The Forces of Evil

M. Scott Peck, the world-renowned psychiatrist, said the following about the most fundamental choice we have to make:

> There are two states of being: submission [of the will] to God and goodness or the refusal to submit to anything beyond one's own will—which refusal automatically enslaves one to the forces of evil. We must ultimately belong either to God or the devil. This paradox was, of course, expressed by Christ when he said, "Whosoever will save his life shall lose it. And whosoever shall lose his life, for my sake, shall find it."[23]

Dr. Peck goes on to quote C. S. Lewis, who, as usual, states the point vividly: "There is no neutral ground in the universe; every square inch, every split second is claimed by God and counter-claimed by Satan."[24] "Every square inch, every split second." Lewis could have added, "Every decision, every choice." It is difficult for us to accept this part of reality. We think our wills are free. We think we allow some of our activity to be in God's domain—how much we give to churches and charities, church or community work, possibly mission trips, and so on. But what we are doing at work on Tuesday morning (as long as we are reasonably nice and obeying the law)—this is a sort of neutral territory, we think, and God and Satan are basically irrelevant to it.

But there really is no neutral territory. The Bible teaches that "whatever" we do, "whether in word or in deed," we are to do it "all in the name of the Lord." It further says that "whatever" we do, we are to "work at it with all [our] heart, as working for the Lord" (Colossians 3:17, 23).

Jesus is Lord of all. He created all things. He sustains all things. All authority is his. He is the Alpha and Omega. As Abraham Kuyper put it, "There is not one square inch of the universe over which Christ does not say 'mine.' "[25] This Lordship is exercised through our obedience of faith—an alignment of our wills with God's by his grace.

Satan fights our Lord for every square inch. Jesus calls him the "prince of this world" (John 14:30; 16:11). The Bible teaches that "the whole world is under the control of Satan (1 John 5:19). Satan seeks dominion over each of our wills through what the Bible calls the "world," meaning not the physical creation but all the patterns of thought and living—social, political, economic, ecclesiastical—that are ungodly. The world is Satan's kingdom here on earth in defiant opposition to Christ.

Satan uses the things of the world to motivate selfish inclinations for us to *will* to live outside of God's *will* for our lives. Satan's method is always from the world to our selves or sinful natures to our wills.

Some of the more obvious tools of the world he employs to

tempt us are alcohol, drugs, sex, money, adulation, and power. I doubt that anyone reading this book has not made choices with his or her will to walk outside the will of God, momentarily or permanently, because of the seductive power of these worldly forces arousing a sinful nature to corrupt the will. We all know people whose lives have been destroyed by them. We all know families that have been devastated by them. All of us have made foolish decisions with our wills because of our selfish desires. We have all damaged relationships with others, perhaps even those we love, because of our self-centeredness.[26]

But Satan is not the only one seeking to gain greater control over our wills.

The Forces of Good

As Satan works through the world and self to control our wills, so Christ works through the Holy Spirit.

Unlike Satan, the Holy Spirit is not coercive. He will not violate our free wills. We must freely choose to submit every choice of our wills to him.

As C. S. Lewis said, "There are only two kinds of people in the end: those who say to God, 'Thy will be done,' and those to whom God says, 'Thy will be done.' "[27] It is good to remind ourselves that Lewis was talking about those who enter heaven and hell. If our wills are not transformed by grace and do not will to do God's will, we are not fit for heaven. On that day Jesus will say to the unwilling: "Depart from me" (Matthew 7:23 KJV).

But though God does not coerce us, he does woo us. He teaches, warns and urges us to follow his will, since he knows that his will is best for us and will bring us happiness. It is always "good, pleasing and perfect" (Romans 12:2).

Certainly, on the surface, the contest does not appear to be a fair one.

Satan uses the addictive power of drugs and alcohol, the enticements of sex, the allure of wealth, the seductions of approval and praise of man, and the accoutrements of power to turn us from Christ and his will. Moreover, Satan is the father of lies and will use every cunning deceit to mislead us. He finds our weaknesses and seeks to exploit them.

On the other hand, the Holy Spirit, ever respectful and considerate of our free will, uses no seduction or worldly enticement and always tells the truth.

But for those God has brought to new life through faith, his love has a compelling quality that has no equal. We begin to sense that his way is best for us. We begin to want what he wants. We choose, in his grace, to obey.

Our Say in the Matter

This is the crucial point in understanding the centrality of our wills to obedience. Neither Christ nor Satan can reign in our lives, nor influence any decision we make, without our consent. And our consent is an act of our wills.

It is with our wills that we consent to the temptation. The boss hits on the assistant and she consents. Or the assistant puts a move on the boss and he consents. Either way, the consent is an act of will.

The temptation to disobey God may be extremely powerful, as when martyrs in the early church were faced with the choice (an act of will) to deny Christ and worship Caesar or face death. Still, the consent is given by the will.

If our Lord, in the garden of Gethsemane, could resist Satan's temptation, then by grace and the power of the Holy Spirit we can resist whatever temptation Satan lays before us. With Christ we can say to God, "Not my will but yours be done." And God assures us that he will not "let [us] be tempted beyond what [we] can bear" (1 Corinthians 10:13).

So the cosmic conflict for our souls comes down to this: through our consent, will Satan reign in our wills through the enticements of the world, or will Christ reign in them through the

Holy Spirit? When Christ reigns in our wills through his love and the Holy Spirit, we have the obedience of faith, and the happiness that flows from it.

Cooperating with Christ

Paul's prayer for the Ephesians was that "Christ may dwell in your hearts by faith" (Ephesians 3:17). And in Galatians he taught that as our old self has been "crucified with Christ," it is no longer we who live but Christ who lives in us (Galatians 2:20). In a sense, *our* wills choose to obey. But most fundamentally, it is Christ's will operating in the will of our hearts through faith that obeys. When Christ becomes the CEO of our lives, we have the obedience of faith. It is the only obedience that pleases God (Hebrews 11:6).

Therefore, in the most fundamental sense, obedience is not something *we* do. Obedience is something *Christ* does through us when his Holy Spirit dwells in our hearts through faith and we consent with our wills to his reign.

We do not obey by learning the Ten Commandments and then disciplining ourselves to do them. This is the self at work. If we succeed, the result will be Pharisaic pride, not the obedience of faith. As George MacDonald says, "In whatever man does without God he must fail miserably—or succeed more miserably."[28]

Obedience without God will lead to misery—a misery flowing from pride. It is better by far that we obey by asking Christ to come into our hearts, where our wills reside. Christ responds to this invitation by sending us his Holy Spirit, through whom we receive the understanding, motivation, and power to obey. How does the Holy Spirit relate to the obedience of faith? That's the subject of our next chapter.

CHAPTER 12
The Power to Obey: The Holy Spirit

LET'S IMAGINE a university, which we will call New Covenant University. New Covenant is endowed with abundant resources, more than enough for every student to receive all that is needed for an excellent and rewarding education. Each student can expect to be equipped to fulfill the whole purpose of his or her life, glorifying God.

But there's more. New Covenant has open enrollment. There are no admission standards. Plus, every student will graduate with straight A's because the grades of the most brilliant student who ever attended are imputed to all students.

What do you think of such a school? It sounds crazy, doesn't it?

And it begs some questions. With the assurance of a perfect report card and graduation, how can the university motivate the students? And with no admission standards, so that students with inadequate preparation or limited natural ability can attend, how can the university equip them to excel?

The only answer is that the university must provide the motivation and build in its students the ability to learn.

This example illustrates how the obedience of faith works in the kingdom. As fallen creatures, we are unable to live obedient lives. We're too weak and prone to laziness on our own. God has to give us his own strength and motivation—through his Spirit.

The Answer to Our Discouragement

One reason most of us don't get excited about the topic of obedience is because obeying God's commands seems to be just plain
hard. We tend to ignore some because we see them as impractical,
such as turning the other cheek or walking the second mile. Others
we may have tried to obey and failed, tried again and failed again.
That kind of struggle is tedious and wearying. It makes us feel bad
about ourselves. *Is obedience to God's will worth it?* we wonder. Maybe we should just give up. Or obey only when it's easy.

The man who knows it's wrong to look at pornography but
can't quit clicking to the wrong kind of websites on his computer.
The woman who has a habit of gossiping and just can't help ferret-
ing out and repeating a juicy morsel. These are examples of people
who have tried to obey and not gotten very far with it. All of us have
been there at one time or another. (Sometimes I wonder if Stoicism—the Greek philosophy I mentioned in Chapter 6 died out
because the Stoics realized that gutting it out for the sake of honor
didn't work in the end. And wasn't much fun either!)

If we are discouraged because hard work in obeying God hasn't
availed much, then the Bible has something to say to us: that's good!
Of course it's not good that we have failed in obedience, but it *is*
good when we come to realize that our own efforts aren't enough to
make us obedient. That's the first step toward finding out how we
really can be happy in obedience.

The apostle Paul was once in our camp. He knew the wretchedness of failing in obedience to God—and the joy of overcoming
his failure. One of the most heartfelt passages in his letters comes
when he gets transparent about his own struggle:

> I delight in the law of God, in my inner being, but I see
> in my members another law waging war against the law of
> my mind and making me captive to the law of sin that dwells
> in my members. Wretched man that I am! Who will deliver
> me from this body of death?

Thanks be to God through Jesus Christ our Lord! (Romans 7:22–25, ESV)

Do you recognize Paul's inner conflict between wanting to do right yet doing wrong? It sounds familiar to many of us, certainly me.

But what relieved the tension for him? It was God, not Paul's own hard work, who provided the solution. And this solution brings us to the first part of learning how to mature in obedience—looking to the Holy Spirit.

When it comes to obedience, self-effort won't do it. Not consistently, anyway. And to the extent that through self-effort we succeed in deed, we fail miserably through pride. We need the Holy Spirit—who brings to us the unlimited power of God—if we want to be faithful in obedience.

Our Power Center

There are four dimensions to the obedience of faith. We've already introduced the first three:

1. *What we do*—obey God's biblical commands as well as his individual leading.
2. *The motivation for which we do it*—partly out of obligation yet mostly out of gratitude to and trust in God.
3. *How we do it*—humbly, patiently, gently, joyfully, and above all lovingly.

Now we're able to add the fourth in the list:

4. *The power by which we do it*—the Holy Spirit. (Of course, the Holy Spirit is primary in the first three dimensions as well.)

If we have an image of the Holy Spirit as a misty and amorphous fog, we need to erase it. The Holy Spirit is a *person*—God himself, the third member of the Trinity—and he is full of *power*.

The prophet Isaiah specifically called him "the Spirit . . . of power" (Isaiah 11:2).

Jesus sent the Paraclete (his word for the Holy Spirit), not just to the first disciples, but to all of us who follow him (John 14:16, 26; 15:26; 16:7; Acts 2:39). One translation of the word *paraclete* is "helper." And so the Spirit helps us, in part, by working through our faith to cause us to want to obey God, then to strengthen us to obey and to guide us in all truth so we know what to do and how to do it. He is the power center for the obedience of faith.

The main word the ancient Greeks used for happiness—*eu-daimon*—is made up of two words: *eu* means "good" and *daimon* refers to a god or spirit. The idea was that if you had a good daimon on your side, then you enjoyed a flourishing, favored life. The amazing thing is that, without biblical revelation, the Greeks were on the right track. Believers really do have an emissary of God—the best Spirit possible, the Holy Spirit—who is on our side and gives us happiness through empowering our obedience toward God.

The role of the Holy Spirit for obedience is perfectly summarized by Saint Thomas Aquinas: "It is the grace of the Holy Spirit given through faith in Christ that is predominant in the law of the new covenant and that in *which its whole power consists*."[29] Catch that? It's one of the most important points in understanding Christian life. The Holy Spirit is the *whole power* we have to obey God's will.

Jesus instructed his disciples not to take their first step after his departure until they had received the promise and power of the Holy Spirit (Luke 24:49; Acts 1:8). The first gift to Paul following his rendezvous with Jesus on the road to Damascus was the Holy Spirit (Acts 9:17). André Trocmé was empowered for his intrepid service of Christ by powerful fillings of the Holy Spirit beginning at Saint-Quentin and Sin-le-Noble.

However God may fill us with his Holy Spirit, and however we may experience him (whether at our new birth, gradually over time, or in re-fillings from time to time), it is still the Holy Spirit alone who motivates and empowers us as fallen, inept, and naturally lazy creatures in the obedience of faith.

Commenting on the fundamental role of the Holy Spirit in the whole of Christian life, John Stott writes,

> Thus the Christian life is essentially life in the Spirit, that is to say, a life which is animated, sustained, directed and enriched by the Holy Spirit. Without the Holy Spirit true Christian discipleship would be inconceivable, indeed impossible.[30]

The Spirit in the Mundane

We receive the Holy Spirit through grace by faith in Jesus Christ (Galatians 3:2, 14), and the Holy Spirit does many things for the people he indwells. For example, when the promised Holy Spirit was poured out upon the disciples at Pentecost, he empowered them for a mighty, evangelistic ministry and for the signs, wonders, and miracles that are recorded in the book of Acts. Similarly, today, the Holy Spirit is at work around the world enabling healing, deliverance, revival, signs, wonders and miracles.

Nevertheless, the *primary* work of the Holy Spirit for Christians following our conversion is to motivate and empower us in trusting obedience. He enables us to align our wills with God's, and then he empowers us to delight in that will and live into it to bring glory to God and happiness to us.

Compared to mighty miracles, this work of the Holy Spirit, largely unseen, might seem to be more mundane and everyday. But it is the Holy Spirit's more important work in all Christians.

Does the idea of the priority of obedience over mighty works seem strange to you? If so, you're not alone. But it's true. Let's consider again a passage near the conclusion of the Sermon on the Mount:

> Not everyone who says to me, "Lord, Lord," will enter the kingdom of heaven, but only he who *does the will* of my

Father who is in heaven. Many will say to me on that day, "Lord, Lord, did we not prophesy in your name, and in your name drive out demons and perform many miracles?" Then I will tell them plainly, "I never knew you. Away from me, you evildoers!" (Matthew 7:21–23, emphasis added)

Apparently it's possible to do great and mighty works apart from God's will. "Many" will do them that way. But Jesus is looking, not for those who do such mighty works, but rather for those who do the will of the Father in heaven.

And, thankfully, God never calls us to a task that he will not empower us to do.

Controlled by the Spirit

The apostle Paul received the revelation of the gospel—the truths that we are justified by faith, that we by no means can earn our salvation through works, and that we are free from any condemnation of the law. But this revelation raised a theological question and a very practical and urgent one for Paul: how, then, will Christians—free from the condemnation of law and saved wholly apart from works—lead righteous lives to the glory of God?

Paul gives his answer to this question most fully in Chapters 6 through 8 of Romans, one that Paul found for his own life.

In Chapter 6 of Romans, Paul makes clear our conflict. We are slaves who obey something or somebody—either sin (or our sinful nature), which leads to death, or obedience (or Christ), which leads to righteousness and eternal life (Romans 6:16-18).

In Chapter 7, in an intensely personal way, he discusses how his own sinfulness kept him from obeying the law, which is "holy, righteous and good," but rather caused him to do what he knew he ought not to do (v. 12). This created the state of wretchedness we noted earlier in this chapter. This dilemma applies to us all, doesn't it? Even though we want to live a good life, we are all too often slaves to our sinful natures.

Who is to deliver us from this body of death? Paul's answer comes in Chapter 8. It is the Holy Spirit. "The law [or reign] of the Spirit of Life" has set us free from "the law [or reign] of sin and death" (v. 2). When we live "according to the Spirit" we are empowered to meet the "righteous requirements of the law" (v.4).

Paul further teaches that though "the mind of sinful man is death, . . . the mind controlled by the Spirit is life and peace" (v. 6). There are a couple of words here that we need to consider carefully. The first is "mind."

The Greek word Paul used for "mind" is *phroneo*, and all commentators agree that *phroneo* applies to all the internal faculties of the soul: will, mind, and emotions. John Stott defines *phroneo* as our "absorbing objects of thought, affection, and purpose...what preoccupies us—the ambitions that drive us."[31] Thus, Paul is saying that the whole of our souls-in-action needs to be controlled by the Holy Spirit, and when they are, we have life and peace.

When we let the Holy Spirit be in charge of our wills, minds and emotions, we see that it is the office of the Holy Spirit not only to equip us with the strength to obey but also to motivate us to obey and teach us the truth we are to obey. We know God's will, desire to do it, and delight in doing it.

But I said there were *two* words we need to look at more closely in Romans 8:6. The first was "mind." The second is "controlled."

The whole of the Christian life depends on our minds, wills, and emotions being controlled by the Holy Spirit. The word "controlled," however, is a tricky one. We almost always associate control with the use of some kind of power or coercive influence. But the Holy Spirit controls us only to the extent that we surrender to him.

Too often we think that life and peace are the result of an emotional warmth felt as the Spirit fills us. This is only a part of it. Life and peace are more the result of the Spirit's controlling the driving forces of our lives, after we surrender them to Christ, causing us to walk in the will of God.

The Virtuous Cycle

In all his work in us, the Holy Spirit is working in concert with the obedience of faith; he joins with faith and obedience in what we can call a virtuous cycle.

You've heard about "vicious cycles." These are downward spirals in which one event contributes in a negative way to the next. Imagine someone who loses his job and becomes depressed. To deal with his depression, he might begin drinking too much. The drinking makes him mistreat his wife, putting his marriage on the rocks, thus leading to more depression. That's a vicious cycle, just one of many we could cite.

Lesser known are "virtuous cycles," those cycles in which the elements feed on themselves in a positive way. Economists, for example, see a virtuous cycle when bankers are confident in the economy and therefore finance more investment projects, which in turn create jobs and income, which in turn boost profits and asset prices, which in turn make bankers even more confident.

There are virtuous cycles in the spiritual realm as well. They are not "virtuous" merely in the sense that they are a positive kind of cycle. They are virtuous also because they have to do with living out godly virtues.

A spiritual virtuous cycle takes place inside us, in our hearts. It begins with faith, a trust in God, and belief in his Word that connects us to God's grace. It includes a regenerate heart that welcomes and receives Jesus Christ. And it includes receiving the Holy Spirit, listening to Christ, responding in obedience, and producing the fruit of good works to God's glory.

Now, it is easy to look at this process strictly in linear terms—moving along a straight line from having faith to receiving a new heart to hearing God to receiving the Holy Spirit to producing good works in obedience. In one sense the process *is* linear in that faith is primary. Faith precedes and nourishes acts of obedience. But in another sense, the spiritual life is cyclical and each of these elements, including obedience, reinforces the other. Through faith and God's grace, we receive the Holy Spirit, who strengthens our wills and empowers us to obey. As we obey, our faith is confirmed and deepens and our fellowship with Jesus Christ grows. Obedience to him becomes more satisfying, even delightful, which strengthens our motivation. And so the cycle goes on. The dynamic work of the cycle is driven by God's grace which flows through faith and is administered by the Holy Spirit. It is not earned or deserved by anything we do, but its enabling power flows more fully into the cycle as we, by grace, trust and obey. Thus, as Stephen, the beloved deacon, we become "full of God's grace and power" (Acts 6:8).

Virtuous Cycle I

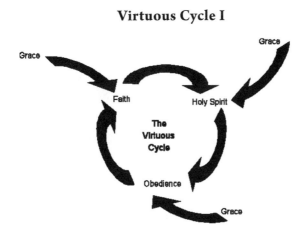

This virtuous cycle produces *external* results in the form of good works that glorify God. It also produces an *inner* reward. This inner reward is "life and peace" or happiness (Romans 8:6). As our faith deepens, our obedience flows more naturally, our fellowship with Christ matures, the fruit of the Holy Spirit manifests itself, and we grow more and more into the abundant life that Jesus came to bring us.

Why do we label our diagram "Virtuous Cycle I"? Because we will have more to add to it as our discussion continues. This is only a beginning.

The Virtuous Cycle in Action

Let's take an example. We can call him Steven.

Steven is president and principal owner of a successful firm of financial planners. His success has come from hard work, a good mind, and exceptionally strong people skills. Steven is a driven man, but underneath a friendly surface, he is very proud. He must be number one at his firm and in his family.

A friend with whom he plays basketball has prayed for Steven for a long time. He shares his faith in Christ with Steven in a "lite" way and asks Steven to try a Bible group. Steven does (thinking of new contacts he can make) but finds more than he bargained for. He is drawn to Christ and prays to receive him as Savior.

At first, one thing is clear to Steven. He cannot agree with the apostle John's declaration that Christ's "commands are not burdensome" (1 John 5:3). The teaching in the Sermon on the Mount seems impossible, plus tithing seems way more than is needed.

So Steven makes small steps at first. He gives up stopping at the "watering hole" on the way home. He cleans up a foul mouth. He reads the Bible for a few minutes every night, and doing so warms his heart.

He comes across Colossians 3:23: "Whatever you do, work at it with all your heart, as working for the Lord, not for men. It is the Lord Christ you are serving." And after discussing it with a successful Christian businessman, he decides to get his senior people together and establish a mission and values for his firm based on biblical principles. The whole process makes him feel good inside. Not only that, but also the process strengthens the team, and they all find that pursuing the mission and practicing the values create a positive work atmosphere for all at the office and produce better results in the marketplace.

Soon Steven is getting up early in the morning to read the Bible, pray, and commit all he does that day to the Lord. A personal fellowship with Jesus is growing. Tithing is producing deep reward in his heart, so soon he and his wife, Helen, are exceeding a tithe—it truly is not burdensome.

Steven takes to heart the teaching of Paul that he is to love his wife "as Christ loved the church," and over time he finds that being Helen's servant through discerning and responding to her needs is far more rewarding than chauvinism. He even agrees that turning the other cheek works better than snapping back when he does not get his way at home. The joy in his relationship with Helen begins to blossom again.

What we find with Steven is three interlocking virtuous cycles. In the center is the spiritual cycle where faith, the Holy Spirit, and obedience are mutually reinforcing. We have two others at the office and in the home where obedience from the heart to biblical teaching is producing both inner rewards and external harmony. The Holy Spirit is the silent partner in, and the power behind, it all.

Steven has found that, after all, Christ's commands are not burdensome but rather combine with faith and the Holy Spirit for great happiness.

Hitting a One-Iron

There is a world of delight, growth and abundance of life that awaits us if we do the work that God has called us to do. And he has given us his Holy Spirit to motivate us and empower us to do this work in a way that glorifies him if we live by the Spirit.

As I mentioned in an earlier chapter, if I wanted to become a better golfer, I could read Ben Hogan's popular book, *Five Lessons: The Modern Fundamentals of Golf*. I could learn the rules and put them into practice the best I was able. But that would only take me so far.

Now, an old man such as I would not go onto the golf course without taking two or three Advils. But what if, instead, I could take a "Ben Hogan pill" that placed in my muscles the ability to naturally do the things that he taught in his book? Thus, when it came time for a one-iron, I could replicate his historic, flawless shot on the final hole of the 1950 U.S. Open, which helped to seal his victory in that tournament. His energies and abilities would be engrained in me. (By the way, I've never even seen a one-iron!)

That is how obedience works under the new covenant, except instead of a "Ben Hogan pill" we have the Holy Spirit. God speaks through his Word and the Holy Spirit to our hearts, and as we hear, the Holy Spirit indwells us and gives us a natural inclination and ability to do what we are told to do, as Christ would do it . . . and to enjoy it.

Power from the Holy Spirit in Real Life

How does this work practically?

Let me say here that we are not talking about miracles in the ordinary sense of the word. Hogan's shot in the 1950 Open was not a miracle. It followed years of practice and PGA competition. The Holy Spirit, in equipping us to do the work God has planned for us, works with characters and skills that have been developed over time. That development requires our work and effort, just as it did for Hogan. He had the most diligent practice habits on the tour.

What the Holy Spirit will do is guide us into the path God has planned for us and walk beside us on that path. That's why we need to get to know the Holy Spirit by regularly reviewing biblical teaching on him. And before anything we do—such as make a telephone call, go on a trip, or start a meeting—we need to ask that he be with us and empower us to be at our best and to act in a way that glorifies God, hopefully after practice and preparation that allow us to perform at a high level of excellence.

Filled with the Holy Spirit

To conclude this chapter, may I tell you about a very personal and important event in my own life, a landmark in my spiritual journey?

When I was forty-three years-old—six years after accepting Jesus as Lord and Savior—I was filled with the Holy Spirit in a way

I never had been before. In Pentecostal and charismatic ministries, my experience would be known as the "baptism in the Holy Spirit." The word for baptism in Greek means to be saturated, completely immersed in something as a towel would be in water when we wash it. That's how it felt for me when the Holy Spirit filled me.

Prophecy foretold a day when the Holy Spirit would be poured out on all of God's people (Joel 2:28–29). Later, Jesus told his disciples not to engage in any ministry until they were filled with the Holy Spirit. This occurred for them on the day of Pentecost (Acts 1:4–5; 2:1–4), and the filling of the Holy Spirit is the gift that is available to us all; in fact, it is one we are admonished to receive (Acts 2:39; Ephesians 5:18).

How did it occur for me?

It started when a friend gave me a book that described the biblical teaching on the baptism in the Holy Spirit. At the time, I was desperate for more of the grace of the Holy Spirit in my life. So I began praying for the baptism of the Spirit.

One Friday afternoon I was praying with a man whom I knew only as Brother Ellis, a Pentecostal. As best I could, I "emptied" myself, meaning I surrendered all I had to Christ: will, mind, desires, career, time, talent, money, and reputation. And I prayed for a filling of the Holy Spirit.

Three days later, and following additional hours of prayer, it happened. I felt "streams of living water" flowing within me (John 7:38). I knew the Holy Spirit had filled the emptiness created by my surrender.

From that point on, there was a radical change in my heart. A new and deeper hunger and thirst for all the things of the Lord became part of my soul. Prayer, Bible study, worship, and fellowship opened up to me and brought me joy and comfort in a way I had never previously imagined.

Twenty-five years later, this hunger and thirst are essentially undiminished in me.

Why it seemed to take two steps for me to be filled with the Holy Spirit, I do not know. I can, however, say with confidence that we all need a time when from the depths of our being we surrender our old selves completely and entreat the blessed Holy Spirit to fill us, to come into our hearts and take over so that our love for Jesus and what he has done for us can be expressed through faith in a life that glorifies him.

If you have not prayed to Christ for the filling of the Spirit, I urge you to do so. It's the first and most crucial part of growing in the obedience of faith. And as we are filled with the Holy Spirit, we find that more and more we are motivated and empowered to do all the "works he has planned beforehand for us to do" (Ephesians 2:10). And that makes us happy.

In studying the Holy Spirit, we have looked at the positive side of the coin. There's a negative side, one that's no less important: self-denial. To that we turn in our next chapter.

CHAPTER 13
It's Not About "Me": Self-Denial

Denying Self

THERE ARE MANY paradoxes when it comes to the subject of happiness, and perhaps none is more stark than this one: for our selves to be happy, we must deny them.

I've found this paradox to be true in my own life, and so have many others. One of these is Malcolm Muggeridge, who said, "I never knew what joy was like until I gave up pursuing happiness, or cared to live until I chose to die. For these two discoveries I am beholden to Jesus."[32]

There is really no way around Jesus' words on the subject: "If anyone would come after me, he must deny himself and take up his cross daily and follow me. For whoever wants to save his life will lose it, but whoever loses his life for me will save it" (Luke 9:23–24).

You see, self-denial is essential to the obedience of faith, the hidden (in this case *really* hidden) key to happiness. If we want to grow in obedience to God, we must surrender our wills to Christ, be filled in the Holy Spirit, and next get our "selves" out of his way. Calvin states plainly, "The denial of ourselves [is] the sum of the Christian life.[33]"

But lest we have pictures of a dull, meaningless future lingering in our mind, we need to first understand that it's not our best self that we must deny. Certainly, God doesn't want to eliminate our

147

identity—the *us* that he created and loves.

It's a particular self that we must deny.

Our "old self."

Goodbye, Old Me

We think of the Christian life as transformational—the old becomes new; the lost is found; the greedy becomes generous and the vindictive, peacemaking. And indeed the Christian life *is* transformational. But one part of our lives cannot be transformed. It must be denied, or more graphically, nailed to the cross and crucified. That part is our *self*, the doorway by which Satan enters to get at our wills. Self is the archenemy of the obedience of faith.

Let's have a brief Q&A about this.

Q: What does it mean to deny self? After all, after I become a Christian, I still have a self. I am still myself. I am instructed to love my neighbor as myself.

A: We need to understand that Christians have two selves.

• *Old self:* This is the self that is controlled by the sinful nature to which we were born captive. When we become followers of Christ, it is impeached as a reigning power in our lives. But unfortunately, it still hangs around as a corrupt force if we allow it to.

We should not think for a second that the will, apart from grace, can overcome the power and seductions of the old self. It cannot. And even if it could, the result would be insufferable pride. Yet with God's help, we can defeat the old self.

• *New or real self:* This is our identity in Jesus Christ. We are given his righteousness and are progressively being transformed into his image. The new self does not grow out of the old self. It is born anew, apart from the old.

Our goal by grace, through faith is to encourage and cultivate the new self so that in time it may eclipse the old self in every way. The new self is actually our real self; it is who we were meant to be, obedient to God and glorifying him through fulfilling his will for our lives.

Because the old self continues to try to interfere with our life in Christ, we must treat it as an enemy. It is helpful to think of it as a third person—better still, as a snake that is bent on destroying the full life that we are to have in Christ. We need to hate it and seek to identify its every guise, thereafter in the power of God to crush it.

Q: What are the characteristics of the old self?

A: The old self has two dimensions.

The first dimension—and by far the most dangerous—is *self-will* which manifests in a *declaration of independence from God*. Because, as we have defined it, obedience is the surrender of our wills to God's will, the self-will is the arch-enemy of obedience. It is the self-will that declares, "I am in charge in determining what is good and evil. I will create my own life to suit me. I will do as I please." This is the independent self that drove the original sin of Adam and Eve.

The second dimension of the old self is *self-centeredness*. It concentrates on "me." Others exist to help me, meet my needs, serve me.

This dimension permeates our lives much more than we can imagine. Because the self is beguiling and deceptive, it is hard to recognize it. Few of us have any idea how self-centered we are. Nor do we want to admit our self-centeredness to others.

The fact is, though, that under the sway of the old self, we care little about the real benefit of others. We can be nice to others, but it is for "me." We can appear humble and meek, we can even be complimentary and generous toward others, but it is still for the acclaim and attention that comes back to "me."

Scott Peck wrote a book on human evil entitled *People of the Lie*. In it, he reviewed his clinical experience with a number of people whom he concluded were evil. They all had three characteristics. (1) They controlled someone else—a parent, spouse, child, or friend. (2) They were impenetrable. They would not allow a counselor to learn anything about their souls. (3) They were all impeccably groomed and well mannered. One never would have concluded that they were evil from their public behavior.[34]

What do we conclude from this? Our old self seeks to control our souls; it hides behind an impenetrable wall (we seldom recognize it); and it is very well mannered on the surface.

Appearing benign, the old self seeks to deceive us into thinking that it is our friend, leading us down a path of success and happiness when, in fact, it is the architect of all disobedience.

When our feelings are hurt, it is the self at work to get us to concentrate on our own righteousness and the wrongfulness of the person who has hurt us. When we enter a party and seek to impress others with our looks or clever conversation, it is the self at work to congratulate us as we bask in compliments. When we flatter another to win favor and reciprocal flattery for ourselves, it is the self who tells us our flattering another is godly encouragement.

The self is present in all greed and gluttony, telling us we deserve our earthly treasures and to enjoy the apparent security and prestige of wealth. The self is present in all anger as we insist on our rights and put down others, whispering in the ear of our hearts that the anger is justified; no need to forgive or apologize. The self is present in all lust as we seek to seduce others for the ego satisfaction it brings when they yield to us.

The self is there to assuage guilt in pornography. "No one sees and it hurts no one," it says.

It is there in sexual liaisons. "My husband (or wife) has deserted me emotionally, and I need and deserve this newfound love."

The guises of our old self are endless. But the point is that it masquerades as a companion when in fact it is the tool of Satan and his door to enter our hearts, take control of our wills, and destroy our lives.

A graphic description of this charming, seductive self that lives within us is found in C. S. Lewis' *The Great Divorce.*

The Lizard and the Stallion

The Great Divorce is a fictional work about a busload of spirits from hell who ride to the outskirts of heaven. One ghost carries something on his shoulder—it is a red lizard who is constantly whispering instructions to the ghost that apparently are irresistible.

An angel appears to the ghost and offers to kill the lizard. The ghost wants it killed but refuses to consent. The angel insists that he will not kill the lizard unless the ghost consents. The ghost puts the angel off, and then the angel says to the ghost that the lizard must die now or he will lose his opportunity to enter heaven. Finally the ghost relents and the angel kills the lizard.

Lewis describes it this way:

> "The burning [angel] closed its crimson grip on the reptile: twisted it while it bit and writhed and then flung it, broken back on the turf." Thereafter, both the ghost and the lizard are reconfigured into an immense, powerful, gallant man and a stallion.[35]

The ghost and the lizard can be seen to correspond to us and our selves. (In *The Great Divorce* the lizard is specifically lust.) We must consent for Christ to work through us to crucify the old self. When we do, we become altogether different persons, stronger and more beautiful, and our selves become something beautiful and powerful as well.

This needs to be understood in terms of doing the will of God. We cannot do the will of God as long as the old self is in control, or more specifically the powers of darkness are in control of the will through the old self by our consent. "Whoever wants to save his life will lose it" (Luke 9:24).

The new self is to the old self as a stunningly handsome, strong, swift stallion is to a beguiling lizard. It is in the new self that we find abundant life and happiness. In the final words of his *Mere Christianity*, Lewis describes the *real* (or new) self Christ will give us and in whom all the blessings of our Lord reside:

> Until you have given up your self to Him you will not have a *real* self. . . . But there must be a real giving up of the

self. . . . The very first step is to try to forget about the self altogether. . . . The principle runs through all life from top to bottom. Give up your self, and you will find your *real* self. Lose your life and you will save it. Submit to death, death of your ambitions and favourite wishes every day and death of your whole body in the end: submit with every fibre of your being, and you will find eternal life. Keep back nothing. Nothing that you have not given away will ever be really yours. Nothing in you that has not died will ever be raised from the dead. Look for yourself, and you will find in the long run only hatred, loneliness, despair, rage, ruin, and decay. But look for Christ and you will find Him, and with Him everything else thrown in. (Emphasis added).[36]

And now we will move to one of those things that is "thrown in" when we deny our old selves for Christ. It is freedom.

Self-denial, on the surface, seems like it must be the death of freedom—we're giving up the freedom to choose what we want for ourselves. But here's another paradox: self-denial actually gives us freedom that we could have in no other way.

False Freedom and True Freedom

Since the Enlightenment in the 18th century, Western thought has tended to define freedom as autonomy—the freedom to create our moral standards and our lives as we choose. Three justices of the United States Supreme Court, in defending abortion, stated the modern, secular understanding of freedom this way: "At the heart of liberty is the right to define one's own concept of existence, of meaning, of the universe, and of the mystery of human life."[37] Of course, this is exactly what we described as the first dimension of the old self that we must crucify: the declaration of independence from God.

Twentieth-century journalist Walter Lippmann says of people who have given up on biblical morality and tried to construct their own ethics, "They are deeply perplexed. They have learned that the absence of belief is vacancy; they know, from disillusionment and anxiety, that there is no freedom in mere freedom."[38] So-called freedom, under the secular view, ends up being no freedom at all.

But in contrast to false freedom, there is a true freedom. And true freedom always has two dimensions. There is a "freedom from" and a "freedom for."

Freedom From

Christ's freedom is first *freedom from the condemnation of the law*. As the apostle Paul said, "There is now no condemnation for those who are in Christ Jesus" (Romans 8:1). Through grace we are set free from any requirement that we must merit our acceptance by God. Our salvation has been bought by Christ and is freely given to us through faith.

In Christ and our new self we also have *freedom from the bondage to sin*. Here's how Paul put it: "We know that our old self was crucified with [Christ] in order that the body of sin might be brought to nothing, so that we would no longer be enslaved to sin" (Romans 6:6, ESV). Living into this freedom we throw off our old self and its sinful nature which destroys our freedom to follow Christ.

These two types of "freedom from" were what Paul had in mind when he wrote, "For freedom Christ has set us free. Stand firm, then, and do not let yourselves be burdened again by a yoke of slavery.... You, my brothers, were called to be free. But do not use your freedom to indulge the sinful nature" (Galatians 5:1, 13).

Freedom For

Most people have little trouble understanding the "freedom from" aspect of our freedom in Christ. But harder to understand, yet still more wonderful, is that there is a positive, constructive side to our freedom.

Though we gain freedom from the condemnation and bondage

of sin in Christ, we are created to use our *freedom for the glory of God*. In our new self, we are now *free to obey* (Romans 6:16). That is no oxymoron in the Christian worldview. Freedom is freedom to do as we ought in an obedient life that pleases God. We are free to align our wills with Christ's will and become a part of his great plan of redemption. In doing this, we bring him great pleasure (which he returns to us in the form of happiness).

This positive form of freedom is what it means to be "free indeed" (John 8:36).

I hope you have begun to glimpse how marvelous—how freeing and delightful—self-denial can be.

Two Powers

Having reviewed the role of the Holy Spirit and the self in relation to the obedience of faith, we can see that the obedience of faith takes place in relation to two powers: the Holy Spirit (through whom God's grace does its work) and the old self (through which Satan does his work). Over a lifetime, as by grace we grow into Christlike character—the obedience of faith flourishes more and more in the wills of our hearts as the old self is denied and the Holy Spirit is given rein.

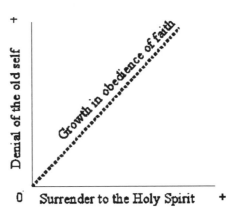

Charles Hodge, the renowned Reformed theologian, writes,

"No man can act independently of sinful nature [or self] and Spirit. He must obey one or the other."[39]

Success Through Self-denial

There is one last question that inevitably comes up when we discuss the subject of self-denial. Can anyone succeed in a competitive world and be self-denied?

Don't we need to have a little anger and greed, a little self-centered chutzpah to succeed in the world? To ask this question indicates that we do not fully understand what self-denial is all about.

- Self-denial does not mean that we are to be weak-willed. Jesus Christ and the apostle Paul were two of the strongest-willed people whose lives are recorded in the annals of history. Yet they both fully understood the meaning of self-denial.
- Self-denial does not mean that we cannot be tough. The offensive tackle on any professional football team can be self-denied as he goes about laying pancake blocks on opposing linemen.
- Self-denial does not mean that we cannot aspire to excellence in whatever calling God has given us. As a matter of fact, if we are not excellent in what we do, achieving outstanding results, how can God be glorified?

Self-denial means that we thwart the old self and do all we can, in grace, to release the full powers, energies, and capabilities of the Holy Spirit flowing through the real self. The self-denied person can win a Heisman Trophy or a Nobel Prize. The self-denied person can be a member of the Augusta National Golf Club . . . or even a five-star general.

Robert E. Lee was one of the greatest generals ever to walk on American soil. He was asked by Lincoln to lead the army up the Potomac and responded that he could not lead an army against his beloved home state of Virginia. As the commanding general of the Confederate troops, he displayed brilliant military leadership that is still taught at the United States Military Academy. Yet these stunning words conclude Douglas Freeman's Pulitzer Prize–winning biography of General Lee:

> If one, only one, of all the myriad incidents of his stirring life had to be selected to typify his message . . . who would hesitate in selecting that incident? It occurred in Northern Virginia, probably on his last visit there. A young mother brought her baby to him to be blessed. He took the infant in his arms and looked at it and her and slowly said, "Teach him he must deny himself."[40]

General Lee was a man who knew the meaning of self-denial. It did nothing to stand in the way of his own excellence in his calling.

On the other side of the equation, if we ask what is the source of most failed careers, we will find that the answer is the old self with its desire for independence and its self-centeredness. Warren Buffett, in speaking to the Washington Business School several years back, told the students there that almost certainly they were going to be successful in their business careers if they didn't "get in their own way." He meant that selfishness could destroy them.

History, both ancient and recent, provides an endless list of people done in by their selfishness. David, the greatest king Israel ever had, permanently impaired his reign through his affair with Bathsheba. The old self, asserting itself in pride, destroyed the Nixon presidency and, expressing itself in lust, nearly brought down Clinton.

I could go on, but I think we get the picture.

Self-denial, far from preventing us from fulfilling our callings, is actually a key to our success. Its opposite—self-centeredness—leads to failure.

That does not mean that the proud, selfishly ambitious, and arrogant cannot be successful in the secular realm. They can. But whatever happiness they have is counterfeit, fragile and fleeting, whereas the happiness of the self-denied is long term—we can even say eternal.

Close to God

So, how do we deny ourselves? What do we do to become self-denied?

This is a tricky question. If we take it on ourselves to deny ourselves, we are in a vicious cycle. The old self will delight in the pride we will engender when we think we have done a good job in denying ourselves. It is only in grace that we can deny the old self. Better stated, it is negated as a force that reigns over our wills when we accept Christ as Lord. Thereafter, it no longer reigns or has dominion except as we consent, and in the grace of the Holy Spirit we can seek to identify it in all of its guises and pray that our consciences will be quickened to recognize its corruption and repulsiveness. As with humility, if we think that we have denied the self, it is very much alive. It loves to be unnoticed.

We have to get our eyes off ourselves and onto the Lord. Dietrich Bonhoeffer said, "To deny oneself is to be aware only of Christ and no more of self, to see only him who goes before and no more the road which is too hard for us. Once more, all that self-denial can say is: 'He leads the way, keep close to him.' "[41]

Close to God. With our wills free to be aligned with God's through the power of the Holy Spirit and the denial of self, we are ready to take up the discussion of the preeminent virtue in the obedience of faith. Herein will lie the source of our deepest happiness.

CHAPTER 14
Love: The Heart of Obedience, Part 1

IT WAS A warm day in Chennai, India, and my friend Anne McCain Brown was sitting in an open-air hut when she heard one of the most astonishing things ever to come to her ears.

That day, she was in India with the International Justice Mission participating in a "legal clinic" in which she was documenting workers who were being illegally held in captivity because of a loan they could not repay. Technically, it's known as bonded labor. In everyday language, it's slavery.

The way it works is like this.

Let's say a poor Indian has to pay for hospitalization or a funeral or some other larger-than-normal expense. The cost of $25 or $50 might seem like little to us, but to this poor Indian, it is more than he has or can borrow from a bank. So he goes to a certain type of moneylender, called a *mudalali*. This shady character lends him the money and requires him to work until the debt is repaid. The man starts working for the mudalali in rolling cigarettes, breaking rocks, or doing some other kind of menial and tiring work.

The problem is, when you are making 75 cents a day, and that is all you have to support your family, it is tough to repay $25. Seventy-five cents is low wages even by Indian standards, so the debtor might think of trying to work somewhere else to earn the money, but the mudalali won't let him work for anyone else. And to twist the knife, he requires that the debt be paid off in a lump sum. So the bonded laborer just keeps working for the mudalali—exactly what the mudalali wants.

Unsurprisingly, many bonded laborers never pay off their debt. They just pass it down to the next generation. As I said, slavery.

But it wasn't these facts that so astonished Anne on that warm day in Chennai. Anne had already heard them many times before. In fact, that's why she was there, documenting cases of this illegal practice so that the local IJM office could present these cases to the local authorities.

No, what astonished Anne were the words that came out of the mouth of a woman we will call Eshani—one of the slaves she was interviewing. Through a translator, Anne learned Eshani's story. At first it seemed much like that of the others.

Eshani was an illiterate woman who had sold herself into slavery for a medical bill and now was working in a brick factory, carrying mud bricks from one side of a field to the other so they could dry properly. She did this all day, every day, six days a week.

The only thing that was unusual about Eshani was the radiant happiness that showed in her face. At first Anne could not account for this radiance, though she was soon to realize that it was the joy of the Lord.

My friend had the pleasure of telling Eshani that IJM was going to present her case to the local police, prosecute her mudalali, and free her. Her debt would be canceled. More than that, she would likely receive $100 in damages from the government—quite a windfall for a person like Eshani.

The radiance in her face faded. And then she said, "Don't do that."

Anne was puzzled. "What did you say?" Anne asked.

"I don't wish you to present my case in court. I don't wish you to prosecute my mudalali."

"Why do you say that?"

"I have been sharing my faith in Jesus with my mudalali," she explained. "He is showing some interest. A few weeks ago, he even asked me to pray for him. If I prosecute him, it will ruin my witness with him. And not only with him but also with others in the brick factory. Four people have come to know the Lord from my witness."

And then she stopped, the full radiance returning to her face.

Meanwhile, Anne was dumbfounded. Here she was, trying to better this woman's life—cancel her debt and help her to get a substantial amount of money, what we would consider a huge blessing and totally within her rights to have—and she was turning it down!

Anne could imagine what her life was probably like. The day-to-day grind of carrying bricks. Living in a one-room hut with no running water, no electricity, no plumbing.

Anne was offering Eshani freedom and a much better situation, and yet she said no. She chose instead to love her enemy—the mudalali who was keeping her in slavery. She wanted him to know Christ and spend eternity in heaven.

She was an amazing example of dying to self and choosing to love others instead.

Love Above All

You may think that, in discussing the various factors in the obedience of faith we have made it unduly complicated. If we need to simplify, we can do that here. Because, as you see, there is in fact a single focal point for all of obedience. A single standard by which we live. A single purpose driving every bit of obedience.

It is *love*.

By the obedience of faith, we abide in God's love; we return God's love; and God's love is made complete in us for us to express in loving others (John 15:10; 1 John 5:3; 2:5). Thus, love becomes the source, the fruit, the organizing principle, and the lifeblood of all obedience. It is the heart of obedience. If we get love right, we get obedience right.

Biblical teaching on the matter is clear.

In the Words of Jesus

Jesus forged the great synthesis of God's commands in love. He did it in response to a question from a critic. Here is how it played out:

Hearing that Jesus had silenced the Sadducees, the Pharisees got together. One of them, an expert in the law, tested him with this question: "Teacher, which is the greatest commandment in the Law?"

Jesus replied: " 'Love the Lord your God with all your heart and with all your soul and with all your mind.' This is the first and greatest commandment. And the second is like it: 'Love your neighbor as yourself.' All the Law and the Prophets hang on these two commandments." (Matthew 22:34-40; see also Deuteronomy 6:5; Leviticus 19:18).

The two commandments to love God unreservedly and to love one's neighbor as oneself sum up all the rest of the teachings of the Bible ("all the Law and the Prophets"). Similarly, in his farewell teaching to his disciples, Jesus twice reduced all his commandments to loving one another as he had loved them (John 13:34; 15:12).

In the Words of the Apostles

The apostle James understood the truth Jesus taught. He gave the central command of love a memorable name: "the royal law" (James 2:8).

In the same vein, the apostle Peter said, "Above all, love each other deeply" (1 Peter 4:8).

The apostle Paul repeated Jesus' teaching when he said, "The entire law is summed up in a single command: 'Love your neighbor as yourself' " (Galatians 5:14).

There is a whole lot more to this matter of love's being the heart of our obedience of faith, and we'll be getting to it soon. But before we go any further, let's consider the source of this love.

Because He First Loved Us

Love is a gift from God. We cannot create it by our own effort.

Instead, we receive it by faith as a grace, undeserved.

In fact, the Bible says that "God *is* love" (1 John 4:8, emphasis added). From eternity, love has characterized the relationship among the Father, Son, and Holy Spirit. And his love is shown to us in that "while we were still sinners, Christ died for us" (Romans 5:8).

It is only because of this love shown to us by God that we can ever hope to love in our turn. "We love because he first loved us" (1 John 4:19).

The gift is administered to us by the Holy Spirit. Through our faith, he pours love into our hearts. It is a fruit that grows from his indwelling presence (Romans 5:5; Galatians 5:22). Without this gift, we are helpless to do anything in the will of God.

Our job is to receive this love, return it to God in our love for him, and pass it on in our love of others. It is not automatic that we receive it, return it, or pass it on. If it were, there would be a whole lot more love in the world, a whole lot more happiness—and a whole lot less misery!

Love needs a heart free of the corruption of self-will to do its work. There is no chamber in a selfish heart into which love can be poured. That's why Paul writes that love comes from a "pure heart and a good conscience and a sincere faith" (1 Timothy 1:5). Where there is rebellion in our hearts, we must first repent and confess in order to open our heart's chambers to receive and transmit the love of God.

Love—for God and for others—is something each of us ought to be asking God for the grace to live out. That is a request he loves to grant. But it is not the only request we humans can make.

The love that God wants to pour in us – and that is of his essence – is not the only love we humans have. There are competing loves that can also be the driving force of our lives.

Competing Loves

There are all kinds of love. Theologian Jonathan Edwards tells us:

The whole world of mankind is chiefly kept in action from day to day, and from year to year, by love of some kind or another. He that loves money is influenced in his practice by that love, and kept by it in the continual pursuit of wealth. He that loves honour is governed in his practice by that love, and his actions through the whole of life are regulated by his desire for it. And how diligently do they that love carnal pleasures pursue after them in their practice! And so he that truly loves God is also influenced by that love in his practice. He constantly seeks after God in the course of his life: seeks his grace, and acceptance, and glory.[42]

Our loves are the energizing forces of our lives. When we love deeply, the object of our love will give us great energy and passion around which our actions (and obedience) will be organized—and our "first" love will be the driving force of our lives. As John Piper puts it, "The worth and excellency of a soul is to be measured by the object of its love."[43]

The Driving Force

I have searched for a good metaphor to illustrate the relationship of biblical love to obedience. It is hard because the role of love is so all encompassing. In nautical terms, love is the polestar, the compass, the first mate (Christ being the captain), the rudder, the fuel, and the engine. Love charts the course, trains and directs the crew, guides the ship and empowers it. We might more simply say that love is the driving force of obedience.

Using another metaphor, perhaps the best way to think of this is to imagine that when Christ is Lord of our lives, he is the CEO seated in the executive suite (really the carpenter's shop) of our hearts. He has a single overarching will for our lives—that we love God and each other. His Holy Spirit pours love into our hearts, and there love becomes Christ's energizing principle, alive with insight and power to organize all our thoughts, motives, and actions.

Harmonizer of the Virtues

Therefore, love is more than just a virtue. It is the virtue that harmonizes—brings together, organizes, and activates—all the other virtues.

Writing to the Colossian Christians, Paul listed a host of the virtues of the new life with which we are to clothe ourselves, including "compassion, kindness, humility, gentleness and patience." Then he stated, "Over all these virtues put on love, which binds them all together in perfect unity" (Colossians 3:12, 14).

Binding them all together in perfect unity. There we have it— love as the harmonizer of the virtues.

What does this mean in practice?

Virtues are internal sources of strength that empower us to bear fruit for God. All virtue is harmonized and ordered by love—a conscious act of will to do what is best for the other person. Paul was teaching, then, that gentleness, patience, kindness, humility, and other such virtues work together in love for the good of another.

Edwards' great treatise on love is entitled *Charity and Its Fruits*. There he shows how the virtues named in 1 Corinthians 13 are the fruits of the love of God living within us. The theme of his teaching is that all Christian virtue, all good works and fruit, grow from love. Love, he writes, is the "sum of the virtues."[44] Thus, when we love someone, that love mobilizes patience and kindness, perseverance and protection, to do what is best for the person we love.

André Trocmé and his fellow Chambonnais give a vivid illustration of this characteristic of love. In Le Chambon love mobilized the virtues of patience, kindness, courage, humility, compassion, and perseverance. It was love at work in a host of other virtues in that small village that saved the Jewish children.

Moreover, Paul teaches in 1 Corinthians 13 that the love that God puts in our hearts casts out all that would poison our relationship with the beloved. Love does not boast. It is not arrogant, rude, or envious. It is not self-seeking or resentful.

And for four years at Le Chambon it was if none of their vices had any strength.

In Galatians, Paul teaches, "The only thing that counts is faith expressing itself through love" (Galatians 5:6). Love flows into our hearts, where by "sincere faith" we are connected to God's grace (1 Timothy 1:5). Then that love mobilizes the best within us (and casts out the worst) when by faith we turn to God and confess and pray, "Lord, let your love strengthen every virtue within me and cast out every vice so that I will do what is best for the beloved."

The Watson Thesis

Another way to understand how love operates in relation to our obedience is to look at the wisdom imparted to us by one of the great business CEOs.

The best book of its type that I have read is *A Business and Its Beliefs* by Thomas Watson. The book is a compilation of lectures given in the 1950s at the Columbia Business School when Watson was IBM's CEO and IBM was the fastest-growing technology company in the world (much like Microsoft in the 1990s). Watson states his thesis for business success in opening his lectures:

> I firmly believe that any organization, in order to survive and achieve success, must have a sound set of beliefs on which it premises all its policies and actions.

> Next, I believe that the most important single factor in corporate success is faithful adherence to those beliefs.

> And finally, I believe that if an organization is to meet the challenges of a changing world, it must be prepared to change everything about itself except those beliefs as it moves though corporate life.[45]

Many great companies have been built around the Watson thesis.

So have other organizations. Effective military units, sports teams, and political parties have kept themselves centered by holding on to their core beliefs with an unshakable grip amid changing times.

The thesis is equally valid for Christian life.

Everything about a Christian can change—geography, employment, health, wealth, loved ones. But the guiding principle for life and obedience, the ultimate commandment from our Lord, must always be love. All Christian "policies and actions" are to grow from love. Love is the polestar of all Christian life and therefore of all obedience.

And driven by love, everything about a *community* can change, even one immersed in poverty and crime.

The Miracle of East Lake

Tom Cousins is a remarkable real estate developer and servant of God. After serving our country in World War II, he entered the real estate development business in Atlanta, starting with urban renewal and ultimately developing some of the largest office buildings and shopping centers in the Southeast. He was very successful at it.

He and his wife, Ann, created a family foundation and looked for ways to help the poorest, especially youngsters in the inner city. They learned that the needs there were multiple. There was no silver bullet. Education (from birth through high school), housing, jobs, health care, and faith were all needed. Victory would come only with a holistic approach to neighborhoods.

Tom had never been shy in taking on enormous challenges and projects, so he and Ann decided to try a holistic approach in the East Lake section of Atlanta, a public housing community known popularly as Little Vietnam. It was the incubator of some 10 percent of all the crime in Georgia.

All of Cousins's friends thought he was crazy, but he was undaunted. It was to take a decade of hard work, overcoming one challenge after another, but today East Lake is a different place. Its crime rate is lower than that of the most affluent residential areas in Atlanta. Students in the East Lake elementary charter school are performing at the level of the best of Atlanta's public school students. The squalor of the Little Vietnam neighborhood has been replaced with more than 650 new housing units, occupied by both the poor and professional-class residents. Adjoining East Lake is a golf course that was bought out of bankruptcy, providing jobs and profits from a PGA tour event held there every year.

What is the ongoing principle behind this magnificent work? God's love written large, not just harmonizing all virtue within the human soul (which it did in Tom's and Ann's souls) but also harmonizing all virtue in a giant community.

It is unlikely that anyone reading this book will be blessed with the business success of a Tom Cousins. But for all of us, our prayer needs to be "Thank you, Lord, for pouring your love into my heart. Now, how do you want me to use it?" Of course, that use begins in the family, extends to our workplaces, and extends beyond to places like East Lake, perhaps as a tutor or a coach or a financial or prayer partner. God has a plan for the use of his love in our hearts. We need to know what it is and walk in it.

We have more to consider on love and the obedience of faith— love for God, love for neighbor, and love in the workplace. This awaits us in Chapter 15.

CHAPTER 15
Love: The Heart of Obedience, Part 2

Love for God

WE ARE TO love God with all we have—heart, soul, mind, and strength. It is this love, above all, that becomes the driving force of obedience.

The Bible leaves us in no doubt about *how* we love God—it's by obeying him. Jesus taught, "Whoever has my commands and obeys them, he is the one who loves me" (John 14:21). His beloved disciple stated it just as clearly when he said, "This is love for God: to obey his commands" (1 John 5:3).

In *The Four Loves*, C. S. Lewis talks of two kinds of love of God. First, there is our "need love" of God. We love him as through grace we lay down our pride and acknowledge our total dependence on God. As Lewis puts it, we come to understand that we are mirrors whose brightness is wholly derived from the sun that shines upon us. The old Baptist hymn captures this idea in its opening line, "I need thee every hour."

We need God because we know that without God, in the most literal sense, the universe will collapse in a nanosecond. And in a spiritual sense, God alone can redeem us from our sin, and he did so by giving his Son to die for us. And God alone will give us the wisdom and power to do the work he has given us in a way that will bring him glory. In this need love we know the goodness of God because he is with us to meet our needs so that all works for the good.

There is a second, more elevated love of God, which Lewis calls supernatural, appreciative love, or adoration. Lewis says, "This is of all gifts the most to be desired. Here, not in our natural loves, not even in ethics, lives the true centre of all human and angelic life. With this all things are possible."[46]

Lewis does not even try to describe this love. He simply knows by faith that it exists and that it will be fully known in heaven. It is the love of God in his holiness, glory, majesty, and beauty apart from what he has done, is doing, and will do for us to meet our needs. In some of the songs of the charismatic renewal, we have imagined it. "Oh, Lord, you're beautiful. Your face is all I see."[47]

Whether it be our need love of God or a foretaste of our adoration of his character, holiness, and beauty (or some combination of these two), this is the fount of all obedience and all happiness. And as we grow in these loves by grace, everything else will fall into place.

Putting first things first is a principle for effective living. The first thing, the main thing, in the Christian life is our love *for God*. In our prayers, our Bible reading, our consciousness, and our daily activity, growing in the love for God should be the primary object of our lives.

More Love for Everything Else

Of course, loving God first—loving him totally—does not diminish the love of other things, people, or purposes. It actually enhances them.

C. S. Lewis, always keen in his insight, writes in a letter to a friend:

> When I have learned to love God better than my earthly dearest, I shall love my earthly dearest better than I do now. In so far as I learn to love my earthly dearest at the expense of God and *instead* of God, I shall be moving towards that state in which I shall not love my earthly dearest at all.

When first things are put first, second things are not suppressed but increased.[48]

Love is the complete opposite of the zero-sum game. One of its primary attributes is plenitude. The more we use it, the more we have of it—and the happier we are. So Lewis is simply telling us that loving God wholeheartedly has the direct result of loving all people more fully.

More Love for God

How do we grow in love for God?

We grow in our love for God in many ways, such as our study of and meditation on Scripture as well as fellowship with God in prayer and in worship. These disciplines deepen our love for God. Obedience crowns it; it makes it mature and complete.

In his first epistle, John writes, "If anyone obeys his word, love for God is made complete in him" (1 John 2:5).[49] No Christian life is mature or complete without the obedience of faith. Until we surrender our wills and align them with God's, we are perpetually adolescent in the faith. More precisely, John is teaching that until we faithfully obey, we are adolescent in our love for God.

John goes on to teach, "This is how we know we are in him. Whoever claims to live in him must walk as Jesus did" (1 John 2:6). The word "walk," in biblical usage, means the entirety of our active life. John has moved from talk about obeying commands to following Jesus' example, a life, as we have seen, that was perfectly attuned to doing God's will in all things. When we "walk as Jesus did," we are "in him," in his love and fellowship.

When we give any thought to love, we know the truth of this teaching. Love for God that is not completed by what we do is essentially useless. The love of a man for a wife and children is completed by what the husband and father does in providing, listening to understand needs, responding in positive support, and putting the interests of the family ahead of his. André Trocmé's love of the

Jewish children and his love for Jesus Christ was "made complete" by leading a community to provide sanctuary for the children.

Our love for God and obedience to God are inseparable as Jesus repeatedly tells us (John 14:15, 21, 23-24). Obedience is joined to loving God in the same way it is joined to trusting God. As we have seen, all three—loving, trusting, and obeying God—are to be done with our whole heart. This can only mean that all three are unified, like three strands of a rope. Do we love God with our whole heart? We do if we trust and obey with a whole heart, never without.

We have seen that faith and obedience reinforce each other in a virtuous cycle. We have added the Holy Spirit. Now we can expand our cycle by adding love for God. Love for God energizes obedience, but obedience deepens our fellowship with the triune God so that we know him more fully and therefore love him more deeply and trust him more profoundly.

Virtuous Cycle II

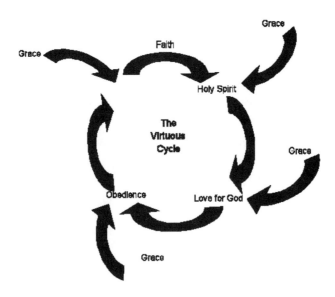

Loving by Obeying

One of the great classics on loving God and its blessings is Bernard of Clairvaux's 11th-century book entitled *The Love of God.* Here Saint Bernard, much like C. S. Lewis, describes levels of love for God moving from need love to adoration. And because obedience is always a part of the loop that expresses and sustains our love for God, Bernard concludes his discussion of loving God by turning to obedience, conforming our wills to God's:

> We read in Scripture that God made everything for His own glory (Isaiah 43:7). So surely all His creatures ought to conform as much as possible to His will. In Him all our affections should center so that in all things we should seek to do only His will and not to please ourselves. *True blessing will come to us then, not in self-gratification, nor in transient pleasures, but in accomplishing God's will in us.* So we pray daily: "Your will be done on earth, as it is in heaven" (Matthew 6:10).

> O pure and holy love [for God]! O sweet and gracious affection [for God]! O *pure and cleansed motive of will purged from the admixture of self-interest, and sweetened in its association with the divine will!* To reach this condition is to be godly.[50]

Where is true blessing? Bernard's answer is that it is in accomplishing God's will as our wills are purged of self-interest and sweetened in alignment with God's. Therein is fellowship with God, love for God, and the Christian's happiness.

Obedience is the natural response to loving God because we know it pleases him and pleasing those we love is at the heart of all love. In the words of Bruce Wilkinson, "Doing is a servant's language of devotion." In our love for God, we covet pleasing him, which means we seek to know his will for our lives and do it.

Chuck Colson wrote a book on loving God. After a thorough analysis, he concluded:

> So we have come full circle—back to where we started. The Christian life begins with obedience, depends on obedience, and results in obedience. We can't escape it. The orders from our commander-in-chief are plain: "Whoever has my commandments and obeys them, he is the one who loves me."
>
> Loving God—really loving Him—means living out His commands no matter what the cost.[51]

D. Martyn Lloyd-Jones tells us, "I am putting this in terms of obedience. Love is not just a sentiment . . . not something you feel now and again in a [worship] service or as you are reading a book. No! Love [for God] is a great controlling passion and it always expresses itself in terms of obedience."[52]

Loving Our Neighbor

The Greek word most often used for "love" in the New Testament is *agape*, referring to a self-giving kind of love. Jesus described this kind of love in many of his teachings and portrayed it vividly in the parable of the Good Samaritan. Most importantly, he lived it out for us.

Billy Graham said that love is "a conscious decision to do what is best for the other person instead of ourselves." Scott Peck defined love as "the will to extend one's self for the purpose of nurturing another's spiritual growth." In short, love focuses on the genuine good of another and wills to meet it as we deny self.

There is a tendency even among Christians to sentimentalize love, to make it something we do because it feels good. If we have a positive feeling about something, even a hot dog, we can say we love it. We also tend to see love as something passive—we "fall into" love. We are told that love is spontaneous, something that flows within us without any human effort.

Love, in fact, does feel good. Usually, anyway. But almost all who have studied the love taught in the New Testament agree that it is a product of the *will*. For instance, C. H. Dodd, the Cambridge biblical scholar, wrote that love is "an energetic and beneficent good will" that "secures the good of the beloved. . . . It is not primarily an emotion or an affection; it is primarily a determination of the will. That is why it can be commanded, as affections cannot."[53] Billy Graham states simply, "The love God wants us to have isn't just an emotion, but a conscious act of the will, a deliberate design to put others ahead of ourselves."[54] This is a pretty good reason for joining Oswald Chambers in calling the *will* the "profoundest thing in man." We may love with a warm affection, but it is a good will that expresses the love in meeting the needs of another.

The love Jesus commands—selfless and sacrificial love—has to be a matter of the will. Jesus certainly did not "feel" like going to the cross to take on the sins of the whole world. His doing so was an enormously courageous act of the will motivated by love of his Father and us. Only the most mature of us *feels* good about taking a stranger into our home (perhaps they did at Le Chambon, but those disciples were mature indeed!), changing the soiled sheets of the elderly, or even getting out of bed at 3:00 A.M. to feed our own baby. Yet we will do such things out of love—a loving gratitude to Christ for what he has done for us and the love of God flowing through our hearts for other people.

But if in our entire "walk" we are to be obedient in love, what about the business world? How can love be the driving force in our business lives?

Love on the Job

Business is tough, down-and-dirty, as one of my mentors once told me. (He was a godly man who ran a business that had a multi-state reputation for great customer service.) Don't we need to leave love at the door when we enter the world of business?

The answer is that we should not and cannot. We should not because we are commanded to love God and our neighbor, and how can we ignore these commands where we spend much of our waking hours? We cannot because anything done without love counts for nothing (1 Corinthians 13:1-3; Galatians 5:6).

How do we love God in the workplace, especially in the midst of the fray? Let's take that as a case study.

The Boss

The first thing we must recognize as we consider love's connection to business is that, in our work, Christ is the boss. We work for the Lord (Colossians 3:23). Whatever we do, including working for pay, whether in word or deed, we do in the name of the Lord, meaning for his sake and kingdom (Colossians 3:17).

In that case, how would we work for a human boss who has done the sort of things for us that Christ has—given us a job out of the goodness of his heart, supplied us with all we need to excel in the job, and stood behind us even when we messed up? We're likely to express our appreciation for such a boss by giving him our very best, seeking to do our part in giving to him a great return on whatever part of the business we are in, supporting him in every way.

At the least, that is how we should express our love for Jesus in our work. We give him our very best, striving for the highest in quality and moral behavior, seeking to do our part in Christ's redemption of this world in all its dimensions. And because he wants to work in partnership with us, we seek his advice and counsel on all decisions and give him the credit and thanks for all successes.

And how do we express love to others in the workplace?

Business, like team sports, operates in two dimensions—the work of the team to prepare to compete and the field of competition.

Teamwork

With respect to the first—that is, teamwork—love is essential. If we look at the virtues characterizing love that Paul gives us in 1 Corinthians 13, we see the most vital components of teamwork: patience, kindness, commitment to the truth, protection, perseverance, trust, and hope. And for effective teamwork, we must drive out those vices that Paul describes as the enemies of love: boasting, arrogance, rudeness, envy, irritability, resentfulness, and bullying.

Any football coach who values team unity would want all of these factors at play within the team as it prepares to compete, and so would any good manager in a business enterprise. In fact, have you noticed how "love" is being used more and more by college football coaches in their talk about teamwork? Patience and kindness are essential to team building. So is a commitment to the truth—that is honesty and a commitment to the business's or team's basic beliefs. Perseverance and protection (I will be at your back) are essential. So are trust (in the program) and hope (optimism for future success). If these virtues are enhanced in a believer because the truth is Jesus Christ and trust and hope are in God, this only adds to the power of the virtues in work endeavors.

How, we might ask, does love influence difficult decisions in business, such as firing someone or reducing the workforce when the economy tanks? Here love operates on the foundation of the biblical virtue of justice. The manager is a steward—a role Jesus understood quite well. The steward operates for an owner and has agreed to be trustworthy in operating the business to produce a return for the owner. Jesus knows the importance of returns (Matthew 25:14–30). Without a return, not just some but all the employees are in jeopardy. Therefore, in the institutional dimension, love must work through justice to be fair to all, difficult as it might be. On a personal level, Jesus calls us to extend ourselves to meet the needs of those who are out of work.

In business, when faced with a difficult decision where disappointment and pain are unavoidable, the question "What would Jesus do?" comes down to how love works fairness through the virtue of justice. Jesus is still on the throne of our wills, and love is his north star to guide us in all we do.

Competition

The second dimension of business is competition. In a free market system, the teams built within a company exist for the purpose of competing. Competition almost always takes place in what we call a win-lose environment, meaning that as one team wins, another loses. People love win-lose games. We play them (golf and tennis) in our spare time. Vicariously, billions of people throughout the world follow their teams avidly in win-lose games. From earliest times, humans both have been thrown into win-lose competitions and have created them in games. Competition is indeed built into the foundation of our world.

Win-lose games have many positives. They build character in youngsters (and adults too!), teaching them how to cooperate on a team, play by the rules, lose with grace, and learn from adversity. They teach us the rule of law. Referees call the game and their decision is final.

In the heat of competition, as regards our adversary, there is little opportunity to love in the sense of helping the weak or being generous to the opponent. When businesses place bids for a contract, the stronger one does not help the weaker by disclosing the bid beforehand. Nor does the stronger retailer raise prices to help the weaker make sales. Here, love must operate through justice which is an elementary dimension of love not its highest expression, but foundational. We play fairly, according to the rules, honestly. The game is limited in time, space and importance and there will be opportunity enough for love to meet legitimate needs after the contest.

Dying for Love

In the midst of the horrors of World War II, a Pole named Franciszek Gajowniczek saw the kind of sacrifice that represents true love for our "neighbor."

Gajowniczek was housed in Barracks 14 at Auschwitz. One night a man escaped from this barracks. And so the next morning, after the prisoners were lined up for roll call, they were left to stand there in the heat of the sun all day.

Finally, in the evening, Commandant Fritsch called out to the men of Barracks 14, "The fugitive has not been found. Ten of you will die for him in the starvation bunker!"

One of the ten chosen to die was Gajowniczek. He began to cry and to say, "My poor children! My wife! What will they do?"

That's when another prisoner stepped out of the ranks. It was Maximilian Kolbe, a Polish monk. He was known in the barracks for ministering to his fellow prisoners, sympathizing with their fears, and making the sign of the cross over them.

Now Kolbe said to the commandant, "I would like to die in place of one of the men you condemned."

The commandant agreed, sparing Franciszek Gajowniczek.

Gajowniczek survived Auschwitz and lived for another 53 years. Until his death at age 95, he delighted in telling everyone about the man who had died in his place.

Love First to Last

In the book of Revelation, Christ criticized those in the church at Ephesus for abandoning their "first love" of God and therefore not doing the things they had done at first (Revelation 2:4–5). How about us? Does our love for God continue to burn strong and through it do we continue to do the things we did at first?

Not many of us will be called to give up our life, as did Maximilian Kolbe. But all of us are called to give up our selfish pursuits so that in delight we will love God by obeying him, and we will obey him by loving others.

Love, as we have learned, is an active principle. It always influences our actions. It determines our obedience.

As Jonathan Edwards said in the quote in Chapter 14, our actions are the best test and evidence of our love for God. So, what are our actions saying about our love?

I know (and those who know me well know better than I) that I have plenty of room to grow in love. Perhaps you do too. But the Holy Spirit stands ready and able to help us grow in love as we surrender our wills to God.

Our next step will be to see that we are thinking rightly so we can understand the path of obedience. Does that mean we just have to learn more or get smarter? No. I'm afraid we need a much more fundamental transformation inside our heads than that.

CHAPTER 16
The Mind of Obedience

WE'VE ALL HAD the privilege of working with some smart people. But we know they're not more obedient to God than anybody else. And they're not happier.

If the key to happiness was what many people think it is—pursuing a life of pleasure—being smart in that case could make us more money to buy more toys and leisure. But if the hidden key to happiness is faithfully obeying God, then we don't need a *smarter mind*. We need a *new mind*. Or as the Bible calls it, a *renewed mind*.

The Call to a Renewed Mind:

> Do not conform any longer to the pattern of this world, but be transformed by the renewing of your mind. Then you will be able to test and approve what God's will is—his good, pleasing and perfect will. (Romans 12:2).

Having a renewed mind enables us to discern God's will (so different from the siren calls of the world) and then to align our wills with his will. That's why having a renewed mind is critical to obeying God.

Changing Our Minds

God is a communicator, and though he speaks in a number of ways, his principal communication is speaking verbally to our hearts through our minds.

- He used Moses and the prophets to beseech his people, calling them to obedient righteousness from the heart.
- Jesus came as a rabbi, or teacher, calling men and women to follow him by using parables and arguments that appealed to their minds.
- Likewise, the apostle Paul was a teacher and advocate for the gospel who spent his entire ministry persuading people through the spoken and written word that Jesus is the Messiah, our Lord and Savior.

In all these messages, God was trying to change people's minds.

Our old ways of thinking are captive to the things of the world and to selfish desires that weaken and corrupt the mind. These old ways must be eliminated. They'll never lead us to the obedience of faith. "The sinful mind is hostile to God. It does not submit to God's law, nor can it do so" (Romans 8:7).

To have a renewed mind means that our mind has been and is being renewed by the Holy Spirit along with the rest of us through faith in Christ. As it is transformed, we can begin to understand God's ways and will. It begins to make sense to us that putting our own desires first is not for the best, whereas falling in with God's plan is.

Michael Novak tells us that the first moral obligation is to think clearly.[55] We like to think the first moral obligation is to obey the Golden Rule or to love our neighbor, but if we think this way we are putting the will—or our choices—before the mind. We can neither obey the Golden Rule nor love our neighbor if we do not have a mind, free of the corruption of pride and worldly passion, that has learned what it means to treat others as we would be treated and to love our neighbor as ourselves.

Therefore, a key to the obedience of faith is to have a renewed mind free of the corruption caused by Satan working through our sinful natures. This is what it means to have the "mind of Christ" (1 Corinthians 2:16).

This renewal of the mind starts when we first turn to Christ in faith, and it continues throughout our lives. From beginning to end, it is a work of grace.

Repentance

Jesus' first word to his disciples—and to all of us—is to repent (Mark 1:15). "Repent" is a translation of the Greek word *metanoia*, which means to have a renewed mind, one that loves God's moral order. Jesus' classic illustration of repentance is the parable of the son who left his destructive, profligate lifestyle when "he came to his senses." The first thought in the prodigal's new mind was to submit to his father's authority (Luke 15:11–32; see especially verse 17).

Some of us by grace receive a new mind so early in childhood that we do not have a personal experience (or at least memory) of *metanoia*. But all of us who come to faith in Jesus Christ in adult years understand the expression "I was blind but now I see." Christ's commission to Paul was to take the gospel to the Gentiles to "open their eyes and turn them from darkness to light" (Acts 26:17-18). Through repentance, by grace our eyes open and we move from darkness to light in our understanding of who God is, who we are, and that Jesus is our Lord and Savior.

This renewal of our mind is by sheer grace. We do not will to have a new mindset. Rather, the repentance that takes place in our mind is the work of the Holy Spirit. It is God's sovereign work and we do not understand it. Twins can hear the same sermon, and one of them can answer the call to repent while the other is completely unmoved.

The Old Testament prophecy that expresses this mystery was quoted again and again by Jesus and Paul. Here's one version of it:

> You will be ever hearing but never understanding;
> you will be ever seeing but never perceiving.
> For this people's heart has become calloused;
> they hardly hear with their ears,
> and they have closed their eyes.
> Otherwise they might see with their eyes,

hear with their ears,
understand with their hearts
and turn, and I would heal them. (Matthew 13:14–15)[56]

Before by grace I was led to repent, I was "ever hearing but never understanding" and "ever seeing but never perceiving." And doubtless you were too. Then we came to "understand with [our] hearts." And at that time our response was the same as Isaiah's: "Here am I. Send me!" (Isaiah 6:8). We were ready to obey.

But we still had a lot of learning to do.

Turning the Light On

Once through God's grace we receive a new mind in repentance, it is the work of the Holy Spirit to illumine and develop the new mind, giving us wisdom and understanding and counsel and knowledge (Isaiah 11:2). As we submit our minds to the Holy Spirit, he shines the divine light on the teaching of the Bible. For our minds to be controlled by the Holy Spirit, we must submit to the authority of Scripture.

Before I became a Christian, I knew something of biblical teachings from my Sunday school as a child and some courses in high school and college. But I considered these teachings mostly human constructions to try to explain things. I considered Jesus to be a great man and a wise teacher, but I thought the Sermon on the Mount was the teaching of a mystic. I basically took a smorgasbord approach to biblical teaching: I accepted that which made sense to me and rejected the rest. My mind, and not God, was my final authority on his truth and who he is. It sounds silly now—so arrogant—but that's where I was.

When I accepted Christ as my Lord at age 37, I was by myself, reading Charles Colson's book *Born Again*. At that time I had no mentor, no one to disciple me. But one decision was clear to me, not through any intellectual analysis but through the Holy Spirit's speaking to me. I was to believe the Bible as it was written. I submitted my mind to the teaching of Scripture. I made the Bible the highest court of appeal in understanding spiritual and moral truth.

I began reading the New Testament under this new regime, and the best way to describe it was "Wow!" Was all this true? Jesus performed real miracles. The devil actually existed. I was a sinner hopelessly lost and separated from God. My salvation was through Christ, not my works. I must admit, the latter took some time to sink in, so accustomed was my mind to thinking that God must like me because I considered myself good, or at least (as my old self assured me) I was above average morally.

This was not to say that I took the Bible literally. (Actually, no one does, because the Bible speaks in metaphor and parable, in poetry and dreams. For instance, we know that Jesus is not a "gate" or a "shepherd"; he is *like* a gate or a shepherd.) But I did resolve never to reject the basic or plain meaning of biblical teaching. There were plenty of passages I did not understand. For those, I accepted them as true, though not comprehending them, and I trusted that, as by grace I grew as a disciple, there would come a day when I would understand.

Though I knew nothing of the work of the Holy Spirit, in retrospect it is clear that by grace he was taking control of my mind to renew it. He was giving me what he gives all followers of Christ: spiritual knowledge.

Spiritual Knowledge

The Christian has two minds. By that, I do not mean that we are double-minded in the sense of being inconsistent in our thinking. Rather, we have *a mind of the head* and *a mind of the heart*. When the Bible speaks of receiving the Word of God or his wisdom, it tells us that this wisdom resides in our hearts (Deuteronomy 6:6; Proverbs 2:2, 10). We can read Scripture and be given only a head knowledge of who God is. As James points out, this is no different from the knowledge the demons have (2:19). The knowledge that leads to the obedience of faith is the knowledge we have in our hearts, a spiritual knowledge that is given us by the Holy Spirit.

This spiritual knowledge was of critical importance to Paul. In almost all of his prayers for his beloved brothers and sisters, he prayed that they have such knowledge and grow in it. His first prayer for the Ephesians was that they be given a spirit of wisdom and revelation so that they might know God better (Ephesians 1:17). In a second prayer for the church in Ephesus, Paul prayed that believers would be strengthened in their inner being with power through the Holy Spirit, so that they would come to know how long and deep and wide and high is the love of God (3:16–19). For the Colossians, he prayed for their spiritual knowledge to know the will of God (Colossians 1:9). For the Philippians, he prayed that love (not study) would abound in knowledge and depth of insight (Philippians 1:9).

It is this knowledge, given to us by the Holy Spirit, that grows through our personal relationship with Christ as we walk with him, talk with him, trust him, depend on him, and obey him. As we learn to know his love and provision, our mind is renewed and our delight in obedience grows.

But this may not happen easily. None of it happens quickly. In fact, it's the work of a lifetime.

Battlefield of the Mind

As we learned in Chapter 11, there is a cosmic battle going on for our souls. The prize is the will. But where is the battlefield? The mind.

What will we believe? Will we believe the truth and go on to obey it? Or will we believe falsehood and follow *that*?

That is the issue at stake in a war that is taking place inside our minds. With a renewed mind, we can grasp the truth and live by it. But by no means is it a foregone conclusion that we will do so.

And now we're in a better position to understand the forces that are engaged in this battle. Not only is it a contest between good and evil; it is also a contest between truth and lies.

The Spirit of Truth

Jesus called the third member of the Trinity "the Spirit of truth" (John 14:17; 15:26; 16:13). Truth-telling is at the heart of the Spirit's ministry to us. He speaks the truth and helps us to understand and accept the truth.

It is the Holy Spirit who works in us to renew our minds, who "teaches us all things" and leads us into all truth (John 14:26; 16:13). "The mind of sinful man is death, but the mind controlled by the Spirit is life and peace" (Romans 8:6).

The Father of Lies

In Satan we have the opposite of the Spirit of truth. Jesus said of him, "He was a murderer from the beginning, not holding to the truth, for there is no truth in him. When he lies, he speaks his native language, for he is a liar and the father of lies" (John 8:44). It is worth pausing to note the part of Satan's character Jesus most emphasized—his deceit. Satan lies. The lie is his mode of entry into our souls to corrupt our lives.

Satan can't force us to believe his lies, but he has his ally, our "old" self, to work through. He can identify our weaknesses still subject to the old self and speak lies to our vulnerabilities so often and so persuasively that it's awfully hard not to believe them and act on them. That's the influence of temptation.

Sin results when we disobey God. But before sin comes temptation. And temptation is nothing more than Satan appealing to our sinful nature by corrupting our minds in thought about what is good for us, or what will make us happy.

Scripture says, "The god of this age [Satan] has blinded the minds of unbelievers" (2 Corinthians 4:4). Sadly, he often does the same to believers.

But it need not always be that way. That's what a tough, middle-aged man with a problem discovered . . .

No Foothold for the Devil

Dave's wife and teenage daughter are starting to grow hopeful at last. So is Dave.

They're hopeful that Dave is learning to control his anger.

It has been a long journey.

Dave grew up in a household where his father habitually berated and physically abused him, especially when his father was drunk. In a perverse way, Dave almost came to accept the violence he received from his father—it was the only time his father showed him any attention at all.

Not surprisingly, Dave grew up with an out-of-control temper and a tendency to get into fights. He lifted weights and worked out to be sure he won those fights. It cost him two teeth and a dislocated shoulder, but most of the time he won. It also got him kicked out of two schools and demoted in the army.

When Dave met Anika and "fell in love," he vowed he would never be the kind of husband and father that his own father had been. But predictably the chains of engrained habits are strong. He fell back into his old ways. He would yell at Anika, shove her, and strike his daughter, Melissa.

Just when none of them thought there was any way out of their misery, Melissa became a follower of Christ at a youth retreat. She persuaded her parents to go to church with her. There they were moved to accept Christ. An older man Dave knew at work began discipling him. Dave confessed his anger and violence and inability to control it. The friend taught Dave Ephesians 4:26–27: " 'In your anger do not sin': Do not let the sun go down while you are still angry, and do not give the devil a foothold."

But as Dave himself feared, the devil already had a foothold in his soul. More than a foothold. The devil was deep inside.

Dave was besieged with voices in his head (they sounded a lot like his father) saying things like, "You're the man—you have a right to get your family to do what you want any way you have to."

The voices in his head were never loud enough, though, to

drown out the truth the Holy Spirit was teaching Dave in his heart: "Love Anika and Melissa."

He was determined to do something about it. So he began learning ways to suppress his anger and find time to calm himself down. He began to experience a deep reward in his soul. The harmony he found with Anika and Melissa when he controlled his temper was becoming the joy of his life. A virtuous cycle began giving Dave both strength and happiness.

And that's why they are all growing more hopeful.

As we see in the case of Dave, our minds in their natural state— that is, before they have been renewed by God—are weak and gullible. They will easily succumb to the deceit of the powers of darkness and the desires of our sinful nature. John Henry Newman was correct when he said, "Moor a ship with thread and quarry granite with a razor blade. It is more likely to do this than for the mind to control the passions and pride of sinful man." [57]

To say that the natural mind is weak, though, is not to say that it is not clever. It will fashion all kinds of rationales for all kinds of sin. Adulterers, those exploiting the poor with shady business practices, those into pornography, drugs, and gambling—all such people have concocted elaborate excuses to justify their wrongful conduct.

Our minds are resourceful when it comes to disobeying God. What will aid the Holy Spirit's work to make them strong to *obey* him? Let me offer some suggestions.

Mind Strengthener 1: The Word of God

The Word of God—the Bible—calls itself "the sword of the Spirit" (Ephesians 6:17). In the battle taking place in our minds, the Word of God is there by our side to give us protection when the tempter comes to draw us from the path of obedience.

When tempted by the serpent in the Garden of Eden, Eve responded by reciting the word of God given to her and her husband: "You must not eat fruit from the tree that is in the middle of the garden, and you must not touch it, or you will die" (Genesis 3:3; compare 2:16–17). But she lacked faith; she didn't really believe God. (We know this because she ate the fruit. And no one in her right mind would eat fruit she believed to be deadly poisonous!) So Eve's lack of trust caused her to succumb to Satan's crafty temptation.

Someone else, however, when tempted used Scripture with full faith in God. Jesus, in the wilderness, responded with a quote from Scripture to each of the temptations Satan threw at him (Matthew 4:1–11). The schemes of Satan fell powerless before Jesus because Jesus wielded the sword of the Spirit in faith.

The Word of God is "living and active" and "sharper than any double-edged sword" to those who have faith in its Author (Hebrews 4:12). Obedience to the Word is always conjoined with faith.

Because of its effectiveness when allied with faith, the Word must become central to our consciousness. We must know it and trust it and practice it consistently so that it becomes second nature to us.

As we have seen in the Shema, Moses said this to the ancient Israelites:

> These commandments that I give you today are to be upon your hearts. Impress them on your children. Talk about them when you sit at home and when you walk along the road, when you lie down and when you get up. Tie them as symbols on your hands and bind them on your foreheads. Write them on the doorframes of your houses and on your gates. (Deuteronomy 6:6–9).

We need to find ways to become immersed in Scripture, to "abide in the word" (John 8:31). It will make an immense difference in the renewal of our minds and in the character of our obedience.

Memorization of Scripture is essential to a life lived to please God.

I was fortunate to come into the faith at a time when the Navigators had a strong influence on discipleship training. This group published wallet-sized memorization cards, and Bible groups using

Navigator training material memorized Scripture systematically. I benefited from these materials, and the verses I memorized more than thirty years ago are still vivid in my mind, helping me to obey God more faithfully.

And I'm hardly alone. Many others have learned the same lesson about the value of memorizing Scripture.

Years ago I picked up a hitchhiker, a young man who was then about 19 years old. His name was Bubba. As we talked, I learned that Bubba had never finished high school. He was on his way to pick up some money by doing yard work.

I quickly noticed that Scripture permeated his talk. His mind was filled with Bible truth. He had memorized hundreds of verses of Scripture. He couldn't talk about baseball without quoting Scripture.

I've kept in touch with Bubba over the years. He is married, has three kids, and holds down a steady job. The Word of the Lord, fortified with the Holy Spirit, has become his strength.

Mind Strengthener 2: Godly Wisdom

In classical thought, wisdom was the most exalted of all virtues. By contrast, in Christian thought, love is the highest virtue, unifying all the others (including wisdom). Nevertheless, wisdom holds a lofty place in biblical teaching. The Bible tells us that wisdom is "more profitable than silver" and "more precious than rubies." Nothing else we desire can compare to wisdom (Proverbs 3:14–15).

Virtues are a source of strength, and a mind that is rooted in the virtue of wisdom has the strength to resist temptation. Thus we are taught in Proverbs that those who walk in wisdom avoid the way of "wicked men" and are saved from the allure of temptation (2:12, 16–19).

The Holy Spirit uses wisdom to strengthen the mind in resisting the cunning deceits of Satan and the world. This wisdom is gained in experience, in heeding the instructions of the Bible, and in putting the words of Christ into practice. Proverbs teaches that "The fear of the Lord is the beginning of wisdom" (Proverbs 9:10), meaning a deep awe and reverence for God's authority and will is where wisdom begins.

Such wisdom is not just good ideas we might run across in the normal course of our lives. It doesn't come from the world. Its author is the Lord.

- "The LORD gives wisdom, and from his mouth come knowledge and understanding" (Proverbs 2:6).
- Christ has been made our "wisdom from God" (1 Corinthians 1:30).
- In Christ "are hidden all the treasures of wisdom and knowledge" (Colossians 2:3).

Without godly wisdom, we are easy prey to the wiles of the devil and the ways of the world that lead to disobedience and death. Take anyone who has squandered the gifts of God in talent or treasure, and you will find the absence of wisdom. On the other hand, find anyone you admire for integrity and honor (whether educated or not), and you will find wisdom at the foundation of this person's life.

Mind Strengthener 3: Our Conscience

Still another faculty that strengthens our mind to obey is the Holy Spirit's whispering to us through our consciences.

Our conscience is a self-regulator in our hearts that helps us know right from wrong and walk in obedience. If we are thinking about doing something that is outside the will of God, then through the communion of the Holy Spirit, our consciences quicken to send a trouble signal to our mind.

The Holy Spirit illumines our conscience through what can be understood as a windowpane. When it is clear, the light of God shines through and the conscience remains sensitive to the Holy Spirit. When we begin to walk outside the will of God, the conscience alerts the mind to guide the will in making a change in course as the Spirit strengthens the will to do so.

If we respond in repentance to the quickening of our conscience, then the window remains clear. But if we ignore the promptings of the Spirit and avoid seeking forgiveness of our sins, the window becomes cloudy. As we begin to rationalize and excuse our misconduct in our minds, there ensues a negative cycle that can result in the window of our conscience becoming opaque—no light coming through at all. The Bible calls this condition a seared conscience (1 Timothy 4:2). We are sold out to sin, our freedom is lost, and the Holy Spirit has relented to our disregard of his promptings.

Thankfully, though, our consciences also act in a positive way. We may have hurt another person in anger or have selfishly declined to meet the needs of another. In prayer, or even in the middle of the night, our conscience may quicken our mind to understand the need to make amends or to move out in love, and as we do, the window to our conscience is cleansed.

Mind Strengthener 4: Our Will

Our wills can help our minds think clearly. Although the role of the Holy Spirit is primary in the battle over what we believe, strengthened by grace, we have our own role to play as well. We can *choose* what thoughts we will entertain in our minds. We can *choose* whether we will dwell on the temptations and fears that come from unbelief or abide instead in the truths of God.

The Bible exhorts us to "take captive every thought to make it obedient to Christ" (2 Corinthians 10:5). That is a call to set our wills into action. We can use our wills to determine what thoughts we entertain and harbor in our minds.

Paul teaches that when we come to know Christ, we must put off the "old self," which is being corrupted by deceitful desires, and be "made new *in the attitude of [our] minds*" (Ephesians 4:22–24, emphasis added). The renewal of the mind is something that the Spirit of God does for us. But also by our wills we must actively cooperate with him.

Mind Strengthener 5: Obedience to God

A renewed mind is crucial to helping us obey God—the hidden key to happiness. But in its turn, obedience strengthens this renewed mind.

As we have seen, George MacDonald teaches us that obedience is "the soul of knowledge." In other words, the Holy Spirit uses our obedience to open our minds to understand the mysteries of God's revelation.

The Christian life is filled with apparent paradox. For example, to save our lives, we must lose them. And in obedience to God's law we find freedom. Because these truths are paradoxical, they are "foolishness" to the natural mind (1 Corinthians 1:18, 21, 23, 25; 2:14). They cannot be learned in any classroom or by reading any book.

We come to confidence in these truths only when we live them out—when we in fact surrender our lives and submit to God's will. And in doing so, we can agree with Oswald Chambers, who says, "The golden rule for understanding spiritually is not the intellect but obedience."[58]

G. K. Chesterton once said that the problem with Christianity is not that it has been tried and found hard but that it has been thought hard and not tried.[59] If we try Christianity and if in faith we move out in obedience, we will learn three things that will yield happiness in the abundance of life.

- We will learn who God is and what his character is—faithfulness and love.
- We will learn the truth of Jesus' teaching and how obedience to it leads to happiness.
- We will learn the joy and peace of fellowship with God.

Apart from the obedience of faith, all the worship, Bible reading and study, and small-group discussion will come up short.

A Beautiful Mind

The movie *A Beautiful Mind* traces the life of genius mathematician John Forbes Nash Jr., who suffered from paranoid schizophrenia. For years, delusional characters left him unable to discern reality from hallucination. Eventually his determination to overcome his illness enabled him to resume teaching at Princeton.

In 1994 a representative from the Nobel Committee met with Nash to assess his mental state and determine whether he would be a suitable Nobel laureate. According to the movie, in their conversation Nash jokes, "I *am* crazy." Then he says more soberly, "I take the newer medications, but I still see things that are not here. I just choose not to acknowledge them. Like a diet of the mind, I just choose not to indulge certain appetites."

Christians need a diet of the mind. We need to guard what we put in it, and we do that with the will. We choose not to "indulge certain appetites" and then the Holy Spirit can get on with the work of making our minds "beautiful." But beyond transformed minds, we must *want* to obey God. We must desire obedience. And so we turn to our emotions in the next chapter.

CHAPTER 17
Emotions in the Obedience of Faith

ROBERT RECORD IS a medical doctor in an inner-city clinic in Birmingham. He could have a successful practice in a first-rate hospital. He was an honors graduate from Rhodes College and ranked high in his class in medical school. He has consummate social grace. Why does he work in an inner-city clinic, then? He is simply called to provide medical care (much of it for free) to the least of our brothers and sisters.

What I find most impressive about Robert, however, is his zeal for his work, for building his clinic, for serving his Lord and his clients. He loves his work. He performs it from the heart, with a smile. For sure, the work honors God, but so does Robert's attitude.

And that's where we are in learning how to grow in the obedience of faith.

In previous chapters, we looked at the will and the mind. Now we come to the third faculty of our souls: our emotions. We have many emotions, ranging from joy to sadness, fear to comfort, affection to hate. In this chapter we will concentrate on three emotions that are particularly important to an obedient life: desire, fear, and pain (or the stress of our souls).

Desires—Eager to Do Good

Our desires drive us and ultimately combine with our wills and minds to define our lives. Every successful person, whether good or bad, is driven by strong desire, and every lazy or weak person is characterized by little desire.

God loves strong and fervent desire. He created our hearts to have such desire. It begins with our love for him, which is to be ardent and wholehearted and ultimately extends to all our service of him. Jesus rebuked the Laodiceans for their lukewarmness, saying that it disgusted him (Revelation 3:16). Paul teaches that we are to "never be lacking in zeal" and that we are to "keep [our] spiritual fervor" (Romans 12:11). He writes that Jesus gave his life for his disciples to be "zealous of good works" (Titus 2:14, ESV). Pause for a moment to meditate on this. Why did Jesus die for us? "To purify for himself a people of his very own, zealous of good works."

"Zealous of good works"—that well describes the output of obedience from the heart. From the mind we decide what is good; from the will we do it; from the emotions we are *eager* to do it.

Who is the worker who pleases the boss? Is it the one who meets minimum standards begrudgingly and resentfully, merely in order to collect his pay? Or is it the one who performs the same task with zeal because in his heart there is a strong desire to do the work well? And between the two, who is the happier worker?

The dwarfs in *Snow White* whistle while they work. Jesus died to create a people of his very own who whistle while they do good works for him, with a strong desire that makes them eager to do so.

John Piper has written an excellent book on desiring God, developing the biblical truth that God wants our desires to be strong and for us to enjoy him and enjoy life out of this affection. He opens the theme of his book with a quote from C. S. Lewis:

> If there lurks in most modern minds the notion that to desire our own good and earnestly to hope for the enjoyment of it is a bad thing, I submit that this notion has crept in from Kant and the Stoics and is no part of the Christian faith. Indeed, if we consider the unblushing promises of reward and the staggering nature of the rewards promised in the Gospels, it would seem that Our Lord finds our desires

not too strong, but too weak. We are half-hearted creatures, fooling about with drink and sex and ambition when infinite joy is offered us, like an ignorant child who wants to go on making mud pies in a slum because he cannot imagine what is meant by the offer of a holiday at the sea. We are far too easily pleased.[60]

Jesus has not called us to be half-hearted about anything we do. Our desire for him and to serve him is to be "with all [our] heart," meaning with enthusiasm and passion (Colossians 3:23).

But where does such fervency come from?

The Ultimate Desire

In the obedience of faith, all emotion should proceed from the ultimate emotion found in the desire for God. The "born again" experience is always filled with intense emotion. Experiences of being filled with the Holy Spirit are profoundly moving. The emotion is a fervent affection for God and his Son rooted in their holiness and beauty. With the "eyes of our heart," we come to see God more clearly for who he really is—holy, pure, unblemished, all loving, all powerful, a great and awesome God who in three persons created, governs, and sustains the universe.

In this experience, we realize that God has forgiven our sins and invited us into fellowship with his Son, Jesus Christ, who loved and died for us. Peter describes the emotion as "inexpressible and glorious joy" (1 Peter 1:8). Our desire to accept the invitation and enter into the fellowship is overwhelming. From this desire, all other desires derive, and they motivate in our wills an obedience pleasing to God.

This movement from a loving awe for God to a desire to obey is shown us by David in the 19th Psalm, which C. S. Lewis described as the "greatest poem in the Psalter and one of the greatest lyrics in the world."[61] In this psalm, David, the shepherd, reflects first on how "the heavens declare the glory of God" (v. 1). Then, from the contemplation of the beauty of God's creation, David moves to meditation on the beauty of God's law (vv. 7–11).

Likewise, Psalm 119 is a love poem on the goodness of God's law. There is no other passage in Scripture that portrays so completely the emotional chambers of the heart in which God's law is written. The psalmist's soul is "consumed with longing" for God's law. He "loves" it, meditates on it day and night, and "delights" (repeated ten times) in keeping it. He sums up his thoughts with "Great peace have they who love your law" (v. 165).

Jesus illustrates how our desire for God's rule should be all consuming with his parables of the hidden treasure and the merchant searching for fine pearls (Matthew 13:44–45). Both the man who found the hidden treasure and the merchant who found the valuable pearl "sold everything," so great was their desire to obtain the treasures. In these parables, Jesus is teaching what the kingdom of heaven is all about. God's rule (and our obedience to it) is something we should desire with such passion that we sacrifice all we own to obtain it.

So our first desire is to love God and know his fellowship, and closely akin to it, and derived from it, is the desire for his law and kingdom. This is at the heart of Jesus' teaching "to seek first [God's] kingdom and his righteousness," and all other things, such as food and drink and clothing, will be given to us (Matthew 6:33).

The problem, of course, is that knowing God and his fellowship and desiring the reign and rule of his law are not our only desires. And for some humans, most or even all of the time—and for all of us, some of the time—they are not our preeminent desires.

Ordering Desire

There are several things we need to remember about our desires.

Our Many Desires

First, let us remember that we have many desires. As John Piper puts it, our soul is a veritable "factory of desires."[62]

Some desires are godly. They are for God and his kingdom and create the passion to walk in his will and finish the work he has for us. Even these can get out of control, such as when a desire for excellence in work, even work in ministry, becomes workaholism. A desire for sufficient income to support our family can easily grow into a sinful greed.

Other desires are always sinful. These include envy and the prideful desire for independence from God.

Happiness comes from the feeling of joy and peace when we desire the right things in the right order and proportion.

The Holy Spirit orders our desires in accordance with God's will through self-control, which ensures that the three faculties of our soul work in harmony. The mind and will control the inordinate and sinful passions of our heart, and our desires motivate our wills to delight in choosing God's path for our lives and to persist in walking in it until our work is finished.

We Live by Faith, Not Emotion

Second, we need to remember that the obedience of faith is a walk of *faith* motivated by strong desires engendered by the Holy Spirit, not a walk of *emotion*. Our emotions are unsteady, here today and gone tomorrow, especially when they are grounded in circumstances.

Tony Campolo used to ask all couples who consulted him for marriage counseling what their relationship would be like when they were no longer "in love." Of course, this question mystified all the couples about to get married, but love in this romantic form is unlikely to last over a period of time, just as the warmth of a "Kumbaya" experience does not last forever.

Believers who are driven by emotion might move from church to church seeking a new and different emotional experience, complaining that the last church "did not feed me anymore." Or they might seek emotional satisfaction in work and move from job to job as the satisfaction from a new job wears off.

But more importantly, emotions that can be ruinous in our lives as passions spring up in a moment and drive greed or sexual passions, which lead to disastrous decisions. These decisions, made in a moment, can have grievous, long-lasting implications as they did for King David when he slept with Bathsheba.

Good Desires Gone Bad

Third, we need to remember that in the cosmic battle for our souls, the will is the prize and the mind is the battlefield. The foothold in our hearts that the devil seeks is in the emotional chamber—our prideful desires for independence and our cravings for those things of the world that will compete with our love for God and doing his will. For instance, Paul teaches that the love of money puts us on the path to "ruin and destruction" (1 Timothy 6:9). James admonishes that evil desires lead first to sin and then to death (James 1:14–15).

Though our emotions are unruly, the life of faith is steady and persistent. Faith is anchored to a God who is unchanging, whose character is founded in love and faithfulness. Its shield protects us from all the temptations to disorder our desires that Satan may throw at us. It grounds us in the truth to see through the cunning deceit of Satan's schemes. It does not rely on circumstances, which may thrill us one moment and depress us the next.

Therefore, whatever the circumstances, whatever the problems and even tragedies in our lives, in faith we are more than conquerors and safe in the love of God.

The Desire for More

But we need to be clear that the Bible does not teach that ambition or the desire to make money are sinful in themselves. It is "selfish ambition" and the "love of money" that are condemned (Philippians 2:3; 1 Timothy 6:10).

Human desire, even our passionate, persistent desire for more, for bigger and better, and for new frontiers is the source of most, if not all, progress in life. And that progress adds to the freedom, justice, health, and improved quality of life of millions, even billions of people. Strong desires for more and better in the souls of statesmen, explorers, inventors, scientists, soldiers, industrialists, salesmen, and most of us have built this country and given us the high standard of living we enjoy. They have given us the power and wealth to defend democracy throughout the world and the means to spread the gospel to every nation and tribe on earth. Where these desires have involved arrogance or greed or gluttony, it is not the desire that is bad but its self-centeredness. It is the desire that is out of God's order, not subordinate to his reign and rule.

The question in moral thought is, how do we keep these desires in proportion for a happy life? As we will see in Chapter 24, God's commission is for us to do our part in this progress. We are to be in the world but not of it. In the roles Christ has assigned for our lives, we need to bring glory to God by doing more than our share, walking the second mile. Indeed, imbued with the desire to please God and carry out his will for our lives and the power of the Holy Spirit, we should delight in doing more than our share.

Let's now turn to two other emotions that have a special place in the obedience of faith.

Pain: The Crucible of Obedience

The psalmist who wrote the magisterial 119th Psalm, which celebrates God's law and the happiness that comes from obedience, emphasizes his sufferings and declares,

> It was good for me to be afflicted
> so that I might learn your decrees (Psalm 119:71).

Isn't that a surprising conclusion to reach? Yet it is one that many faithful followers of God have arrived at over the years.

In C. S. Lewis's book on suffering, *The Problem of Pain*, he writes that God uses suffering to break our pride and lead us to surrender our wills to God's. For Lewis, pain is "God's megaphone to arouse contented creatures from the 'illusion of self sufficiency'" to an awareness that God is Lord, we are his creatures and all sufficiency is from him and in obedience to him.[63]

This is certainly true of me. I keep a diary (really, my personal "psalms" and prayers), and as I look back on it, I realize that I made ninety percent of my entries when the going was tough, when a problem threatened, and when my anxiety and fears were high. Whenever I feel pain, I turn to God with a fervency and urgency lacking in the good times. On the other hand, when things are going well, my "illusion of self-sufficiency" is elevated and I am less likely to pour out my heart to God in prayer. To borrow the words of Lewis, in the good times I am likely to become "content with my profane life."[64]

And it is true of my friends as well. The financial panic of 2008 brought several of them down financially. These were men who had been highly self-sufficient when times were good but who searched for their sufficiency in God when in their pain they realized that life was more than money and the pleasures and ease it might buy.

One of the most eloquent spokesmen for Christ in the 20th century was Malcolm Muggeridge, a journalist and editor for the English magazine *Punch*. His insight on suffering, given in an interview, aligns with Lewis': "Imagine human life being drained of suffering! If you could find some means of doing that, you would not enable [life]; you would drain it. Everything I have learnt, whatever it might be—very little I fear—has been learnt through suffering."[65]

We may to disagree with Muggeridge. We can learn multiplication tables without suffering, for example. But I have found that those who know and love God most deeply are those, like the Psalmist, who have known what the ancients in the faith called "the stress of the soul."

The writer of Hebrews lifts our understanding of suffering and obedience to a higher level when he teaches that the "author of [our] salvation" (Jesus) was made "perfect through suffering" (Hebrews 2:10). In this suffering "he learned obedience" and became the "source of eternal salvation for all who obey him" (5:9).

Of course, in the Hebrews passage just quoted, "salvation" means the progressive strength to overcome the power of sin that follows our adoption into our Father's family. But its main import here is to teach us that even Jesus learned obedience by his suffering. Certainly, therefore, should we.

Scripture says we "rejoice in our sufferings" because they produce character (Romans 5:3). Pain causes us to cast aside our illusion that happiness consists in the abundance of possessions or even our "life" on earth. Rather, for those who have turned to Jesus for our salvation, it causes us to grow in our trust that our sufficiency is in his grace (2 Corinthians 12:9).

There is no more graphic illustration of this basic truth than the testimony of Aleksandr Solzhenitsyn, who was imprisoned for eight years in one of Stalin's gulags. Reflecting on his life there, where he came to know Jesus Christ, the 20th century prophet wrote:

> It was granted to me to carry away from my prison years on my bent back, which nearly broke beneath its load, this essential experience: how a human being becomes evil and how good. In the intoxication of youthful successes I had felt myself to be infallible, and I was therefore cruel. In the surfeit of power I was a murderer and an oppressor. In my most evil moments I was convinced that I was doing good, and I was well supplied with systematic arguments. It was only when I lay there on rotting prison straw that I sensed within myself the first stirrings of good. Gradually it was disclosed to me that the line separating good and evil passes not through states, nor between classes, nor between political parties either—but right through every human heart. . . . That is why I turn back to the years of my imprisonment and say, sometimes to the astonishment of those about me: "*Bless you, prison!*" I . . . have served enough time there. I nourished my soul there, and I say without hesitation: "*Bless you, prison, for having been in my life!*"[66]

It was through back-breaking toil and sleeping on nothing but prison straw that Solzhenitsyn was delivered from his pride and turned to Christ as Lord.

It is interesting that C. S. Lewis's most extensive comments on obedience are found in *The Problem of Pain*.[67] Lewis finds the strongest defense of God's creation which allows suffering is that pain is required to cause the rebellious soul to "lay down his arms" and as the prodigal son to turn to his father and say, "Thy will be done." Such pain, Solzhenitsyn tells us, turns inhumane prisons into blessings.

Fear of the Lord: The Impetus to Move Forward

The stress of our souls from suffering plays an important part in our obedience. So does another emotion: fear—specifically, fear of the Lord.

Fear with Faith

We want to dismiss fear of the Lord in our understanding of obedience because sermons that dwell on a vengeful God, angry at sin, are counterproductive to most of us. They also miss the most central teaching about the obedience of faith in the Bible—we obey not out of fear but because through faith we know the love of God.

But we should not dismiss a proper understanding of the fear of God. It is fundamental to both obedience and happiness. In the messianic prophecy in Isaiah 11, we learn:

> The Spirit of the LORD will rest on [the Messiah]—
> the Spirit of wisdom and of understanding,
> the Spirit of counsel and of power,
> the Spirit of knowledge and of the fear of the LORD.(v. 2)

And then the passage concludes with the observation that the Messiah "will delight in the fear of the LORD" (v. 3).

This summation is not what we would expect. Why wouldn't the delight of the Lord be in wisdom or understanding or the power of God?

What does it mean for the Messiah's delight to be in the fear of the Lord? Certainly the fear of the Lord is almost everywhere associated with obedience. The Bible teaches that to fear God is to keep his commandments (Deuteronomy 5:29; 6:2, 24) and obey his voice (Haggai 1:12). It is to walk after him (Deuteronomy 10:12; Psalm 128:1) and to serve him (Deuteronomy 6:13; 10:20). What the passage in Isaiah teaches us is that the delight of the Messiah is in a reverence and honor for God's will and authority that galvanizes a life of obedience.

Isaiah 11:2-3 is messianic prophecy. And does it not hit the nail on the head? What was the delight of Jesus' life? What was the food of his soul? It was to know God's will and to do it.

Wisdom and understanding, counsel and power and knowledge, were important parts of Jesus' life, too. But they all served the purpose of his knowing the will of God and the courage to do it in a way that honored his Father.

The greatest source of "delight" for Jesus was doing his Father's will. It should be for us as well. We serve an omnipotent, omniscient, holy God. Therefore, we come into his presence with fear, an awe and reverence for his majesty and will. But we also serve an all-sufficient God. Our faith is in his love and sufficiency. And moving out in this faith to please him is the delight of all of us.

Fear Without Faith

On the other side of the coin, in the absence of faith in an all-sufficient God, fear paralyzes us. It was such paralysis that caused the servant who received one talent to bury it. He feared a master whom he thought was a "hard man" harvesting where he had not sown and gathering where he had not scattered seed. So he was "afraid." His rebuke was as severe as was the commendation of those who served the master well. "Throw that worthless servant outside into the *darkness*" (Matthew 25:24–25, 30, emphasis added). His fear in the wrong way led to misery.

The fear that leads to our shrinking back in the face of the risks of doing God's will produces a disobedience from lack of courage grounded in faith. Such a fear deprives us of enjoying the promises of God to his children. It results in a life of "darkness" (Matthew 25:30). In Hebrews we read that we are to "persevere" so that when we have "done the will of God, [we] will receive what he has promised." By courage in faith we can persevere. If in the lack of faith we "shrink back," God is not "pleased" with us. But, thank God, "We are not of those who shrink back and are destroyed, but of those who believe and are saved" (Hebrews 10:36–39).

The craven impulse to quit, to leave a course we have chosen in faith, is almost always of Satan. That impulse comes when the going gets tough and Christ is poised to strengthen our faith and character and provide us with the strength to succeed or the courage to honor God in the way we persevere in the trial. The words of God to uphold us in such circumstances are many, but perhaps the best are those he gave an anxious Joshua, who was to lead the children of Israel into the promised land: "Be strong and very courageous. . . . Do not be terrified; do not be discouraged, for the LORD your God will be with you wherever you go" (Joshua 1:9). And we would also do well to remember the preceding two verses, which instruct Joshua to "be careful to obey all the law. . . . Be careful to do everything written in it" (vv. 7–8). God is beside us to strengthen and guide us as we walk in his law.

Oswald Chambers said, "It is the most natural thing in the world to be scared, and the clearest evidence that God's grace is at work in our hearts is when we do not get into panics. . . . The remarkable thing about fearing God is that when you fear God you fear nothing else, whereas if you do not fear God you fear everything else."[68] We need to ever be aware of this contrast. If we don't fear God, we will be consumed with fear of something else; we will not obey and we cannot be happy.

Going back to Isaiah 11, it is the Spirit of God that teaches us the fear of God, and this is not a fear that paralyzes and causes us to shrink back but a courage grounded in the faith of an all-sufficient and loving God that empowers us to move forward in obedience and in the victory that comes from this obedience.

The League of Anti-Laodiceans

Happiness comes from the joy and peace we have when we desire the right things in the right order and proportion. This situation exists when, through faith, we put Christ on the throne of our lives and, with the Holy Spirit working through a renewed mind and submitted will, we order our desires.

This does not mean that we subdue our desires. Indeed, our desire for God and for the advance of his kingdom is to be passionate; so should be our desire to be good spouses, parents, and workers. Unlike the Laodiceans (Revelation 3:14-21), we are to burn hot with love for God and the doing of his will, not lukewarm!

Let's always remember that our desires, when purified by the Holy Spirit, are good. They will make us, not just *willing* to do what God asks, but *eager* to do it.

We have now reviewed the three faculties of our soul, will (Chapter 11), mind (Chapter 16), and emotions, in relation to faithful obedience. But for our lives to glorify God they need to be rooted in fertile soil which is a Christlike character. We examine character in our next chapter.

CHAPTER 18
Obedience Becoming Natural: The Character of Christ

THE BASIC THEME of this book is that the hidden key to happiness is obedience. But a more precise way to say it is that the hidden key to happiness is becoming a person whose character is to faithfully obey. That is, happiness relates not to just *what we do*; but also *who we are*.

It's having a character that naturally obeys.

Character is not something that just happens. We need to work at it and see that our character is developing in the right kind of direction—namely the direction of joyful obedience to our wise and loving God.

Two Very Important Questions

Character is a big topic and a very important one. So before we dive into any theology or practical discussion about character, let's first answer two fundamental questions.

What is Character?

The *Oxford English Dictionary* defines character as "a distinctive mark impressed, engraved, or otherwise formed." When we talk about character, then, we are referring to traits that lie deep within us, engraved in our hearts and souls through practice as an artisan engraves a design in silver or stone.

A more popular way of putting it is that character is how we behave when no one is looking. That definition might not be in the *Oxford English Dictionary*, but it's not bad. When no one is looking, there is no restraint—no police to arrest us, no proof that might convict us, no friend or neighbor before whom we might be ashamed. So we are free to behave as our characters, good or bad, would guide us.

In this sense, character is very important to all Christians because, as the apostle Paul teaches, we are free from the condemnation of the law (Romans 8:1). Yet God expects us to obey him—indeed, he expects us to be "perfect" (Matthew 5:48).

Which leads to a second basic question . . .

How is Character Formed in Us?

Aristotle—whose insights are a foundation of our Western understanding of character—gave the answer in its simplest form: "Moral goodness is the result of habit."[69]

As the dictionary definition quoted above indicates, our habits, good and bad, engrave behavior traits in us and they form our characters. We call good habits (such as love, courage, or faith) *virtues*, and we call bad habits (such as greed or anger) *vices*.

Our wills do not operate on a blank slate. In each of us they have been trained over the years so that they work in predictable ways. An honest person—one in whom the virtue of honesty has been engraved into his character—is likely to tell the truth. Likewise, a lazy person—one in whom the vice of laziness is engraved into his character—is likely to be unmotivated.

In a speech given at a Fordham University commencement ceremony, President Ronald Reagan gave an eloquent summary of how character develops and displays itself in our lives.

> The character that takes command in moments of crucial choices has already been determined. It has been determined by a thousand other choices made earlier in seemingly unimportant moments. It has been determined by

all those "little" choices of years past—by all those times when the voice of conscience was at war with the voice of temptation, whispering a lie that "it doesn't really matter." It has been determined by all the day-to-day decisions made when life seemed easy and crises seemed far away, the decisions that, piece by piece, bit by bit, developed *habits* of discipline or of *laziness*; *habits* of self-sacrifice or self-indulgence; *habits* of duty and honor and integrity—or dishonor and shame[70] (emphasis added).

President Reagan was passing on the wisdom of the ages. Crises reveal our character, and the character revealed is the product of habits developed through the years, good and bad, as we have moved through life. These habits strongly influence our wills.

Jesus concluded the Sermon on the Mount with the metaphor of building a house on the rock rather than sand. He told us that if we want our moral lives to have a strong foundation to withstand the storms that threaten them, we must take his teachings and put them into practice (Matthew 7:24–27). Like the golfer who practices the Ben Hogan fundamentals, we should practice and thereby habituate the teachings of Jesus so that obeying them becomes natural, even spontaneous, flowing from a character shaped in the image of Christ.

And Moses taught in the Shema that, living the obedient life comes from a life of training. Under the new covenant, as we put Jesus' teachings into practice, we grow into a Christlike character. That fundamentally is what discipleship is about (Matthew 28:20). But, as we saw in Chapter 12, the power for living the obedient life comes from the grace of the Holy Spirit, whom we receive by faith in Christ. How, exactly, do the Holy Spirit and character relate?

The Holy Spirit and Our Character

We know that all power in the physical realm needs to be harnessed and directed if it is to be effective. An automobile engine harnesses the energy in petroleum to power a car. A dam and a dynamo use water power to create electric power. A sail captures the power of the wind to move a sailboat.

There is a spiritual lesson in this.

The Wind and the Sail

Using a biblical metaphor, the Holy Spirit is like wind (John 3:8). And the "sail" that catches this wind is our character resulting from practicing obedience to biblical teaching.

To see all this more clearly, let us take the example of a prisoner—we'll call him Joe.

Joe

He is a man who was deserted by his mother at six months and turned over to foster parents. His foster father abused him; his foster mother paid scant attention to him. At 18 he was convicted of robbery on the false testimony of a gang buddy attempting to evade his own responsibility. Released from prison eight years later, he killed the witness who falsely testified against him. Now he is in for life.

Responding to a sermon at a prison "revival," Joe's heart is moved by the Holy Spirit and by faith he receives Christ as Lord and Savior. He becomes justified before God, born again. He loves Jesus Christ and is committed to following him.

Joe has a new heart. His affections are powerfully transformed. He is deeply sorrowful for his sins. His mind has a new orientation—he now sees all things through the lens of faith.

But the scars, or engravings, in the old heart will not go away easily. The Holy Spirit has much work to do in transforming his character and his heart.

In the power of the Holy Spirit, Joe needs to begin the process of building his house on rock—or in the words of Paul, putting off his "old self and its practices" and "putting on the new self, being renewed in the image of God." With a life being built on rock, the decisions of Joe's heart will flow into good deeds more naturally.

Joe's example shows how the Christian ethical life is a synergistic, interactive partnership of the Holy Spirit, a willing heart and Christlike character. If Christ by the Holy Spirit lives in our heart through faith, we will in obedience bear good fruit. From that obedience there ensues both a fullness of fellowship with God and a Christlike character, each nurturing the tree of our life to bear more fruit.

We, average Joes (and Janes), become not so average after all.

The Virtuous Cycle's Purpose

The virtuous cycle of faith, the Holy Spirit, love for God and obedience we talked about earlier produces its intended result as it builds up a character of obedience in us.

In time, as the virtuous cycle operates in our lives, we will reach a point where we are naturally and joyfully obedient to God. Not that we never fail again. We *will* fail. But joyful obedience is our permanent primary orientation—it is who we are.

This is what we want, isn't it? To please God by doing his will today, tomorrow, and forever? I believe it is. And we can become that kind of person but only as our character is transformed. So let's add Christlike character to our virtuous cycle.

Virtuours Cycle III

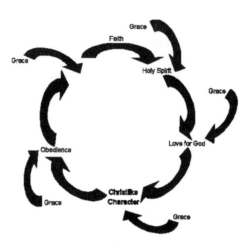

We have now completed our virtuous cycle. The most important insight we gain from it is that obedience is not just the output of an righteous life. Obedience is a vital organ in the life of our souls. In the depths of our souls by grace it combines with faith, the Holy Spirit, love for God and Christlike character to enhance their goodness and vitality and to give us abundance of life. Through the virtuous cycle we not only bear fruit for the glory of God but we come to know the true happiness we can only have in Christ.

Virtues for Obedience

What are the character traits—we can call them virtues—that need to be engraved by practice into our souls so that our natural inclination in all decisions is to obey God? There are many virtues in the character of an obedient Christian. We will look at three virtues essential for obedience. These virtues are found in a passage in Philippians. This passage is very familiar to many, but it is not often recognized as a teaching on obedience, even though, most centrally, that is what it is. In it we are exhorted to take on the character of the most obedient child of God ever—Jesus Christ himself—in order that in obedience we can "work out our salvation" (see Philippians 2:12). Here we learn in succinct terms those habits that are to be engraved in us so that our wills may naturally and spontaneously obey the teachings of scripture and the promptings of the Holy Spirit.

> Your attitude should be the same as that of Christ Jesus:
> Who, being in very nature God,
> did not consider equality with God something to be grasped,
> but made himself nothing,
> taking the very nature of a servant,
> being made in human likeness.
> And being found in appearance as a man,
> he humbled himself
> and became obedient to death—even death on a cross! . . .
>
> Therefore, my dear friends, as you have always obeyed—not only in my presence, but now much more in my absence—continue to work out your salvation with fear and trembling, for it is God who works in you to will and to act according to his good purpose (vv. 5–8, 12–13).

Here Paul tells us that the virtues that empowered Jesus in his obedience "to death" were these:

1. Humility
2. Self-emptying
3. Servanthood

These virtues may not be trendy. But these three traits are *all* strengths that need to live deep inside if we want to be faithfully obedient.

Moreover, humility, self-emptying, and servanthood are beautiful and desirable in their own way. They are internal strengths—virtues fundamental to obedience—and as such are the foundation to the abundant life and happiness. And they can lead to success in whatever career or calling we have.

Paul is telling us about how to have the same *attitude* as Christ Jesus so we can obey. The Greek word translated "attitude" is the same word, *phroneo*, as is translated "mind" in Romans 8:5–7, referring to our whole heart, our mind, will, and emotion. Therefore, Paul is teaching that humility, self-emptying, and servanthood should be engraved into all dimensions of our soul so that we can be obedient as was Jesus.

These virtues start low—with humility—and only go lower. But let's remember as we discuss these three virtues. In God's economy, the last becomes first and the lowly is exalted.

Humility: Having a Realistic View of Ourselves

Humility is an absolute prerequisite to the obedience of faith. All Christian character and all the other Christian virtues are built on it. This has been recognized throughout the history of the church. Saint Augustine, (5th century) for example, said that "humility is the foundation of all other virtues."[71] And Edwards (18th century) called humility "the most essential thing in true religion."[72]

But I get ahead of myself, historically speaking. Let's go back to Jesus—what did he teach about humility? We'll hit some highlights.

- When Jesus chose to describe his own character, this is what he had to say: "I am gentle and humble in heart" (Matthew 11:29).
- The first of the Lord's Beatitudes is "Blessed are the poor in spirit" ("poverty of spirit" being another way to refer to humility) (5:3).
- He also taught that humility—like that of a little child— is the mark of "the greatest in the kingdom of heaven" and that "he who humbles himself will be exalted" (Matthew 18:4; Luke 18:14).

With an example and statements like this coming from our Lord, we can hardly avoid trying to understand humility and acquire it.

Humility is a widely misunderstood term. It is fundamentally a virtue of the mind. It is seeing reality clearly—namely the reality of our unworthiness, smallness, and dependence in light of a holy and infinitely powerful, wise and providential God. The humble heart that takes in the truth of our utter dependence on God is filled with gratitude for the multitude of gifts that are lavished on us, most especially salvation, and from that gratitude obedience flows.

How, then, we can ask, could Jesus be humble? After all, he *was* God!

The answer is, he *became* humble. Paul says in Philippians, "Being found in appearance as a man, [Jesus] humbled himself." He made himself subject to the physical and moral laws of the cosmos and the governmental laws of his time and place. He became dependent on God for the body he was given and the air he breathed. He became a human being with all human limitations, subject to hunger, thirst, fatigue, temptation, betrayal, and even death on the cross—all of this even though, as Paul wrote, he was "in very nature God" (Philippians 2:8, 6).

As Jesus' example shows, humility is not related to position. We can see many other examples of this truth as well. People in powerful positions can be humble.

As General Washington became our nation's first president, he observed,

> No people can be bound to acknowledge and adore the Invisible Hand which conducts the affairs of men more than those of the United States. Every step by which they have advanced to the character of an independent nation seems to have been distinguished by some token of providential agency.[73]

Being keenly aware that the destiny of the nation was in God's hands, Washington was humble enough to realize that his own authority was limited.

Admiral Hyman Rickover, the father of our nuclear submarine fleet, had on his desk a plaque that read, "O God, thy sea is so great and my boat is so small."

Even in the top levels of business, humility can be found. *Good to Great,* a book investigating why some companies achieve stellar results, came up with the surprising conclusion that the CEOs of such companies are typically humble people.[74]

People like these—people with humility—stand out. Their characteristics are different from those of the general run of humanity.

- The *humble heart* says, "I don't deserve it. I have it by gift—thanks be to God! What can I do in return?"
- The *proud heart* says, "It's mine; I earned it and am entitled to it. It's not enough. I owe nothing in return."

- The *humble heart* is dependent and obedient.
- The *proud heart* is independent and rebellious.

- The *humble heart* delights in duty and service to others. It respects authority and order.
- The *proud heart* attends to duty and service only when made or paid to do so or to achieve applause. It cares for authority only when it is in charge.

Faith that believes in scripture and trusts the triune God revealed in the Bible is planted in the soil of humility. It is only in humility that we have the obedience of faith.

Our response. How, then, do we grow in humility? How do we loosen our grip on what we perceive to be our rights and entitlements? How do we see ourselves in proper perspective?

We simply open our eyes to reality.

First, we have to look at God and ourselves. We look at the stars and contemplate the grandeur of the God who made the universe. We try to understand the fourteen billion years it has existed in comparison to the fourscore years we hope to live in God's grace. We consider the incredible order and complexity of physical matter. We contemplate our bodies and how "fearfully and wonderfully made" they are (Psalm 139:14). We have learned our bodies have one hundred trillion cells of immense complexity, each one organized internally by a DNA bank of instructions more detailed than the thirty-two volumes of the *Encyclopedia Britannia*.

And then, also, we have to look at ourselves in relationship to others. For most of what we enjoy, most especially our freedom and our prosperity, is nothing that we produced ourselves but rather has come from others who have lived and worked down through the ages as well as in our own day. We need to observe the people cleaning the rugs and scrubbing the bathrooms and give them thanks. We ought to look at the products that make our lives better, such as our laptop, and marvel that thousands, if not millions, of our fellow human beings on this earth contributed to making them.

And most importantly we need to read the Bible and pray to be filled with the Holy Spirit. That's how we may understand more fully who God is, who we are, and how much he loves us—so much that he gave his Son to die for us.

In the grace of God, humility—a true assessment of who we are in our sinful and redeemed state—gives birth to obedience. But humility is not all we need engraved in our character if we are to be obedient from the heart. We also need to be self-emptied.

Self-Emptying: Leaving Behind Whatever Doesn't Serve God

Self-emptying—that's a strange-sounding idea, isn't it? It's not something we hear about every day. It might seem a little worrisome (is it the erasure of our identity?) . . . or even painful.

It's none of that. But it is part of having the attitude of Christ. Paul wrote that Jesus "made himself nothing," or more literally from the Greek, "emptied" himself (Philippians 2:7).

Self-emptying is somewhat different from self-denial, or the crucifixion of our sinful natures that we discussed in Chapter 13. We see this different quality of self-emptying in Jesus' example. In coming to earth, he emptied himself of his sovereignty—he simply left it behind in order to live obediently into the purposes given him by his Father. There was nothing ungodly or sinful about the abandoned attributes. Quite the opposite: they were divine. Nevertheless, they had to be left behind for Jesus to be obedient to the purpose of his incarnation.

This was by no means an automatic thing—it was what the Spirit led Jesus into the wilderness to work out in his heart through forty days of fasting. The temptations he encountered there were for him to invoke his divine powers to achieve worldly success and acclaim (Matthew 4:1–11). But he said no. He had left all this behind to walk the path of obedience to the will of his Father.

Likewise, self-emptying for us does not mean just the crucifixion of the "old self" but also the willingness to leave behind everything—even the good things—in our lives when Christ calls. These things can include our professions, our wealth, positions of power, situations of comfort. Any of these might become expendable when we choose to follow him wherever he leads us (Luke 14:33).

This has been the pattern throughout the history of faith.

Hebrews 11 recounts example upon example of self-emptying. Abraham obeyed God by becoming "a stranger in a foreign country." Moses "refused to be known as the son of Pharaoh's daughter" but "regarded disgrace for the sake of Christ as of greater value than the treasures of Egypt" (vv. 9, 24, 26).

Peter, likewise, left behind everything—his family, his work, his community (Luke 18:28–30). None of these was sinful, but Jesus' calling on his life required that they be abandoned.

And biblical examples are not all. We can review the lives of Christian martyrs, of the Reformers, of the Pilgrims who settled in our country, the Moravians we discussed in Chapter 8, and thousands of other missionaries who have left all behind to obey the call of Jesus. All these examples show self-emptying, some kind of "leaving behind."

Does that mean that each of us is called to leave *all* behind? Not necessarily. There is also a biblical principle that we are to bloom where we are planted, to follow Jesus in our native village or chosen profession (1 Corinthians 7:20). The important thing for each of us is that our hearts respond to God's will for us, whether that means leaving or staying.

Our response. Most often we do not need to leave home or give up our job. A leader can renounce the trappings and accoutrements of leadership; a wealthy person can live a simple life; a college professor can teach little children on the weekends. Simplicity, humility, anonymity, quietness are expressions of self-emptying and should be the witness of everyone.

The point here is that is we are to lead obedient lives. If we are to hear Jesus and follow him, our attitude always must be that regardless of what he asks us to renounce or leave, we must be willing to do so. We are to be ready to empty ourselves of it all for his sake. That's the self-emptying that leaves us free to be filled with God's purpose in our lives and his life in our souls.

We've stepped down from humility to self-emptying. But there's one step still lower to descend to: being a slave.

Servanthood: Exchanging Getting for Giving

The third character trait of Jesus that fostered his obedience was a servant's heart.

Even though Jesus was "in *very nature* God," he took on "the *very nature* of a servant" (Philippians 2:6–7, emphasis added). And who is a servant? One who does the bidding of a master. The "very nature" of Jesus was to obey. Think about it.

The word for "servant" here was used to describe a slave in the ancient Roman world. If we think clearly, we are shocked that the God of the universe would stoop to such a role. Yet he did.

In one sense, we shouldn't be surprised. It was foretold in the prophecies of Isaiah, which made it clear that the Messiah was to be God's servant (Isaiah 42:1–4; 50:4–9; 52:13–53:12). Jesus was "formed . . . in the womb to be [a] servant" (49:5). So are we.

Jesus understood this. He knew he was on earth to serve and to suffer death for our transgressions. In his own words, "The Son of

Man did not come to be served, but to serve, and to give his life as a ransom for many" (Matthew 20:28).

He modeled this servant's heart with a towel when he knelt before his disciples and washed their feet. He made it clear that we should follow in his footsteps: "I have set you an *example* that you should do as I have done for you" (John 13:15, emphasis added). The symbol for the life of a disciple of Jesus is a towel.

Another symbol is a hoe. This one comes from Saint Bernard, who said, "Learn the lesson that, if you want to do the work of a prophet, what you need is not a scepter, but a hoe."[75]

Carrying a hoe and not a scepter is antithetical to attitudes of the prince of this world. Scripture tells us that Satan was an angel of light, one of the elevated angels in heaven. He was expelled and fell "like lightning" from the heavenly realm, landing on earth with an army of minions (Luke 10:18; see also Isaiah 14:12–22 and Ezekiel 28:12–19). Satan is a rebel, not a servant. In *Paradise Lost* Satan brags, "Better to reign in hell than serve in heaven."[76]

To reign or serve, to wield a scepter or dig with a hoe—it's a basic choice. In the wilderness Satan tempted Jesus with the scepter; Jesus chose the hoe. And he said that in his kingdom "the greatest among you will be your servant" (Matthew 23:11).

Next to the command that we love God, the requirement that we serve (obey) God is the strongest determinant of a right relationship with God in Scripture. Moses puts it to the children of Israel like this: "O Israel, what does the LORD your God ask of you?" And he answers: "To fear the LORD your God, to walk in all his ways, to love him, to *serve* the LORD your God with all your heart and all your soul" (Deuteronomy 10:12, emphasis added).

Here, by the way, is a fourth activity to which we commit with "all [our] heart." We can add service to love, trust and obedience, although serving and obeying are functionally equivalent.

We serve God, not simply because being a servant was the very nature of our Lord whom we emulate, but also because, as Paul teaches, we are not our own; we have been "bought with a price" (1 Corinthians 6:19–20). Jesus has died for us; we belong to him and the God-given purpose of our lives is to serve him wholeheartedly and with gladness.

Our response. How do our hearts grow into the heart of a servant? Surely this is the work of the Holy Spirit. But as we have seen, the Spirit needs a sail. We need to practice servanthood, so that it becomes a virtue, something we do naturally.

In the company where I spent the majority of my working life, servanthood was one of the three core values. We tried to create a culture where everyone was a servant, not just to our customers and shareholders, but also to each other in our work—highest to the lowest and vice versa.

In our families, in our work, in our communities, and in our world vision, we need to ask ourselves how we are serving others. Are we creating harmony? Are we peacemakers? Are we there to carry burdens?

As we pray, as we abandon selfish agendas, as we are filled with the Holy Spirit, we will develop a servant's heart, willing to obey our Lord whenever and however he speaks.

The Upward Spiral

Are the three virtues of humility, self-emptying, and servanthood engraved in our characters? If so, the virtuous cycle is likely spiraling ever upward in our hearts, and as was the case with Steven in Chapter 12, intersecting with virtuous cycles elsewhere in our relationships.

These virtues were certainly engraved deeply in André Trocmé's soul. One of the most courageous soldiers (though not in uniform) in World War II, he sought no ribbons; his name appeared in no headlines; it was only by coincidence (perhaps not in God's eyes) that a Jewish professor of moral philosophy ran across the heroism of the saints he led. He had a towering intellect and could have lived in the United States with our wealth and safety, yet he emptied himself of such luxuries, chose to follow Christ in poverty and became his slave in the love of desperate Jewish children. His spiritual virtuous cycle intersected with hundreds, even thousands, of others at Le Chambon.

If we want to be more like Trocmé, possessing the character of Christ and an eager willingness to obey God, then there's one last discipline we need to develop. To become sensitive to God's leading, we need to learn to hear and respond to his whispers in our ears.

CHAPTER 19
"Speak, Lord!": Discerning the Will of God, Part 1

IF YOU PASS through the Five Points traffic circle in my hometown of Birmingham, Alabama, you will see the statue of a man on his knees, looking up toward heaven. The man depicted in this local landmark is known as Brother Bryan.

The Reverend J. A. Bryan, inspired by George Mueller, was a Presbyterian minister who pastored a blue-collar congregation in Birmingham. Brother Bryan lived by faith, never asking anyone for a nickel, yet he led the balloting for the *Birmingham News's* first Man of the Year, more than doubling the votes received by the runner-up. Until his death in 1941, he worked tirelessly to meet the needs of working-class people and the poorest Birminghamians. He is still widely remembered in the city today. As the statue suggests, prayer was the basis of his productive life of service to God and humanity.

When I see the statue of Brother Bryan kneeling in prayer, I think of the biblical line "Speak, LORD, for your servant is listening" (1 Samuel 3:9–10). And that is the true attitude of obedience: listening to God with an attitude of ready submission, of willingness to do whatever he asks.

The words for "to obey" in both biblical languages—Hebrew and Greek—mean simply "to hear." All obedience begins with hearing God.

Jesus said, "My mother and my brothers are those who *hear* the word of God and do it" (Luke 8:21, ESV, emphasis added).

227

I don't know what God will say when he speaks. But I do know one thing: he is speaking. And what he speaks will be just right for each of us. His will is "perfect" for us (Romans 12:2).

And I know one more thing: God's guidance won't do us one bit of good, and it won't lead us one step closer to happiness, unless we develop the capacity to hear it . . . and then go on to obey it.

Listening Prayer

Listening is no easy thing. That's true for listening in general, and more true for listening to God.

When others speak, my mind can be fixed on another issue of the moment, or I may be more interested in making my point than in hearing another's. Habit 5 in Stephen Covey's *The 7 Habits of Highly Effective People*—"Listen before being heard"—is not one that comes easily for me.[77] Just ask my wife!

How about you? How good a listener are you? In particular, how good are you at picking up on what God wants to say to you?

Long ago, the Lord said to Isaiah, "Come now, let us reason together" (Isaiah 1:18). He invites each of us into his presence for mutual communication. We are to listen as well as speak. And if we are to listen to God's specific words for our lives, then we must do so in the context of a personal relationship with him.

We enter into the fellowship to hear God's words for our lives through prayer—specifically, through what Leanne Payne calls "listening prayer."[78] The Holy Spirit is our prayer partner, and in the "fellowship of Holy Spirit" he guides us into all truth about God's plans and purposes for our lives (2 Corinthians 13:14; see also Romans 8:26–27; John 16:13). As God invites us into his presence to "reason together" with him, we ask him for guidance:

> Show me your ways, O LORD,
> teach me your paths;
> guide me in your truth and teach me,
> for you are God my Savior,

and my hope is in you all day long (Psalm 25:4–5).

The entire objective of seeking God's guidance is to discern his plan or will for our lives. We ask him to show us *his* ways, *his* paths, *his* truth. We are to discern God's purposes for us.

In all likelihood we will not hear specific instruction from God in an audible way. But in faith we may nevertheless know that God will guide us every step of the way. If we are trusting in the Holy Spirit and have denied ourselves, then he will show us his path for us.

Discovering God's Path

In Leo Tolstoy's short story, *"Two Old Men,"* Efím Tarásitch Shevélef and Elisha Bódrof, while young, vow to God that one day they will make a pilgrimage from their homes deep in Russia to Jerusalem, there to worship Christ.[79] Years later and late in their lives, at significant financial sacrifice and no little inconvenience to their families, the two men set out on foot.

After traveling five hundred miles, Elisha is delayed when he stops at a cabin for a cup of water and finds a family that has been devastated by a drought. The family is at death's door, unable to buy food, with all of their property mortgaged. So Elisha, recalling Scripture, uses the money he had saved for the pilgrimage to buy the family food and clothing, to redeem their property from foreclosure, and to reestablish them so that they can prosper in the good weather that is to follow.

Penniless, Elisha returns home, never having completed the pilgrimage—except in spirit.

The two men had planned their pilgrimage for years in prayer and with much preparation, but as Elisha and Efím set off on their walk, the Holy Spirit diverted Elisha presenting him with an unexpected opportunity to love. And this man simply did the right thing as God led him. Knowing the Word of God, spiritual discernment, and circumstances combined for Elisha to bear fruit that was pleasing to the Lord.

As you and I are going along in life, what path might God be calling us to take? What might he want us to do?

Can we discern his guidance? And if we do, are we willing to lay down our own plans and do what he asks?

The Character That Hears

There is much teaching in the Bible on how God instructs us. Most of it essentially is teaching on how we keep our fellowship with him pure and intimate so that we are in a position to hear the loving, wise advice and guidance of a father for a child. What are the keys to this relationship and to discerning God's will?

1. Humility

Humility, we have seen in Chapter 18, is a key virtue for obedience. It is also the first key to following God's guidance. As David states in Psalm 25, "He guides the humble in what is right and teaches the humble his way" (v. 9). Thomas à Kempis tells us that a humble knowledge of self is a surer way to God than a deep sense of learning. As we have already seen, humility is simply understanding who God is, magnificent in his power, sovereignty, and love, and who we are in our sinfulness and insignificance apart from him.

If the prayer posture of the obedience of faith is "Speak, Lord, for your servant is listening," we can hear only as humble servants of the Lord of the universe.

Humility's ultimate epiphany is that in all creation the one supreme will is the will of God, a will infinitely greater than the sum of all created wills. In humility we realize our wills are to be totally surrendered to and aligned with his, as Jesus' was. We were created for no other purpose. Humility is the soil in which all obedience grows.

Without humility, we can perhaps learn in our head but not discern in our heart. We can know the Ten Commandments and the Sermon on the Mount, and we can hear sermons and go to Sunday school, but until we have humility, we pay scant attention. As Jesus emphasizes, it is easy for us to hear and not understand (Matthew 13:13). When we understand who God is, how totally dependent we are on him for all blessings, and how infinitely wise, powerful, and loving he is, we are ready to listen, understand, and respond in the obedience of faith.

The attitude of the humble heart that can discern spiritually is seen in the young widow Ruth of the Bible. In committing her life to following her mother-in-law, Naomi, she said, "Where you go I will go, and where you lodge I will lodge. Your people shall be my people, and your God my God. Where you die I will die, and there will I be buried" (Ruth 1:16–17). Ruth's will was surrendered to Naomi's in humility. She was able to say to Naomi, "Speak, for your servant is listening." Such is a perfect model for our relationship to God.

When we pray for guidance, therefore, we need to acknowledge God and his majesty and our total dependence.

It is helpful to memorize the scriptural doxologies that express God's sovereignty and majesty and to commit them to our hearts as we pray for guidance. Among these doxologies, or brief hymns of praise, are Romans 11:33–36, Philippians 2:5–11, and Revelation 4:11: 15:3–4. As we recite them in our prayer for guidance, the Holy Spirit will lay them on our hearts as we enter into the fellowship of our God for his counsel.

Nehemiah's prayer on behalf of a sinful and broken people returning to Jerusalem from exile is a good example for us. He begins, "O LORD God of heaven, the great and awesome God . . ." Then he continues by calling himself "your servant," and the Israelites "your servants," as he confesses the nation's "sins . . . against you" (Nehemiah 1:5–11, ESV).

We need in humility to confess our sins before we seek God's guidance. Our "iniquities" separate us from God (Isaiah 59:2). They destroy our fellowship with God. It was only after David "acknowledged [his] sin" to God and "did not cover up [his] iniquity" that God responded with the words that give his followers solace even today: "I will instruct you and teach you in the way you should go; I will counsel you and watch over you" (Psalm 32:5, 8).

So in humility we pray, "Instruct me and teach me" and "Counsel me and watch over me." And certainly God will give us the wisdom and instruction for the challenges we face and dilemmas we encounter. Further, he will give us his hand, walk beside us, and keep his eye on us as we bear fruit.

Humility opens our minds to know that the mind of God is infinitely greater than our own.

Perhaps the most penetrating teaching on how to listen to God is Paul's instruction at the end of Chapter 11 and beginning of Chapter 12 of Romans. In a paean of praise that concludes Chapter 11, Paul declares that God's mind is "unsearchable" and his plans "beyond tracing out." He asks rhetorically, "Who has known the mind of the Lord?" and "Who has been his counselor?" All this to make clear that God's plans and will are often inscrutable, far from what we might want, expect or understand with our natural mind. As Isaiah had recorded the word of the Lord,

> My thoughts are not your thoughts,
> neither are your ways my ways. . . .
> As the heavens are higher than the earth,
> so are my ways higher than your ways
> and my thoughts than your thoughts. (Isaiah 55:8–9)

2. A Sacrificial Attitude

In light of the immensity and inscrutability of God's mind, Paul teaches in the first two verses of Chapter 12 that if we are going to be able to "test and approve what God's will is," we must (1) "offer our bodies as living sacrifices…." (2) "no longer conform to the patterns of this world," and (3) "be transformed by the renewing of our mind." Paul is teaching us that, to hear God as he leads us in his will, we must first offer ourselves in our relationship with God as "living sacrifices," emptied of self-centeredness, just as Jesus was humbled and self-emptied as he sought and understood God's will in order to walk in it.

God desires to communicate his will for our lives in fellowship with us, but nothing so sours this fellowship as our selfishness. This is true of any relationship where one of the parties uses the fellowship for selfish purposes. In these circumstances the relationship will be strained, and over time it will fail.

This selfishness may manifest itself in materialistic greed—the grasping for more money or an upper hand in a partnership or in neediness for more time, attention, and affirmation (and sulking when it is not obtained). Such strains the integrity of the relationship.

Thus Paul teaches that our body, as an expression of our material, sexual, and psychological needs, must be sacrificed if we are to hear God. If we seek God's guidance in our business, our focus should be on the benefits of those we serve (our customers, fellow workers, and the business owners), not our selfish needs. If we need guidance in the use or investment of money, likewise the focus needs to be on those—other than us—that it is God's will for the money to serve. As we focus on serving God first and in his will serving others, our needs will be met, to overflowing. "Seek first his kingdom and his righteousness, and all [we need] will be given" us (Matthew 6:33; see also Matthew 19:29).

3. Renunciation of the World

Paul goes on to instruct that, if we are to hear God's will, we must no longer conform to the patterns of this world (Romans 12:2). The "patterns of this world" are the patterns of thought and living—social, political, economic, ecclesiastical—that are ungodly. Satan is the ruler of this world, and when our lives are conformed to its patterns, we are in no position to have fellowship with or to hear God.

We all have preconceived ways of perceiving reality, and these preconceptions close our minds to receiving advice contrary to them. John describes worldly preconceptions as "the desires of the flesh and the desires of the eyes and pride in possessions" (1 John 2:16, ESV). When our worldly passions create the preconceptions through which we measure advice, we cannot hear God.

We see this in the natural realm all the time. Marriages break up because of sexual passion for another partner. All reasonable advice is rejected. Not only is the adultery sinful, but it is also foolish and almost always leads to misery. Likewise greed, gluttony, and a host of other worldly mindsets cut us off from fellowship with God and ever hearing his advice.

4. The Renewed Mind

Paul teaches that we must be transformed by the renewing of our minds (Romans 12:2). As we have discussed, it is with our wills that we will obey God, and it is with our renewed minds that we will discern his guidance. Our old ways of thinking that were captive to the things of the world and our selfish desires that weaken and corrupt the mind must be eliminated. The natural mind is hostile to God. (Romans 8:7). It cannot follow his counsel.

Finally, Paul gives us a critical instruction on guidance. We must "test and approve" what God's will is, his "good, pleasing and perfect will" (Romans 12:2). The implication here is that there are many counterfeit signals coming our way. Satan, who is committed to our not hearing God or doing his will, is masquerading as an "angel of light," seeking to deceive us or seduce us into false truths and wrong paths (2 Corinthians 11:14). Thus, before we can approve any guidance we might perceive as coming from God, we must "test" it, most especially by God's written Word. God's specific instruction for our lives will never contravene it.

5. Trust

Possibly the most prominent of all guidance scriptures is Proverbs 3:5–6, which teaches,

> Trust in the LORD with all your heart
> and lean not on your own understanding;
> in all your ways acknowledge him,
> and he will make your paths straight.

God stands ready to "make our paths straight," but he gives us this kind of direction as we trust in him with all of our heart. David expresses the same idea in his prayer for guidance in Psalm 25. After asking God to teach his paths and lead in his truths, David adds, "You are God my Savior, and my hope is in you all day long" (v. 5).

The same theme is taken up by James when he teaches that God is ready to generously provide "wisdom" to us whenever we ask, provided that we not "doubt," for those who doubt will not "receive anything from the Lord" (James 1:5–7).

This teaching should not be surprising. We will not listen to advice from someone we do not trust. It is nonsensical to seek a relationship or a deeper fellowship for others' counsel and instruction if we do not trust them to be wise or know what they are talking about.

Here we again see the coupling of obedience and faith. If we are to discern God's paths for our lives, so that in his grace we might walk in them, we must first trust him wholeheartedly.

6. Love

Finally, if we are to hear God, love must be a foundational principle of our lives. Paul's Philippians prayer is that our "love may abound more and more in knowledge and depth of insight, so that [we] may be able to discern what is best and may be pure and blameless until the day of Christ" (Philippians 1:9–10). This is merely the other side of the coin to self-emptying and renunciation of the world. Our selfishness and our craving for things of the world get in the way of our hearing and understanding of God's guidance. Love, on the other hand, is the perfect lens through which we will be able to see clearly all that God is asking us to do. Love will focus our hearts on the needs of others and the true calling of our lives to serve God by serving others in all that we do.

Isaiah 58:10–11 gives us the same insight.

If you spend yourselves in behalf of the hungry
and satisfy the needs of the oppressed,
then your light will rise in the darkness,
and your night will become like the noonday.

The LORD *will guide you always;*
he will satisfy your needs in a sun-scorched land
and will strengthen your frame.
You will be like a well-watered garden,
like a spring whose waters never fail. (emphasis added)

As we in sacrificial love spend ourselves on behalf of the hungry and the least and satisfy the needs of the oppressed, we have put ourselves in a position to hear God so that he might guide us and at the same time satisfy all our "needs" so that we overflow "like a spring whose waters never fail."

Where love is the lens of our spiritual eyes, we will see clearly. All of the law—an expression of God's will—is summed up in love. It is in perfect harmony with the character of God, who is love. It binds all virtue together in perfect harmony. Therefore, when we in love reach out to the least of our brothers and sisters, God delights in making his will known to us.

One Who Heard God

Is there any wonder how André Trocmé so clearly heard God's call and followed his will in his life? Recall his life story.

He was a humble man living in a forgotten part of a conquered country. He offered his body as a living sacrifice to God, willing to die in his love and care for the strangers in his land. Early in his life, he renounced the things of this world (though he worked in the house of Rockefeller) and vowed to pursue a life of poverty in impoverished French villages. His mind was transformed at an early age as he sought his God's face with all his heart. His trust was wholeheartedly in God because he had no wealth on earth to support him nor weapons to protect him. And then love: his church's arched doors bore the words of his Lord, "Love one another," and in one accord, those who belonged to it spent themselves "in behalf of the hungry" and "satisf[ied] the needs of the oppressed."

I'm no Trocmé and I doubt you are. But here is a beautiful

example of a character that was in a position to hear God.

We have looked at how we in God's grace position ourselves so that God can lead us. In the next chapter, we turn to how he guides us.

CHAPTER 20
"Speak, Lord!": Discerning the Will of God, Part 2

THE BIBLICAL RECORD tells us of men and women who heard words directly from God in various ways. Adam and Eve walked with God in the garden. Abraham was God's friend and talked with him. Jacob and Joseph had God-sent dreams. Moses heard God speaking from a burning bush. Isaiah had a vision of the divine throne in heaven. Peter, James, and John heard God speaking on the Mount of Transfiguration.

Can we hear from God too?

Yes, we can. (Though I doubt from a burning bush!) God uses at least five modes of guidance to lead us. Knowing about each one enables us to better discern his will so that we may obey it.

1. Through His Word

Scripture is a permanent expression of God's will. It tells us what he wants and doesn't want us to do.

If the Bible prohibits a course of action, that should put an end to it. For example, the apostle Paul repeatedly listed categories of conduct that are forbidden to us (Galatians 5:19–21; Ephesians 4:31; Colossians 3:5–9).

On the other hand, if a path we are considering is commended by the principles of Scripture (such as serving one another in love or carrying one another's burdens), and if it is consistent with the fruit of the Holy Spirit, then it is open for further prayer and consideration.

Our response. If we want to hear what God is saying to us in Scripture, then we need to know it; not just have some familiarity with it but be fully immersed in it (John 8:31). It needs to "dwell in [us] richly" (Colossians 3:16). We need to read Scripture daily, memorize it, pray it, and consciously conform our lives to it. As we put its teachings into practice, we will more and more come to live it spontaneously and naturally.

You should use any technique for immersing yourself in Scripture that works for you. But allow me to mention a couple that have worked for me.

Long ago I collected a series of Scripture verses that I entitled "Words of the Lord for Daily Living," which I typed out and put in a small three-ring binder I carry with me everywhere. I have committed many of these verses to memory, and when I have time—say, in a hotel room or on an airplane—I refresh my recollection of them. (I have collected them in Appendix C.)

In addition, I have developed a prayer list I have prayed through on the weekends for some two decades. This is not a list of personal requests, such as that Cousin Bob will find a new job or Aunt Martha will start feeling better. No, this prayer list is about God's will for the kind of character a disciple is to have. It lists a number of verses relating to such topics as guidance, servanthood, self-denial, humility, purity, faith, flesh, God's plan and purpose, joy and peace, prayer, and will. Not only do these verses allow me to pray about these subjects once a week, but also the prayer keeps them freshly on my mind (and hopefully in my heart).

2. Through His Spirit

Just as God spoke to his friend Abraham, so the Holy Spirit communicates with us in a personal way.

The Holy Spirit is "the Spirit of wisdom and of understanding" (Isaiah 11:2), and as the Paraclete, he walks alongside us to guide us in every choice we make. In our hearts, he applies the truth of Scripture in practical ways. Sometimes he even speaks directly to us about what God wants us to do.

Our response. We'd be foolish to miss anything the Spirit wants to say to us. This is why we must develop spiritual discernment. We have to tune the ears of our own spirits to hear what the Spirit of God is saying to us.

Nearly every day for years now I have prayed a prayer based on Paul's prayer in his letter to the Colossians:

> Lord, may I have knowledge of your will through all *spiritual wisdom* and *understanding* so that I might live a life worthy of you, pleasing you in every way and bearing fruit in every good work.[80] (Based on Colossians 1:9-10, emphasis added)

Paul's prayer teaches us that if we are to live a life worthy of our Lord, we must have spiritual discernment of God's will—a discernment that is deeper and more profound than we can have through the human brain.

We may not always discern the Spirit's leading clearly. A Pentecostal pastor once told me to beware of "led poisoning." It is easy to think our personal agendas have been confirmed by the Spirit when they have not. For that reason, we need to "test" our sense that the Spirit is leading us with all of the guides discussed in this chapter.

3. Through Our Conscience

It doesn't show up on x-rays. No surgeon can put a scalpel on it. Yet each of us has a spiritual "organ" known as *conscience*, which defends or accuses us over different decisions we make (Romans 2:14–15).

In Chapter 16 we discussed our consciences as one of our "mind strengtheners." It also guides our spirits in their communion with the Holy Spirit.

Our conscience does not give us detailed instruction from God. But it is one means by which the Spirit speaks to our spirit. If we pay attention to our conscience, it can act like guard rails that will keep us from straying over one side or the other of God's path for us.

As Paul says, if we have a doubt about a practice or course of action, we should avoid it even if it is not scripturally condemned. If our conscience says no, we should assume that it is God's Spirit speaking to our spirit and then refrain—it is not God's will for us (Romans 14:22–23).

A troubled conscience gives us an uneasy feeling. But a contented conscience gives us a sense of peace in our spirits.

As Paul says, "Let the peace of Christ rule in your hearts" (Colossians 3:15). If a course of action is not prohibited by Scripture and is consistent with its general principles, and if in our spirits we have a peace about it, we may well proceed with it.

Our response. Recognizing that we have a conscience means that we can learn to consult it. Before acting, we can stop and ask ourselves what our conscience is saying to us. Is our conscience troubled or peaceful?

The conscience is easy to ignore, and our old selves hanging on will prompt us to ignore it—for money or position or recognition. But we must remember that the more we ignore the conscience, the more it withers. If we will listen to and heed our conscience, then it will grow more robust and become a stronger guide to what God wants from us.

4. Through Circumstances

Teresa was an elementary school teacher in a suburb of Birmingham who thought she felt a calling from God to devote her career to inner-city ministry. She did not know if this prompting in her spirit was really from the Holy Spirit, but she began praying about it.

That's when a principal she had previously worked for called her. This principal said that she was now with Cornerstone Schools, a Christian K-8 school in Birmingham's inner city, serving children from poor and disadvantaged homes. Would Teresa have any interest in working there?

Today Teresa is teaching the fourth grade at Cornerstone. The principal's calling her out of the blue that day was just the thing she needed to not only confirm God's call but also let her know specifically where she was to serve in inner-city ministry.

This illustrates another way God communicates with us: through circumstances.

God has planted each of us in a certain time and place. All that has gone before has put us on a certain path. God, who is sovereign, will use, allow, and create circumstances to guide our future paths.

Our response. God doesn't always use circumstances to guide us as clearly as he did in Teresa's case. But he always orchestrates circumstances to accomplish what he wills. Our part is to try to read the circumstances in our lives to see what God might be saying to us through them.

There is no foolproof way to read circumstances. But what Oswald Chambers calls the "quiet persistence" of circumstances is a good indication that God is speaking. (3.28)

5. Through the Counsel of Others

I don't want to leave the impression that spiritual discernment of God's will is strictly a solitary activity. Nothing in Christian life really is. That's why God made the church! Why shouldn't we submit our uncertainties to others and bring their spiritual wisdom to bear in finding the course of obedience to God? As Proverbs teaches us, "Plans fail for lack of counsel, but with many advisers they succeed" (15:22).

When we are faced with a difficult decision, we may have a peace about it in our hearts, and Scripture and circumstances may allow it, yet it is still helpful to seek the counsel and ask for the prayer of wise Christian brothers and sisters and even others, who are wise but do not know the Lord, before we set out. As Proverbs also teaches, "Do you see a man wise in his own eyes? There is more hope for a fool than for him" (26:12).

We are all capable of making foolish decisions that squander the time, talents, and resources that God has given us because we do not seek the counsel of those older, more experienced, and wiser than we. God can use them to either check our plans altogether or refine and modify them in a way that allows us to proceed more fruitfully for the Lord than we otherwise could on our own.

Our response. If we don't have some wise, mature, godly people in our lives, there's no time like the present to look for some. And if we haven't made a practice before of seeking advice, we need to learn vulnerability, and trust in submitting our challenging decisions to others for their advice.

So let's add it up. We've got the Bible, the Holy Spirit, our conscience, circumstances, and wise counsel to help us hear what God is telling us. A confluence of these guides will confirm God's leading. Yet even if we are sincerely trying to hear God through all of these channels, and even if we are preserving our relationship with him in holiness, we still may not necessarily hear him clearly.

What then?

When You're Still Not Sure You've Heard Him . . .

I can point to some ten major decision points in my life where Christ's presence became palpable to me and his direction inescapable. Each of these occasions was in relation to the spiritual dimension of my life, not work. In decisions relating to work, I have received no specific leading, though I have prayed and prayed for it.

For instance, one time I was trying to decide whether to change my career path, leaving law practice for a job in insurance. The night before I had to make that decision, the factors for and against the career change seemed to me to be in equipoise. Some advisors said yes; others, no. So, what did I do? I told God that if I slept soundly that night, I would take the insurance job. I slept soundly that night, and I did leave law practice. In retrospect, I am sure this was the Lord's will, but his guidance was not manifestly clear to me at the time.

I'm grateful for every time God chose to plainly direct me in my decision making. But my experience has not been unusual, I think, in that most of the time I have had to make decisions without such clear guidance.

The simple fact is that God does not give us specific guidance on all that we do. It is not God's will that we should be puppets directed and guided in minute detail. He wants to develop godly character in us so that, abiding in his Word with a regenerate will and a renewed mind, we naturally do the right thing.

We will have strategic decisions and quandaries and challenges, and for these we will seek his fellowship and receive his guidance. But as the expression has it, "life comes at us fast," and often we will be on our own to react in a godly way on the basis of the virtues engraved in our characters.

The Christian life is more like a golf game or tennis match than it is like a football game. In football, the coach sends in every play—offense and defense. With golf and tennis, though, all the coaching is before and after play, not during.

We have our time to read, study, digest, and memorize Scripture, which has instruction to guide us in all circumstances. We have our time to grow into Christlike character by putting Christ's teachings into practice. We have our time to enter our prayer chambers and seek God's guidance. But then the decisions we make, the actions we take, and the words we speak often have no direct, recognizable input from our Lord.

Surely, through his Spirit and his Word, Christ lives in our hearts through faith, walks with us, and counsels us (Ephesians 3:17). Apart from our being consciously aware of it, he is orchestrating events, giving us energy, thoughts, and words to help us through. His providential hand is surely upon us, but in ways we will understand only when in eternity we see things clearly. Our part is to keep seeking him and serving him the best way we know how.

And there's one more thing. Though we may not always have as clear guidance as we would want, the process of seeking him is a beautiful thing in itself.

Looking back over many years as a Christian, I can honestly say that the times I have spent praying for God's guidance (especially when praying the guidance scriptures I referred to earlier in this chapter) have been among the sweetest I have had with my Lord. Even when I have not "heard" him in a specific way, I have loved the Spirit-given attitude of a heart that keeps on saying, "Speak, Lord, for your servant is listening." And by faith I have known he has been beside me every step of the way.

Real-Life Obedience

We have completed our walk through the garden of the obedience of faith, observing its blooms that create the fragrance and beauty of Christ. Now we leave the garden to consider the challenges and routines of our daily lives.

A major objective of this book is to anchor the obedience of faith to practical daily living, for it makes sense there or not at all.

In the final set of chapters, we will consider what the obedience of faith looks like in areas of life that are basic to all of us, particularly our careers and how we order our days. And just as in Part 3 we have looked at the village of Le Chambon as a rough template for how to mature in the obedience of faith, so next let's begin by paying attention to an individual who can serve as an inspiration for us in living faithfully obedient lives in the 21st century in America.

PART 4

Obedience In Our Daily Lives

CHAPTER 21
Obedience in Our Daily Lives

I WAS PRIVILEGED to meet Truett Cathy—best known as the founder of the Chick-fil-A restaurant chain—two years ago. I was struck by what an understated man he was, despite his extraordinary business achievements. I was also impressed by his solid faith in Jesus Christ and his faithful obedience to God as a businessman, husband, father, grandfather, teacher and philanthropist. And make no mistake: nearing the end of his career, this is a man enjoying the deep satisfaction of a life aligned with God's will. This is a very happy man.

The Making of a Christian Businessman

Some successful business people come from privilege and position, while others work their way up on their own. Truett Cathy belongs to the latter variety.

Truett was born in northeastern Georgia in 1921. His father was in real estate and insurance sales, and when the Depression destroyed this livelihood, the family moved to Atlanta. There, at the age of eight, Cathy learned to buy Coca-Colas for four cents a bottle, put them on ice, and sell them for a nickel. During the Depression, he threw newspapers in the afternoon and in the evening helped his mother operate a boardinghouse so the family could make ends meet. She cooked the meals, and Truett shucked corn, shelled beans, and washed the dishes.

In the days before credit cards, the Cathys had an "account" at the local grocery store. Truett's mother would send him to the store to purchase groceries to feed the boarders. There were days when the account was "full" and Truett, a twelve-year-old, would come home to his mother empty-handed. Those were not easy times.

Straight out of high school, Truett joined the Army, where he served during World War II. (Truett never went to college.) When he was discharged, he and his brother Ben decided to go into the food service business—the only business they knew.

From The Dwarf House to Chick-fil-A

Truett sold his car, and he and his brother came up with $4,000 cash, to which they added a $6,600 bank loan. With this capital, they bought a small piece of property in a good location for a restaurant, near the Atlanta airport and a Ford assembly plant. They built a short-order restaurant with seven stools, four tables, a jukebox, and a cigarette machine and named it The Dwarf House. They operated it twenty-four hours a day, six days a week, each taking a twelve hour shift.

Truett lost his brother Ben two years after they opened The Dwarf House when he died in a plane crash. For the next nineteen years, Truett flipped hamburgers, served eggs and bacon, mopped floors, and gave the best and friendliest service of any short-order restaurant in Atlanta.

He could have continued as a modestly successful small-time restaurant owner, but God had bigger things in mind for this humble yet entrepreneurial man.

In the early 1960s, Truett began to buy chicken scraps from a food service business providing chicken breasts for meals served on the airlines. First, he served what we now know as "nuggets," and soon he was serving a chicken fillet sandwich. These offerings were almost unknown in the restaurant business at the time.

After twenty-one years of operating the Dwarf House, Truett opened his first Chick-fil-A store. From such a small beginning, he parlayed the idea of a chicken sandwich into a business that today has 1,500 restaurants, more than 50,000 employees (Chick-fil-A calls them "team members"), and approximately $3 billion in annual sales.

The winds of the fast-food business have been at Truett's back. As Americans have become more conscious of cholesterol, we have eaten more chicken—just as Truett's billboard cows insist we do. He also became one of the first to provide fast food in the indoor malls that grew rapidly in the last third of the 20th century.

But more importantly, Truett has had the wind of God at his back.

Principled Business

Truett was raised in a Christian home. His parents taught him biblical principles and sent him to church regularly. In church, he benefited from the mentorship of Sunday school teachers and pastors.

Later, he married a devout Christian woman, Jeannette. He credits her with teaching him the meaning of being truly committed to Christ. It was she who convinced him to be consistent in tithing—a practice he has kept up all his life since then.

Commitment is a virtue Truett never tires of preaching. He says, "When we're fully committed, strange and unusual things happen."[1] That's how he explains his remarkable success story. God put unexpected opportunities in his way; in faith, with hard work and a strong will, he grasped those opportunities.

The Bible verse that Cathy keeps coming back to as representing his business philosophy is Proverbs 22:1: A good name is more desirable than great riches; to be esteemed is better than silver or gold. Business success is important. But more than that, he wants to live his life with integrity, bringing honor to God and his family through sound ethics, caring, and generosity.

From the day Truett and his brother opened The Dwarf House, his business life has been governed by the basic tenet to "invite God to be involved in every decision."[2] He has sought to apply the Golden Rule to every customer, employee, and supplier the company has.

In 1960, though, he went through what he calls a "crisis of faith." In a short period of time, his restaurant burned and he had to undergo two life-threatening surgical operations. Sitting in the car before the second operation, he did business with God.

> In those moments I came to realize that the material things I had acquired, the success I had enjoyed with The Dwarf House, meant nothing. What mattered was my relationships with Jeannette, Dan, Bubba, Trudy [his children], my friends, and most of all, my relationship with God. I experienced a new peace in the car that morning, knowing that whether I lived or died I would be with God.[3]

Since then, Truett has lived in the peace that comes with doing God's will. And his signature obedience has to do with the Fourth Commandment.

Bringing the Sabbath to the Restaurant Business

Chick-fil-A is widely known for being closed on Sundays. Back when Truett started his restaurant career, in the 1940s, it was not particularly unusual for a restaurant to close its doors on Sunday. But it is unusual for a national restaurant chain to *still* be closed on Sundays in the 21st century. After all, many restaurants do their best business on Sundays.

Truett says, "Never have I intended to make a big issue out of being closed on Sunday. It amazes me that other people bring up the subject so often. In almost any gathering when anyone mentions Chick-fil-A, someone says, 'And you know, they always close on Sundays.'"[4]

He isn't critical of other restaurants that stay open on Sundays. He even admits that he and Jeannette often eat Sunday dinner in someone else's restaurant. But he says that, from the beginning, he felt that closing on Sundays was an act of obedience that God was calling him to.

In one book, he tells how the practice started:

> When Saturday came during our first week of business back there in 1946, Ben and I sank exhausted into a couple of chairs after the dinner crowd had thinned. Between the two of us, we had covered six 24 hour shifts.
>
> "What do you think, Truett?" my brother asked.
>
> "I think we ought to close tomorrow," I replied.
>
> The thought of working around the clock on Sunday and then starting all over again on Monday was just too much. From then on, we told customers, "We're open 24 hours a day, but not on Sunday."
>
> Closing on Sunday has become a distinctive principle of my Christian background. From my infancy, my Sunday school teachers and pastors stressed that Sunday is the Lord's Day. I see another reason. God commanded, "Six days you shall labor and do all your work" (Exod. 20:9). God told the Israelites to work only six days so that the seventh could be used for rest. . . .
>
> While I was growing up, Sunday was an important day for family times together; often Mom and Dad would take us to visit kinfolks. I believe God gave His laws not to make life hard but to make it better. Our bodies and our minds need time off to recharge. I've accepted that as a principle and honored God by doing it. God has honored us and the business because of it.[5]

Of course, the results of Chick-fil-A are outstanding. Though all the chain's restaurants are closed on Sunday—something no other national chain does—the sales per square foot that Chick-fil-A accomplishes in six days exceed that of almost every competitor working seven days a week.

Acts of obedience like this don't necessarily guarantee that life will always be easy. In fact, in 1982, Truett Cathy went through a second "crisis of faith," this time one his whole company shared in. As God would have it, though, this crisis wound up settling the company more firmly on its base of biblical principles.

Corporate Purpose

Eighteen years after Truett began to expand under the Chick-fil-A name, the tailwinds in the business turned into headwinds. Much larger fast-food chains began to compete head-on with their own chicken sandwiches. In the early 1980s, the cost of Chick-fil-A debt exploded when short-term interest rates rose above twenty percent. In the recession of 1982, sales declined for the first time in the company's history, and Truett cut his own pay to zero.

He felt personally responsible for the business's woes. He later recalled, "I spent many days and nights in prayer that year asking God, 'Where have I failed You?' The downturn in the business, I believed, was a result of my actions or inaction."[6]

Truett took his executive committee on a retreat to plan how to meet the company's challenges. There, his son Dan asked the most basic and important question any business can ask. "Why are we here? What is our purpose?"

This is the way that Truett describes the ensuing discussion:

> My first response was to put aside such questions and stick to the matter at hand—our difficulties in the business and our response to those difficulties. We had a business to run.

But Dan was not being rhetorical. He really wanted us to consider the purpose of Chick-fil-A, and he believed the answers to his questions might lead us to solutions to our more immediate problems as well. . . .

The discussion quickly focused on our individual priorities. We were unanimous in our belief that each of us wanted to glorify God in all we say and do. It was only natural that we would also want to glorify God through our work. . .

My style has always been low-key with regard to my religious convictions. I hope that people see something attractive in the way I live that leads them to seek the One who leads me. In my own personal way I had committed the company to His purpose but had not done so publicly.

It became obvious that the Committee was moving toward doing just that. By the end of the day we had developed two statements, which became Chick-fil-A's Corporate Purpose:

To glorify God by being faithful stewards of all that is entrusted to us.

To have a positive influence on all who come in contact with Chick-fil-A.[7]

There is much that all working people who desire to grow in obedience of faith can learn from Chick-fil-A's purpose.

The Glory of God

The first part of the Chick-fil-A Corporate Purpose is a perfect expression of the primary purpose of the work of every Christian in the business world.

We are there first to glorify God in all we say and do—in every decision we make. Of course, none of us (most especially I) can live up to this standard perfectly, but for the believer, there are no other purposes that come before glorifying God and then being a faithful steward of all resources entrusted to us.

A Positive Influence

The second part of the Chick-fil-A Corporate Purpose is simply the Golden Rule stated to apply to everyone who comes in contact with the company. This is not just lip service at Chick-fil-A. It is immersed into the culture of the company and the character of its leaders, starting at the top with Truett Cathy.

For instance, the company describes all of its service as "second mile" service. This is taken from the Sermon on the Mount, where Jesus uses the illustration of walking a second mile with soldiers if they make us travel the first (Matthew 5:41). Chick-fil-A employees are expected to go above and beyond in serving each customer who comes their way.

Truett's son Dan explains that "second mile" service is not just a biblical idea; it is good business. Exceeding expectations creates repeat business and loyal customers, which is the foundation of Chick-fil-A's success.

In addition, anytime a Chick-fil-A employee is told "Thank you" by a customer, the employee responds, "My pleasure." The idea here is that serving well is a pleasure, something we do because we want to, not because it's a duty we perform because we have to.

Imagine what it would be like if every company had such values.

Personal Ethics as Business Ethics

Truett Cathy got the opportunity to spread his business philosophy to the wider world in 2002 when the United States Congress invited him to speak to a committee looking into business ethics. This was in the wake of financial scandals at Enron, WorldCom, and other big public companies. Congress was wondering what to do about the problem.

Here is a portion of what Truett had to say to the congressional committee:

> After agreeing to appear before you today, I had to ask myself, "What is the meaning of *business ethics*?" I concluded that there is really no such thing as business ethics. There is only personal ethics. I believe no amount of business school training or work experience can teach what is ultimately a matter of personal character. Businesses are not dishonest or selfish, people are. Thus, a business, successful or not, is merely a reflection of the character of its leadership.
>
> I am deeply disturbed, as you are, by the lack of character I see in the marketplace. In order to satisfy the increased pressure for greater profits, some business leaders are making bad choices that ultimately hurt thousands of employees, stockholders, and the economy. We all know that the scorecard of any business is the profit it produces. Without profit, we cannot take care of our employees, our families, or contribute to the betterment of our communities. The question is, How do we balance the pursuit of profit and personal character? For me, I find that balance by applying Biblical principles and good business practice.[8]

I think we would all agree Truett has it right. Business ethics depends most fundamentally on character, something that cannot be shaped in a classroom but depends on virtues engraved in us— generally when we are young—by practicing the biblical precepts taught and exhibited in the home. The Shema (see pages 95-97) got it right 2,500 years ago.

Truett has a noble record of practicing what he preaches. It's this that gives him satisfaction with his life and peace in his relationship with God.

And Truett's service of the Lord does not stop at Chick-fil-A. He has taken the wealth that a chicken sandwich and outstanding service have given him and used it to serve God. He has taught Sunday school faithfully for over fifty years to twelve-year-old boys. He has opened sixteen foster homes in Georgia, Tennessee, and Alabama. He has provided hundreds of scholarships at Berry College to young Americans who could not otherwise afford college. And he has paid for many more scholarships for his own employees. Indeed, no other company its size gives as much in scholarship money as Chick-fil-A.

The Chick-fil-A business is one of the simplest in the world. It has always been operated by the Cathy family. They have never sold an interest in the business to the public. It does not have fancy five-year growth plans. It simply keeps getting better day by day. It is empowered by the grace of God that comes through faith, a passion to glorify him, and a willingness to go the second mile with all its customers.

When Truett retires and his stock is transferred to his three children, the foundation of the company will not change in these fundamental respects. The children—Dan, Bubba, and Trudy—have entered into a covenant with Truett and Jeanette:

> We will be faithful to Christ's lordship in our lives. As committed Christians we will live a life of selfless devotion to His calling in our lives. . . .

> We will be faithful to carry on our family and corporate heritage. Because of our respect for our parents' commitment to touch peoples' lives in a unique way, we covenant to carry on the purpose and the mission of Chick-fil-A. . . . Recognizing that our humanitarian and philanthropic interests are predicated on a strong and healthy business, we commit to operating Chick-fil-A restaurants with standards of excellence in our products, service, and cleanliness. The basic core philosophies and values with which we were raised, including our policy of being closed on Sunday, will be upheld and protected. Consistent with our past we will

continue to provide opportunities for others by growing the business conservatively, moderating our growth and creating employment stability. We will fund the growth of Chick-fil-A with internally generated capital and debt rather than going to the public market. We will work to maintain the entrepreneurial spirit and professional development from our Chick-fil-A Operators and our corporate staff.[9]

The Cathy family and Chick-fil-A will glorify God for years to come.

The Chapters Ahead

Truett Cathy is a man who has sought through faith to be obedient to God in every path where Christ has led him. We all can learn from him.

Remember our discussion back in Chapter 2 where we saw happiness in terms of living a purpose-driven life and being able at its close to turn to our Father and reflect as did Jesus that "I have brought you glory . . . by completing the work you gave me to do" (John 17:4)? Truett is such a happy man.

In Part 4, we will look at pursuing our calling, doing our work, being good stewards of time and bringing out the best in all through servant leadership . Truett is a model for us.

- We can be obedient in our everyday lives . . . *in our calling.*

Truett Cathy understands that his calling is ultimately not to the restaurant business but rather is to belong to Jesus Christ.

- We can be obedient in our everyday lives . . . *in our work.*

Truett always worked hard and used his work to make the world a better place.

- We can be obedient in our everyday lives . . . *in how we spend our time.*

Truett is a disciplined man who orders his life to make time for the important things: personal devotions, Sunday school teaching, family (including many foster children), work, and more.

- We can be obedient as leaders by following Christ's teaching to be servants.

Truett exemplifies servant leadership.

CHAPTER 22
Obedience in Real Life: Calling

FOR MORE THAN 400 years, we in the West have had a tendency to understand biblical calling in terms of our work. In fact, the word we routinely apply to our work—*vocation*—is a translation of the Latin *vocare*, which means "calling." And certainly work is a crucial arena for our obedience—we'll be getting to it in the next chapter. But while our work is closely related to calling, it is not our calling. The call of Christ is to commit to a person, not to a job, a role, or an assignment.

God initiates his relationship with us by calling us. He even called Jesus for his earthly work. "Out of Egypt I called my son" (Matthew 2:15). Jesus calls us to follow him with two words: "Follow me," the same way he called his disciples.

Our response is in faith; it is the obedience of faith. It is not logical nor rational. It works in us as it did in Abraham. "By faith Abraham, when called . . . , obeyed and went, even though he did not know where he was going" (Hebrews 11:8). A call, obedience. No conversation, no analysis, no rationale.

The same was true for Peter and Andrew. Jesus said, "Come, follow me." And "at once they left their nets and followed him" (Matthew 4:19–20). They gave up all to follow a thirty-year-old carpenter from Nazareth. Such made no sense. They responded in faith with obedience and with all they had. So should we.

We could add Paul to the list. When Paul was on the road to Damascus in his persecution of Christians, the last thing that would have been rational to him was that he surrender his life in obedience to Jesus Christ and spend the rest of his days persuading Gentiles to turn to Christ and accept him as Savior. Yet when Jesus appeared to him and called him, his immediate response was "What shall I do, Lord?" (Acts 22:10, ESV).

And Isaiah, too. When this prophet-to-be came into the presence of the Lord and all his holiness, he would answer the call with "Here am I! Send me" (Isaiah 6:8).

Those who wanted to discuss the terms of their calling got nowhere with Jesus. One wanted to first bury his father. Jesus responded, "Let the dead bury their own dead." Another wanted first to say good-bye to his family. Jesus replied, "No one who puts his hand to the plow and looks back is fit for service in the kingdom of God" (Luke 9:59–62).

If calling means following the Lord, how can any response but immediate, wholehearted obedience be appropriate?

My Call

It is interesting for me to ponder how I was called. In one sense, my calling was unique to me. In another sense, it has much in common with every "call" of our Lord.

It might be said that at first I missed Jesus' call.

Born Again

When I was in college, I read (really, read at) Albert Schweitzer's *The Quest of the Historical Jesus*. This is a book by a devoted servant of Christ who gave up a career in Europe as a great musician and physician to become a doctor to the poorest of the poor in Africa. This book has been criticized for seeking to remove the supernatural content from the miracles. But its last paragraph touched my heart so much that I typed it (there was no photocopying in 1960) and put it in my wallet, where it remained for the better part of a decade. It read:

He comes to us . . . as of old by the lakeside He came to those men who knew Him not. He speaks to us the same word, "Follow thou me," and sets us to the tasks which He has to fulfill for our time. He commands, and to those who obey Him, whether they be wise or simple, He will reveal Himself in the toils, the conflicts, the sufferings which they shall pass through in His fellowship; and, as an ineffable mystery, they shall learn in their own experience Who He is.[10]

Whatever faults there may be with the rest of the book, this conclusion speaks biblical truth. Yet I was not then moved by God's grace to turn to Christ and accept his call—that would come some five years after I had thrown the quote away. That's why it can be said that I let the Lord pass me by.

It was when I was 37 that Christ's call came to me irresistibly. I was certainly not "listening" for it. To use Schweitzer's words, it came to me "ineffably."

At this point in my life, I was keeping a distance between myself and church and was comfortably pursuing a career as a lawyer. I had no idea what it meant to "belong" to Jesus Christ nor to turn to him as Lord and Savior. I had grown up in the liberal, mid-20th century Christian culture that knew little of what it meant to be born again or to be saved or damned.

But I was keenly interested in the Watergate scandal that brought the Nixon administration down. And on a quirk, at a local barbeque restaurant owned by a Christian man, I bought Chuck Colson's *Born Again* to read one more account of that saga.

While I sat on my sofa reading the book one Saturday afternoon, I came across the part where Colson, having pled guilty to being party to a cover-up to protect the President in the Watergate investigation, was led by a friend to turn to Jesus Christ and accept him as his Lord and Savior. As I read about what happened to Colson, I was drawn compellingly to turn to Christ. I prayed something like this: "Dear Jesus, whatever happened to Chuck Colson, let it happen to me."

There was nothing rational about this decision. In fact, everything rational in me rejected the supernatural. I was much like Schweitzer, reluctant to see anything supernatural in Jesus Christ. But the Lord had truly called me, and I answered.

I will not say that I gave up everything, as did Peter and Andrew, nor that I left my home, like Abraham, not knowing where God might lead me. But I can say that, from that point forward, there was "no looking back." Never once since then have I doubted that Jesus is Lord of the universe and the only Savior of a human race that is otherwise hopelessly lost. And on a personal basis, my life was no longer my own but belonged to him.

In retrospect, I can conclude that whatever was happening to me in college as I read the Schweitzer passage and put it in my wallet was not a "calling." I believe that the call of Jesus is irresistible and permanent, as it was for Abraham, Peter, and Andrew.

Total Commitment

However and whenever the call comes, whether it is on the shores of Galilee, on the road to Damascus, on a motorcycle (C. S. Lewis) or in a garden (Augustine), it is a call to total commitment. We are called to deny ourselves and take up our crosses, wholeheartedly and passionately. Our Lord hates lukewarmness. When we answer the call, as a matter of theological fact but also as a matter of the transformation of our lives, we are no longer our own; we belong wholly to another.

Os Guinness, who has written the best single book on calling of which I am aware, gives this definition: "Calling is the truth that God calls us to himself so decisively that everything we are, everything we do and everything we have is invested with a special devotion and dynamism lived out as a response to his summons and service."[11] Calling, in this sense, is the largest context—and ultimately the most practical—within which we consider the topic of obedience.

Called to Jesus Christ

We are called fundamentally to belong to Jesus Christ, not to a job or a cause. Paul begins his letter to the Romans by referring to "those who are called to belong to Jesus Christ" (Romans 1:6).

Chuck Colson illustrates this point with a story of Mother Teresa:

> A few years ago a brother in the order came to [Mother Teresa] complaining about a superior whose rules, he felt, were interfering with his ministry. "My vocation is to work for lepers," he told Mother Teresa. "I want to spend myself for the lepers."
>
> She stared at him a moment, then smiled. "Brother," she said gently, "your vocation is not to work for lepers, your vocation is to belong to Jesus."[12]

That is our vocation. We are called, primarily, not to the work or even to missionary service that Christ has assigned us, but to Christ himself. We belong to him.

The calling on Truett Cathy's life was not most fundamentally to the restaurant business but to Jesus Christ. Christ had a plan for Truett that included marrying Jeanette, working with her to raise three children devoted to Jesus Christ, flipping hamburgers, swabbing floors, and ultimately running a nationwide business employing more than 50,000 people that joins in Christ's redemptive work and brings his Father much glory.

The calling on your life and mine is not first of all to a business career but to the Lord of all creation. Once we fully grasp that, our response is "Speak, Lord, your servant is listening," to discern Christ's plan and purpose for our lives, to trust him and through that trust and the obedience that flows from it to be connected to the grace that will "fulfill every good purpose . . . and every act prompted by . . . faith" (2 Thessalonians 1:11).

Calling and Purpose

Calling is always connected to purpose—God's purpose for our lives. (We can just as easily say God's will for our lives.) We are called "according to his purpose" (Romans 8:28). God has called us so that by his Holy Spirit working within us we may play our part, small as it is, in his plan as he "works out everything in conformity with the *purpose of his will*" (Ephesians 1:11, emphasis added). If we are to live obedient lives in accordance with God's calling, then, we must begin with an understanding of purpose.

God is a purposeful God. He had a purpose when he created the universe, when he called Abraham and made him patriarch of a great nation, when he called Moses to lead the children of Israel out of Egypt, when he sent his Son to die for our sins, when he sent Paul to spread the good news to Gentiles, and when he created and gave life, both biological and spiritual, to you and me.

The Bible makes plain that God's overarching purpose for our lives is that by his grace we may be "conformed to the likeness of his Son," that we might live for his glory (Romans 8:29). As Rick Warren puts it, "The ultimate goal of the universe is to show the glory of God."

Under this central, overarching purpose of every life called to God, there are specific purposes for our lives. "We are [God's] workmanship, created in Christ Jesus for good works, which he prepared beforehand, that we should walk in them" (Ephesians 2:10, ESV). It is as if God has, through his calling, assembled an orchestra, and from Abraham and Moses to Peter and Andrew and down through each of us, we are assigned parts to play in a great symphony that brings him glory and works toward the redemption of the world (See Hebrews 11:39-40.).

Christian obedience is based on the foundation of calling, and it is always connected to the purposes for which we were created.

Does that seem intimidating? Perhaps overwhelming? Too high a calling for the likes of us? Fear not. God gives us not only the purpose but also the means to fulfill it. And the most humble among us can, by God's grace, accomplish great things.

Maria Sackett – Called to Pray

We can learn much from the life of Maria Sackett, an unmarried, unemployed woman whose faithful labor for her Lord resulted in the spiritual revival of Stephentown, New York.

Maria's story is told by the renowned evangelist, Charles Finney, whose preaching ministry spawned revival in many towns and cities in the Northeast after the Civil War.[13] In 1868, he was preaching at New Lebanon, New York in an engagement that was to last many weeks. After preaching one Sunday, Maria came up to him and, choked with deep feeling, asked him if he could come to a town a few miles from New Lebanon named Stephentown. Finney put her off as his preaching responsibilities in New Lebanon required all his energies.

But Finney inquired as to Stephentown and found that the town had but one church whose minister had been a complete failure resulting in his becoming an infidel, hostile to Christianity. As a result the church closed its doors and according to Finney, "the whole town was in a complete moral waste and state of impenitence."

The next Sunday, a tearful Maria again pled with Finney to come and preach at Stephentown. Finney found her pleas irresistible so he agreed to preach Sunday evening the next week.

The service was well attended but nothing extraordinary occurred and Finney stayed that night at Maria's parents' home in a room under Maria's. Finney remembers the night:

> "This Maria seemed to be praying nearly all night. I could hear her low, trembling voice interrupted often by sobs and manifest weeping. I had made no appointment to come again, but before I left in the morning she pleaded so hard that I consented to have an appointment made for me at five o'clock the next Sabbath."

Finney returned and at that service, "the Spirit of God was poured out on the congregation."

Finney goes on to record how well-nigh all the leadership in Stephentown came to receive Jesus as Lord and Savior. Years later he checked back and wrote, "The converts turned out to be sound and the church has maintained a good degree of spiritual vigor… ever since."

Maria had no special skills. She just had a heart for the lost and for the advancement of the kingdom. Through her courage to ask the evangelist to come to Stephentown, but more importantly through her heart-felt labor in prayer, the Lord used this young woman to turn the spiritual life of a town "from darkness to light, the power of Satan to God" (Acts 26:18).

Do you remember André Trocme's description of his ministry as an "ethic of combat"? Maria, too, was called to an "ethic of combat" though she may never have so described it. And, indeed, in one way or another, we all are, and in obediently living into it we have great happiness.

The Will and the Equipping

One of the texts I have prayed daily for years is at the conclusion of Hebrews: "May the God of peace . . . equip you with everything good for doing his will, and may he work in us what is pleasing to him" (Hebrews 13:20–21). The thought of this prayer is that God "equips" and "works in us" for the doing of his will. When we walk in that will, the plan of his purpose, his grace is there to provide all we need, and by faith we can be assured that we will have it. The grace is not there to equip us to walk outside God's plan. If God has assigned us the work of a pastor, he will equip us for that assignment and not for that of a politician, and vice versa.

The words of Andrew Murray, in his commentary on this prayer (which I have modified to make it fit the NIV translation) are provocative indeed. He writes:

The God of peace [equip you] to do His will. To do His will. This, then, is the object of all that God has done. That the Son, who is God, should be our Redeemer; that the stupendous miracles of the incarnation and the atonement, the resurrection and the seating of a man on the throne of God, should be wrought, that the Holy Spirit of God should be poured out from heaven—all was with one view, that we should *be brought to do the will of God.* The whole relation between God and the creature depends on this one thing: without it there can be no true fellowship with God. It was for this Jesus became man: *Lo, I come to do thy will, O God.* [Hebrews 10:7] It was through this He redeemed us. It is to make us partakers of the power to do this, that, as Mediator of the covenant, He puts the law in our heart, that we may do the will of God on earth as in heaven. *It is for this alone He lives in heaven:* the only proof and measure of the success of His work is *that we do the will of God.* Without this, all His work and ours is in vain.[14]

Has Murray overstated it? No, Murray is speaking truth. We need to continuously remind ourselves that obedience to the will of God is the reason we were created. Jesus "gave himself . . . to purify for himself a people eager to do what is good" (Titus 2:14). Unless we obey in faith and do the will of God, our lives are in vain.

Another great theologian, Jonathan Edwards, agrees. Looking at the new birth in relation to the "end," or purpose, of Christian life, Edwards wrote,

"The new birth, which is the work of God in grace, is directly related to the fruit of good works, for good works are the end to which the whole work of new birth is intended. All is calculated in this great change in the soul so as to directly tend to good works. Yea, the fruit of good works is the very end of redemption in Christ."[15]

Empowered to Fulfill Every Good Purpose

The principles of calling are summed up in the oft-overlooked prayer of Paul for the Thessalonians.

> We constantly pray for you, that our God may count you worthy of his calling, and that by his power he may fulfill every good purpose of yours and every act prompted by your faith. We pray this so that the name of our Lord Jesus Christ may be glorified in you . . . according to the grace of our God and the Lord Jesus Christ. (2 Thessalonians 1:11–12)

Paul alerts us to the fact that with calling comes accountability. It was his desire that the Thessalonians—and the rest of Christ's followers—be "counted" worthy of God's calling. We are to "live a life worthy of the Lord," to quote Paul's Colossians prayer (Colossians 1:10). The calling of God is the most exalted invitation in all creation, in all eternity. By faith we need to discern, and by God's grace carry out, the purposes for which we are called to be "worthy" of such an honor.

When we in faith respond to the assignments God gives us in our calling, God's "power" will "fulfill every good purpose" he has given us "and every act" that flows from our faith. By his Spirit, God works in us to accomplish his purposes; he will provide all we need, not merely for our work to be adequate, but also for it to be fulfilled to overflowing. As we have seen, our responsibility is through faith, by grace to grow in Christlike character. It becomes the sail and God provides the wind. And we might note that to the prayer Paul adds that God's power working in us will accomplish our ultimate purpose, that the "name of our Lord Jesus Christ may be glorified" according to God's grace.

Summing it Up

There are four basic conclusions we can draw from this brief overview of calling.

1. We are called to belong to Jesus Christ, who assigns us the work he has for us. Most fundamentally, I am not called to be a lawyer, husband, father or grandfather. I am called to Jesus Christ for his good purposes and glory as I do the work of a lawyer or husband and so forth.

2. The plan and purpose for our lives are God's, not ours. He is the one who calls. He is the one who has assigned us the purposes he has for us.

3. When we discern the "works God has planned beforehand for us to do" and move out in faith, God through his power and grace will "fulfill every good purpose" he has given us to the glory of Jesus Christ. God will be beside us working with us. We are his "workmanship"; he is conforming us to the likeness of Jesus Christ; he is equipping us to do all that he has called us to do. Our role is to "work at it with all [our] heart, as working for the Lord" (Colossians 3:23).

4. Calling gives life and work rich meaning and from that meaning much happiness. It allows us to understand that there is purpose in our lives, a worthy and eternal purpose, assigned to us by the Creator of the universe. We work, ultimately, not for some company or human boss, but for the God who has called us and assigned us the work he has created us to do for his kingdom even if it be in a secular marketplace. And we are accountable for carrying out the work assigned to us. Jesus was, and so are we.

With this background, we can now look at work in relation to obedience. But here we'll see that "work," biblically understood, is broader than what we normally think. It's not just what we do for a paycheck.

CHAPTER 23
Obedience in Real Life: Work

WE'VE SEEN THAT calling is ultimately to a person—Jesus—and not fundamentally to any activity we might do. But what does that mean, practically? How do we live into our calling? We do so through work. We can even say we do so *only* through work.

It is common for Christians to separate "Christian service" from work. We are prone to think we serve God in the church, with volunteering in community work, or in the family, but not in the workplace. Properly understood, however, Christian life in all its dimensions has everything to do with work. Work is central to the biblical worldview and to obediently living out the assignments given us by the One who called us and to whom we belong.

Linda Clare, a woman from Oregon, wrote in a magazine article,

> My long hours working as a childcare provider often tempted me to complain about my job. Although I didn't know what work God wanted me to do, I was sure it must be something other than "just" babysitting.
>
> Then one day, a father who came to pick up his toddler commented, "You taught Kasey to pray. She says grace at home now, and my wife and I are thinking of attending church."
>
> God's direction suddenly became clear. Now, when others ask what I do for a living, I smile and say, "I 'just' babysit for the Lord."[16]

This is a woman who gained a new perspective—one that we all need. Through work, we live out our calling and obey God's will for our lives.

Heaven and Earth at Work

Webster's dictionary defines work as "sustained physical or mental effort to overcome obstacles or achieve a result." There may be exceptions, but as a general rule, nothing worthwhile in human life takes place without work. God likes it when his people work. And more than that, he sets the example by working himself.

"Impossible!" we might say. After all, the dictionary defines *work* as a "sustained physical or mental effort to overcome obstacles or achieve a result." And God needs no "sustained physical or mental effort" to do anything. He needs no work to "overcome obstacles."

Yet the first thing we learn about God in the Bible was that he created the universe. At the end of six days of creation, God "finished the *work* he had been doing," so that "on the seventh day he rested from all his *work*" (Genesis 2:2).

As we have seen, the biblical understanding of how God accomplishes results through us is by work. We are God's "workmanship" (Ephesians 2:9). He "works" in us "to will and to act according to his good purpose" (Philippians 2:13). He "works" all things for good (Romans 8:28). He is the Potter and we are the clay (Isaiah 64:8; Jeremiah 18:6).

Jesus worked for profit for all his adult life until he was 30 years old. He worked as a carpenter—work that for all time, in all places, has been sweaty, difficult, and requiring "sustained physical effort."

And there was nothing easy about his ministry. In a most literal sense, it was all work—walking dirt roads in a hot, dry land; dealing with crowds and beggars, the sick and the poor; debating the scribes and Pharisees; and ultimately being crucified on a cross. Jesus described his ministry as work. "My food," he said "is to do the will of him who sent me and to finish his *work*" (John 4:34, emphasis added).

Likewise for Paul. He "worked night and day, laboring and toiling," so as not to be a burden (2 Thessalonians 3:8). As a laborer, he held himself out as a model and taught, "If a man will not work, he shall not eat" (v. 10). And as with Jesus' ministry, Paul's missionary journeys required enormous sustained physical effort and entailed immense suffering.

Paul associated work with the most lofty of godly virtues, speaking of "work produced by faith" and "labor prompted by love" (1 Thessalonians 1:3).

In fact, the Bible teaches that man was created to work. Even before the Fall, God "took the man and put him in the Garden of Eden to work it and take care of it." And before that, God had decreed that man was to "rule over" all creation and to "subdue it" (Genesis 2:15; 1:26, 28).

Following the Fall, work became a toilsome burden. "By the sweat of your brow you will eat your food" (3:19). So work, which was at first a noble commission, became one filled with problems and challenges. The life of work is always difficult.

The parable of the talents gives us important insight into Jesus' view of work. The amount of money the rich master gave his servants was very large. The *ESV Study Bible* tells us a talent was a measure of money worth about twenty years of a laborer's wages, or about $500,000 in U.S. currency.[17] Five talents would have been worth over $2 million. The one who received the five talents "went at once and put his money to *work* and gained five more" (Matthew 25:16, emphasis added).

Obviously, there was no Nazareth Stock Exchange or Jerusalem Commodities Exchange. So, to double $2 million, the servant would have "to put money to work." Perhaps he opened a kiosk and traded in rugs or clothing. Or maybe he bought a vineyard and cared for it or invested in livestock and worked in that trade. But he didn't call up a broker and put the money in Microsoft. He worked and took risks in a competitive, unregulated marketplace full of thieves and shysters, and for this work he was rewarded with the right to "share your master's happiness!" (25:21).

We are called to Jesus Christ, and he has work for us to do. We do it through the obedience of faith. For most of us in our adult years, this work is in the competitive marketplace. Paul says, "Whatever [we] do"—in sales, manufacturing, administration, "whatever"—we should "work at it with all [our] heart, as working for the Lord" (Colossians 3:23). Like Truett Cathy, who found ways to bring glory to God in the fast-food business, we all can serve God in our work. All work is high and lofty because it is assigned us by the Lord of the universe—indeed, a more exalted assignment could not be imagined. But also, in the most fundamental sense of the word, it is work for the "good."

The Need for Redemption

For me, the word *good* has always been rather insipid. "Good" is a compliment of faint praise. How about "excellent" or "outstanding"? Maybe better still, "superb"? Not so for God. He created a good world. That was his mark of excellence. Everything about his creation was "very good" (Genesis 1:31).

In a lovely insight, St. Augustine marvels at the goodness of God's creation:

> *And you saw all that you had made, O God, and found it very good.* We, too, see all these things and know that they are very good. In the case of each of your works you first commanded them to be made, and when they had been made you looked at each in turn and saw that it was good. I have counted and found that Scripture tells us seven times that you saw that what you had made was good, and when you looked for the eighth time and saw the whole of your creation, we are told that you found it not only good but very good, for you saw all at once as one whole. Each separate work was good, but when they were all seen as one, they were not merely good: they were very good.(emphasis in original)[18]

But something catastrophic happened when our ancestors

declared their autonomy from God and decided to determine for themselves what was "*good*" and "evil." What God had created and was very good became infected; beauty was soiled; truth became twisted. Jesus spoke of his own generation (like any generation, including ours) as "evil" (Luke 11:29), and Paul wrote that "the creation was subjected to frustration," so that it has been "groaning as in the pains of childbirth right up to the present time" (Romans 8:20, 22). It still is.

It is against this background and in these circumstances that we are called to Jesus the Redeemer, and it is Jesus the Redeemer who gives us work. The work to which Jesus assigns us in whatever sphere is the work of redemption, to play a role in restoring the goodness of God's creation. This is most fundamentally what the Bible means when it speaks of "good works"—they are works that are redeeming creation from the bondage to decay.[19]

Science has a law to describe this bondage to decay—the second law of thermodynamics, or entropy. This law says that lifeless physical processes (and we might add all biological life as well) tend to run down. Scientists say that all matter in the universe is constantly in a process of degradation, heading toward an ultimate state of inert uniformity billions of years from now. Though Jesus Christ "[sustains] all things by his powerful word," in part he uses our work to keep entropy from happening (Hebrews 1:3). We get sick; doctors heal us. Wood rots. We replace it. Metal rusts. We treat the corrosion. Weeds spring up. We kill them. In his wonderful novel *Cutting for Stone*, Abraham Verhese remarks, "We are all fixing what is broken. It is the task of a lifetime." This is a pretty good description of Christian ministry.

And, of course, human civilization has heaped more decay into the laws of nature. Human envy, greed, and evil are constantly tearing down the goodness of God's creation. The 20th century saw more human evil by far than any previous century, with Hitler, Stalin, Mao, Pol Pot, and genocide in Rwanda. Today, drug cartels, traffickers in sex slaves, and corruption in government destroy God's good creation. And the sin that infects the lives of each one of us inflicts its own destructiveness.

The task of the Christian is in God's grace through faithful obedience to combat these destructive forces, first in ourselves and then in creation, as we participate in the ministry of our Lord, the Redeemer. Therefore, all the work Jesus calls us to do is fundamentally redemptive.

The Work of Restoring Creation

Jesus' first concern, and the most vital of redemptive work, is redeeming people. This was the primary work of Jesus' own ministry. He came to seek and save the lost (Luke 19:10). And his parting words in the Great Commission direct us to make disciples of all nations, baptizing them in the name of the Father, the Son, and the Holy Spirit (Matthew 28:18–20). We all have a role to play in carrying out this commission. We may not be evangelists or missionaries, but whether it be with prayer, witnessing, financial support, or volunteer work, we can all do our part.

Beyond seeking and saving the lost, Jesus assigns each of us a portion of the work of restoring God's creation to its intended goodness. We can this divide this work into five basic categories.

1. Parenting

For those of us called to be parents, we know it's work! And there is no more important work. It is in the family that our children develop the character, both spiritual and practical, necessary for any successful endeavor to which God may call them. Character is formed early in our childhood, and it becomes deeply engraved in our souls at a fairly early age. Thereafter, whether the character be good or bad, it is very difficult to change. As we have seen in Chapter 9, in God's economy the training of our children in the faith and in obedience to God is assigned the highest priority.

2. Asserting Dominion

The first commission in the Bible, and certainly one of the most important, is that we be fruitful and multiply, fill the earth, subdue it, and have dominion over all creation (Genesis 1:26–28). We are stewards of planet earth to make all that God has given us productive.

Almost all the work we see is carried out under this commission. Construction of houses and buildings, farming, transportation, manufacturing, communications, drugs and chemicals, plastics and metals, conquering and treating disease, financial and janitorial services—the list is almost endless. For those called of Jesus to do it, this is sacred work carried out under divine sanction in obedience to divine assignment.

I met Hubert Juneau, a Haitian, some twenty years ago in New York City, when he drove me from the LaGuardia Airport to a Manhattan hotel in his cab. He was listening to Christian radio and we struck up a conversation, which ultimately led to his moving to Birmingham and working for our company, delivering the mail internally. It was not a high-paying job, but a year later I received a long, handwritten letter from Hubert thanking me for giving him the opportunity to serve Christ by delivering the mail at our insurance company. He explained that his work was vital to the company's functioning (policy billings and premium checks were then handled in the mail). He was honored to be at the center of the process. Hubert ultimately left Birmingham to go back to New York, and he now lives in Florida, where he drives a school bus. We remain good friends and he calls every year on my wife's birthday to check on us.

Hubert has it all right. He knows that he belongs to Jesus Christ, and whether he is driving a cab in New York, delivering the mail in Birmingham, or driving a school bus in Florida, Hubert is part of Christ's redemptive work, laboring at it with all of his heart as working for the Lord. He lets us know what the poet George Herbert meant when he wrote:

Teach me, my God and King,
In all things thee to see;
And what I do in anything
To do it as for thee. . . .
A servant with this clause
Makes drudgery divine;
Who sweeps a room as for thy laws,
Makes that and th' action fine.[20]

3. Establishing Justice

A third category of work carried out under God's original commission is establishing and maintaining justice. Justice is the very foundation of God's throne. The Lord loves justice and requires it of us. Prophecy makes clear that justice is to be at the heart of the reign of the Messiah (Psalm 89:14; Isaiah 9:7; 11:4; Micah 6:8).

The first commission of taking dominion cannot be carried out without a rule of law that supports fair play in the marketplace, enforces promises, and punishes corruption. The justice that Jesus is most concerned with, however, is justice to the poor and weakest in society. Consider this description of the Messiah:

> I will put my Spirit on him
> and he will bring forth justice to the nations. . . .
> In faithfulness he will bring forth justice;
> he will not falter or be discouraged
> till he establishes justice on earth.
> In his law the islands will put their hope
> (Isaiah 42:1, 3–4).

All who follow this Messiah, Jesus, are to likewise be engaged in bringing forth justice.

Establishing justice for the poor and weakest has taken centuries and much bloodshed. Historians might date its beginning in Anglo-American history with the Magna Carta in 1208. By that measure we've been at it 800 years. The process certainly includes our Civil War, the most deadly in the nation's history, which brought forth the emancipation of slaves. The modern civil rights movement, from about 1950 till 1975, was an important part of the process.

The list of leaders who contributed to this process is a long one. William Wilberforce, who, following the call of Jesus, led the battle to abolish the slave trade in England, played a major role. Martin Luther King Jr., likewise responding to Jesus' call, was another who contributed greatly.

Of course, on a worldwide basis, there is much still to be done, as corruption in government in Third World nations results in great oppression and little or no opportunity for the weakest in those societies.

Those who work in government, in the courts, and in the practice of law, and especially those who defend the cause of the indigent and unpopular, are carrying out the work of the Lord.

4. Making Peace

Next, there is the category of work we can call peacemaking or community building. Perhaps a better title could simply be love. The idea is that little worthwhile progress can take place in asserting dominion over the earth or establishing greater justice without strong communities, whether they be towns, cities, or nations, companies, partnerships, or families. To accomplish great things, people must work together, and it takes much work and patience to lead us to work together.

The Old Testament Scriptures have a word for this kind of community: *shalom*. This word is most simply translated as "peace," but scholars say that it refers more widely to wholeness or unity within a community, to harmony, tranquility, security, friendship, agreement, and prosperity. Find any strong nation, city, company, team, or family, and you will find at its foundation leaders who are peacemakers, who have created or built *shalom*. Certainly my wife, Fairfax, is the peacemaker in our family. We might call such people servant leaders, those who sustain great effort over long periods of time to overcome obstacles to community.

The United States has had many such leaders. When the institution of slavery was tearing the country apart, President Lincoln was a great peacemaker who would not let a great nation ("the last great hope of earth") be split apart. In his magisterial Second Inaugural Address, he concluded:

> With malice toward none; with charity for all; with firmness in the right, as God gives us to see the right, let us strive on to finish the work we are in; to bind up the nation's wounds; to care for him who shall have borne the battle, and for his widow, and his orphan—to do all which may achieve and cherish a just, and a lasting peace, among ourselves, and with all nations.[21]

5. Pastoring and Teaching

Some are called to pastor or teach full time. In our adult lives, all of us are called to help others by imparting through instruction and example whatever good habits, knowledge or wisdom we may have that can equip others in the work to which they are called. We may pastor and teach as parents, in the workplace, in the church, or in the community. To those who are called to this work full time, such is a high and worthy calling, as no other calling can be successful without good coaching and teaching.

Of course redemptive good works are not limited to these categories. Christians are spontaneously engaged in Christ's redemptive work as Good Samaritans in improving the well-being of others in untold ways—in the street, in restaurants, in airports, in service stations, and in the home.

Serving God As We Are

At the heart of a biblical understanding of calling is the idea of a radical uprooting such as that of Abraham, Peter, or Paul. In fact,

I have found that the reluctance that many of us have to enter fully into an unconditional response to the summons of our Lord to follow him is that it might entail giving up those things that we hold dear—job, training, career, perhaps even home and community. We cannot rule it out, and we can say that if such is the assignment of Christ, it is only in undertaking it that we will ever find our happiness and that Christ will equip us to do it well.

The calling most times, however, is simply to honor Christ, to let him reign in our wills and lives in the situation we were in when the call to follow him came. In fact, it is likely that all that has gone before by way of relationships, character, schooling, training, and talents is in Christ's plan for our future life under his lordship in the place and work we were in when he called.

Certainly, that was true for André Trocmé. From Sin-le-Noble to the University of Paris to his marriage to Magda and to his ultimate assignment to Le Chambon in its strategic location—all this coalesced for the work in Christ's redemption that Trocmé was called to lead. It is true for Truett Cathy as well.

Paul, in one of the most prominent teachings on calling in the Protestant tradition, says that "each one should remain in the situation which he was in when God called him" (1 Corinthians 7:20).

For many of us, when we turn to Jesus Christ, receive him as Lord, and are filled with the Holy Spirit, we want to go into "full-time ministry," as if a calling into such work is more "full time" for the Lord than building a bridge, working in a bank, or selling insurance. I think most of us, if we were asked to do so, would rank missionary work in Africa, or full-time work on a ministerial staff, more highly in spiritual terms than practicing law, being a policeman, or working as a chef.

This attitude has a lengthy tradition. In the Middle Ages, service in a monastery was exalted work, whereas other work in the world was viewed as second-rate, even debasing and demeaning. The Protestant Reformation radically changed this view. According to Luther, God pays no attention to the greatness or insignificance of the work being done but looks at the heart that is serving him in the work. "This is true even of such everyday tasks as washing dishes or milking cows."[22] From this time forward (at least in the Protestant tradition), the only thing that was important was working for Christ "with all of our heart" wherever he called us to work.

After I received Christ as Lord at age 37, my desire was to go into full-time ministry. But circumstances dictated against this, in terms of my obligations to both family and my employer. The doors simply did not open to make "full-time ministry" possible, and I was very frustrated, thinking in the traditional mode, that my service to the Lord was second-rate. After several years with this attitude, it changed altogether with a word from the Lord spoken deep in my spirit to this effect: "You ingrate, I have given you a wonderful job and a wonderful family, and I will equip you and enable you. Now, serve me in this situation with all your heart and quit trying to flee from it."

It is my hope that we can all begin to understand better the calling to himself that Christ has for all his people as well as the specific work he has for us to serve him in faithful obedience. As we accept and respond to this calling and do the work, we can be obedient in the broadest and best sense. Now let us narrow our focus and take a look at how we use our time to obey our Lord day by day and week by week, in the tasks he has assigned us.

CHAPTER 24
Obedience in Real Time

KIRBY SEVIER IS my prayer partner. We have been covering each other, our families and our major challenges in prayer for over a quarter of a century. Kirby is what everyone should want for a prayer partner. He's well nigh a saint. He is also one of the best wills and estate lawyers in the country and our firm's hiring partner. He has filled this role since the firm was formed in 1984.

Kirby is well known for his family, six children and now ten grandchildren and growing. He also has a large surrogate family. In 1992 he was one of the organizers of an evangelical youth meeting in Birmingham and befriended two young men, African Americans, who received Jesus Christ at the meeting. He began taking them to his church every Sunday and then to lunch – picture this, Kirby and his wife, Becky, six children and Eric and Derrio. And Eric and Derrio soon asked six of their neighbors to come along. So far, the next eleven years the Sevier van was carrying eight inner-city kids to church and to lunch afterward. Kirby remains the mentor of these eight. Though Kirby found them in poverty and vulnerable to many risks, by God's grace they overcame the obstacles of inner-city life, graduated from high school or college, and became committed Christians. They now have thirteen children and Kirby is their God-parent, and he stays in regular contact with them all.

Kirby is also an eloquent spokesman for the biblical principles of parenting; and he is the guardian of the firm's founding principles, which form the moral compass for all the firm's activities.

Kirby's hour-long presentation on how every noble endeavor and worthy institution must be founded on immutable moral principles is always the highlight of firm retreats. We never tire of the message.

I do not know anyone who more fully integrates a faith in Jesus Christ with an obedience that permeates every aspect of living. He is a disciple 24/7 and by God's grace excels at all he touches. He is also a very happy man.

Organizing Life

One of the quandaries almost all of us face is how we should spend our time. Though we have much technology and machinery that allow us to be more productive than our parents, we all seem to be busier and under more time pressure. How should we organize our time if we are to lead obedient lives and enjoy the happiness and blessings that flow from them?

There is no single answer to this question, as our lives are so varied, but there are patterns that can help most of us. Let's consider how we might look at some of the most important and time-consuming responsibilities for those of us seeking to be faithfully obedient to our Lord: personal devotions, work, family, ministry, self-improvement, and rest.

Time with God

Old-timers called prayer, Bible reading, and the like "means of grace" because they are channels through which God's grace flows into our souls. The means of grace are exactly that—means. They are not the end of life, the purpose for which we were created. But they are essential because they are the means through which we are endowed with the wisdom, motivation, and power to achieve our purposes.

Of all the preparation we can make to live an obedient life of faith for the glory of God, a daily study of the Scriptures and prayer are probably the most necessary. We have seen how a total familiarity with the Word and an ongoing reference to it throughout the day are part of the fundamental teaching of the Shema (Deuteronomy 6:4). God admonished Joshua, as a condition of his success as a general, to "meditate" on Scripture day and night, meaning that he was to keep it ever before him, never absent from his trust in God and his decision making (Joshua 1:8). The Psalter opens with the observation that the man who is "blessed"—that is, happy—is one whose "delight is in the law of the LORD" and who "meditates day and night" on the law (Psalm 1:1–3). Jesus was equally clear that only those who "abide in [his] word" could be his disciples and that his "word" is to "abide" in us, conveying perhaps even more vividly that biblical teaching needs to completely saturate our minds and shape our obedience (John 8:31–32; 15:7–8).

The grace we receive, and the fellowship with God we experience through Bible study and prayer, are as necessary for us as believers as sunlight and rain are to an orange grove. They are essential to its fruit. So although regular devotion is not the most important thing we will do in a day (that will be bearing fruit that glorifies God), it is crucial to bearing fruit. We must have prayer and Bible reading.

Good Morning, Lord!

When should we have our devotions?

For most of us, the early morning is the only time of day—and the best time—when we can pray and devote ourselves to Bible study effectively. We can always begin the day earlier, but we cannot always find time during the day for personal devotion. And at the end of many days, we are simply too tired.

Jesus rose early to pray. We should too.

What if we find rising early to pray and read difficult, as we simply would rather sleep? If such is the case, one of two things will occur (neither of them good): we will quit the practice or we will continue with a stoic determination to do our duty. And mere duty is hardly conducive to a good relationship with anybody, especially God.

We need to understand that praying and studying are supposed to give us pleasure. We should enjoy them as much as, even more than, we enjoy other pleasurable pursuits.

If rising early for devotion is arduous and not something we enjoy, we must seek a larger filling of the Holy Spirit. It is part of the Holy Spirit's ministry to give us an appetite to pray and to be fed by the Word. Down through the ages, getting up early to be with Christ has been a delight for those who are filled with the Holy Spirit. It can be for us, too.

Too Busy Not to Pray

How much time should we spend in devotions?

It depends on how busy we are and how much we have to do. The heavier our responsibilities and the more formidable our trials, the more time we need to take for prayer and the greater our need for the wisdom and courage that God's grace will give us.

Does that surprise you? Martin Luther's comment is informative: "I have so much to do today that I shall need the first three hours in prayer." A busy and challenging day means more prayer at its beginning.

When I was my busiest, I would try to find thirty minutes early in the day for prayer and Bible study and a couple of hours on Sunday. After I "retired," I spent four years working in a city ninety miles from home, and that opened up much more time for prayer as I drove to and fro. (The automobile makes a great prayer chamber. Often prayer is by far the best thing we can do while driving alone, far more productive than most radio or even teaching CD's.)

I would not have prayed in this way unless I wanted to, and I wanted to because the Holy Spirit birthed such a desire in me. No one should conclude that I was given such an appetite because I was good or deserved it. Far from it! God generously gives us such a desire if we want it and ask him for it. And I can say what Jackie

Gleason used to say: "How sweet it is."

I may add that, as we begin our day with prayer, so should we continue it in prayer, not necessarily on our knees or formally, but in our consciousness. Paul tells us that we are to "pray without ceasing," meaning that throughout the day we need to maintain a prayer-consciousness of God (1 Thessalonians 5:17). So as we enter meetings, make telephone calls or speeches, or do our daily work, we should be continuously asking God for his guidance, wisdom, and power. In this way, we may keep our will aligned with his in faithful obedience.

Core Responsibilities

After our morning devotions, most of our hours need to be devoted to our core responsibilities, which for almost everyone through the ages have been family and work. How can we get our obedience right in these core areas?

I have heard many times that the priorities of our lives should be God first, then family, and finally work. I've heard it, but I don't think it's quite right.

Of course, God comes first. But he is also last. In fact, he is "all in all" and "the Alpha and Omega" in everything we do, whether in family or work or any other endeavor.

And then, as between family and work, from time to time either may come first. We continually need to seek God's will as to where we ought to spend our time and energy. There will be times when family will require all that we have, such as when a spouse or child or parent is sick or in trouble. And there will be times when our work will require all we have, such as when a crisis arises on the job. Therefore, focusing on work more than family is not always the wrong choice.

My maternal grandfather, whom we called D, was one of the most godly men I have known. When I was in law school, I had no picture of him, but I put a big "D" on a piece of paper and taped it on the wall of my room to remind me of his character and principled life.

D was a traveling salesman, selling Munsingwear underwear all over the Southeast. He would get into his Oldsmobile and leave home for three and a half days a week almost every week. Yet his family—wife and daughters—remained the most harmonious family I have known. His daughters (one of them my mother), although deprived of his presence by his work half the time, loved him deeply and grew into wonderful ladies, bearing much fruit for God's glory. Of course, my grandmother, also a godly person, was left at home with her daughters—and she deserves even more credit than he for the way the girls turned out.

It never occurred to D or his wife and daughters that he was putting work ahead of family. He was a God-fearing man who did what he had to do in order to support his family, then he gave them the time that was left. What was important was that he loved them dearly and manifested in his character all of the fruit of the Holy Spirit.

Commission Work

Of a lower priority in terms of our time and energy is what we do beyond our core work.

With the spare time that most of us have today (we would likely not have had nearly as much 100 years ago), we need to find a way to serve the Lord with what we can call commission work. By "commission work," I refer to two commissions—one that Jesus left for us and another that guided his life.

You can easily guess what the first commission is.

The First Commission: Disciple Making

The last words of Jesus in the Gospel of Matthew are:

> All authority in heaven and on earth has been given to me. Therefore go and make disciples of all nations, baptizing them in the name of the Father and of the Son and of the

Holy Spirit, and teaching them to obey everything I have commanded you. And surely I am with you always, to the very end of the age (Matthew 28:18–20).

In light of these words, known as the Great Commission, we know making disciples is work all of Christ's followers are to take up. Jesus calls us to make disciples of our children by word and example at home. Perhaps we make disciples as well as teachers at church or in small groups. How we represent Christ at work and elsewhere can have a profound effect on those who are early in their discipleship development or who do not know Christ at all. We have ongoing opportunities, if we look for them, to bear witness to Christ in telling others of the hope that is in us (1 Peter 3:15).

The Second Commission: Mercy

We all know the Great Commission. Yet there is another commission that was Christ's vision for his own life. It is in Isaiah 61, Jesus' commission for his earthly ministry.

After fasting in the wilderness for fourty days, seeking the strategic will of his Father for his work, in his first sermon Jesus opened a scroll and read from what we call Isaiah 61:1. We don't know if he read from the next two verses or not. And even if not, they are certainly among the most inspiring in our Scripture.

> The Spirit of the Sovereign LORD is on me,
> because the LORD has anointed me
> to preach good news to the poor.
> He has sent me to bind up the brokenhearted,
> to proclaim freedom for the captives
> and release from darkness for the prisoners,
> to proclaim the year of the LORD's favor
> and the day of vengeance of our God,
> to comfort all who mourn,
> and provide for those who grieve in Zion—
> to bestow on them a crown of beauty

> instead of ashes,
> the oil of gladness
> instead of mourning,
> and a garment of praise
> instead of a spirit of despair.
> They will be called oaks of righteousness,
> a planting of the LORD
> for the display of his splendor (Isaiah 61:1–3).

After reading from Isaiah, Jesus said, "Today this scripture is fulfilled in your presence" (Luke 4:21). It was this work that was Jesus' food. And since we are his disciples, these words are our commission and spiritual food as well.

Isaiah 61 ministry explicitly embraces the evangelism of the Great Commission, since it refers to preaching good news. But it has a broader focus on ministries of mercy to the poor and outcast. And, of course, properly carried out, these ministries are easily joined with the Matthew 28 ministry of disciple making.

But are we fulfilling these two commissions?

The Joy of Commission Work

From time to time, I have interviewed people looking for a job. And I find that one of the best questions I can ask is "What is your greatest passion outside of work and family?" We can discover much about ourselves by asking this question. Is it woodcarving or gardening, reading or fishing, tennis or golf? For Christians, I would submit that the answer needs to be some kind of Matthew 28 or Isaiah 61 endeavor.

Again, what if we don't enjoy such work and therefore don't want to do it? As with early morning devotion, if that is our attitude, we will either soon burn out in it or do it with stoic determination, which does not honor God. If we don't truly enjoy the tasks of these commissions, we simply need more of the Holy Spirit, as preaching good news to the poor, making disciples, binding up broken hearts, and freeing those in bondage is the Holy Spirit's commission as well. (Remember the opening words of Isaiah 61, "The Spirit of the Sovereign Lord is on me.") He awaits our self-emptying and our prayer to Christ that he fill us (or re-fill us) in the Holy Spirit.

Of course, our commission work is likely to be "behind the lines." Many of us will not have time to spend months in the mission field nor the speaking skills to preach good news to the poor. But we can serve as an usher in a Great Commission church or keep the books for a recovery ministry. We might cook and wash the dishes in a soup kitchen or serve on the board of an inner-city ministry.

As we carry out the Matthew 28 and Isaiah 61 commissions of our Lord, we can know that we are doing God's will for us. We are being obedient. Our wills are aligned with his.

So commission work is important and an exceedingly great joy. But it is not so important that it takes precedence over our core work.

Resolving the Conflict between Core and Commission

Many Christians feel conflict between core and commission work. We rightly see sacred activities to be of eternal significance but wrongly see secular work as of little lasting consequence. So someone might believe that he can slight his job in order to spend more time in ministry. Or someone might think she should neglect her family in order to evangelize or serve the needy. Is this God's will?

If this is how we are thinking, we need to keep in mind that core work is a high and noble calling and that, without it, it would be almost impossible to take the gospel message to all nations or deliver the oppressed from bondage. Without strong families without the transportation, communication, and all kinds of other advances created in secular work, without efficiencies in manufacturing and distribution without a strong government, and without the wealth created by commerce, where would we be?

In the early days of foreign missions, a lifetime of work by great missionaries, such as Hudson Taylor, made little relative progress in China compared to the immensity of that nation, as precious as was every soul that was saved and all the seeds that were planted. Travel to and from China took months, and so did communications. Now the servants of God have an easier time in many ways—and it's due to people working in secular callings who have made technological advances.

Those who work full-time for the Lord need the support of secular work and vitally depend on the rest of us.

There is much talk today of moving from success to significance, the idea being that after we succeed in the secular world and have enough savings to retire, we should turn more and more to commission work, where we can engage in work of eternal significance. To be sure, some of us who start in secular core work are later called to full-time commission work. But for most of us, isn't it better to think in both/and terms? While in secular work we can do much of eternal significance in commission endeavors. Might the kingdom of God not be better off if we remain in such work and earn income even when we could retire and then give the extra income to those already called to full-time commission work?

Of course, we must make these decisions based on the will of God for each of our lives individually, and we must fervently seek that will. But the desire to leave the world of secular work altogether for commission activity is not necessarily of God and therefore is something we should consider carefully before acting.

Furthermore, while our core work is in the secular realm, we need to keep clear the line between core and commission work. Commission work should not crowd into core, whether it be occupational work or family. So great is the passion of many for commission work, this is easy to do.

Yet we do not glorify God when we let commission work crowd out our family responsibilities or core work. If it reduces our reliability or excellence in either, those who suffer will take note. If they are Christian, they will regret that God's name is being dishonored, and if they are not, they will resent the worker or family member who is letting them down. Letting commission work infringe on the effectiveness of core work is not putting God first but rather is dishonoring him.

There was a time, some twenty-five years ago, when my passion for commission work was putting a strain on family responsibilities. I went to a priest for advice, and he told me that I had made commission work an idol and was putting it ahead of God. This stunned me. But I came to understand that he was right. Putting God first meant putting core responsibilities (love) to family first and commission work second.

Sharpening the Saw

We might think that after we have completed our core and commission work, we are ready for our rest. But before we get to "Sabbath time," there is another aspect of any life that glorifies God, and it is what Stephen Covey calls "sharpening the saw."[23] Simply put, this is continually getting better at whatever we do—getting better and better in the quality of our work for God.

In Christian terms, if we wish to "sharpen our saw," we learn, practice, and exercise so that we can make better use of our talents in whatever Christ calls us to do. To serve Christ well in most of our work, we need minds that understand how to achieve excellence in the tasks to which he calls us and healthy bodies that are ready to work long and hard.

For example, if we teach the Bible, we need to be very good at it. That involves study. For any work, we need to study to keep apprised of the best practices and latest technology. We need to keep feeding and challenging the minds God gave us.

Likewise, we need good diets and physical exercise so that our bodies are prepared to run "the race marked out for us" (Hebrews 12:1). You might say this is taking it too far, that Christianity is strictly a spiritual thing; it's not about our bodies. But the Bible does not teach that. In light of God's mercies, we are to present our "bodies as living sacrifices, holy and pleasing to God" (Romans 12:1). To be sure, the race we run and the enemy we engage are spiritual, but our spiritual callings take strong bodies if we are to "finish" his work.

Whether it has to do with our bodies or our minds, our Lord is not glorified by lazy people who do not do their best, as the parable of the talents makes vividly clear (Matthew 25:14-30). Sloth has been considered a serious sin down through the ages. Whatever we do, we should do it with all of our heart (Colossians 3:23). And that's a hallmark of the most obedient and effective Christians.

British evangelist George Whitefield (1714–70), who crossed the Atlantic to America thirteen times, preached until he had no more breath. On his way to bed the night he would give up his soul, he paused on the staircase and preached to onlookers until the candle he held in his hand had burned away into its socket. His last sermon that day lasted two hours.

Whitefield's cohort in their early years at Oxford, John Wesley (1703–91), delivered some 40,000 sermons and rode approximately a quarter million miles on horseback over the English roads.

These were men who honed and practiced their skills. They were not lazy but made the most of the gifts God had given them.

Let us remember that the principle of the second law of thermodynamics (stating that lifeless physical processes tend to run down) applies to humans as well. Our minds, our spiritual faculties, and our bodies are constantly losing their effective edges unless we continuously sharpen the saw. The vigor, effectiveness, and impact we will have in Christ's redemptive activity depend on our sharpening the saw, and there is no retirement of this need.

Though George Bernard Shaw was no Christian and had his share of disputes with Christians, he did express a thought that (with a couple of changes I have made in brackets) is thoroughly biblical as to how we are to complete our life of obedience to the Lord:

This is the true joy in life—that being used for a purpose recognized by yourself as a [worthy] one . . . . I am
of the opinion that my life belongs to [Jesus Christ] and
as long as I live it is my privilege to do for [him] whatever
I can. I want to be thoroughly used up when I die. For the
harder I work the more I live. I rejoice in life for its own
sake. Life is no brief candle for me. It's a sort of splendid
torch which I've got to hold up for the moment and [by
God's grace] I want it [to] burn as brightly as possible before handing it on.[24]

Or as Paul indicates, a Christian's life is to be a "poured out" offering of sacrifice to our Lord (Philippians 2:17).

R&R

So let's sum up what we've covered in our survey of obedience
in real time: We begin the day in prayer and study, and we spend the
day bearing fruit for God in our core responsibilities and commission work. Then we take care to keep our performance edge in all
we do by sharpening the saw of our spiritual, mental, and physical
faculties.

After that, we are ready to rest.

As our spiritual, mental, and physical capabilities need to be
continually sharpened, so they also need rest one day in seven—
and, I might add, every night.

I said early in the book that, in writing about obedience, I am
writing about something I had thought about a lot but not necessarily something that I am good at personally. This is certainly true
in the area of Sabbath rest.

I must admit, I have made liberal use of our Lord's teaching that
the Sabbath is made for man, not man for the Sabbath, and Paul's
that we are to let no one judge us as to how we observe the Sabbath
(Mark 2:27; Colossians 2:16). I attend church almost every Sunday
and use Sunday afternoons for more extensive prayer and meditation.

Nevertheless, when I was more fully in the workplace, I would work and even schedule meetings on some Sundays. Sometimes I would travel on Sunday to be available for a meeting or would spend a part of Sunday preparing for a difficult assignment, such as a board meeting, that would take place on Monday. And in my family life as well, I would not always reserve Sunday for rest and worship. My children played competitive tennis, and when they were young, I would travel with them and often missed church as they played on Sunday. I have played many a match on Sunday myself. I go to movies with my wife on Sundays and on occasions shop.

To sum up, I have worked occasionally and sought the service of others who must work on Sunday. Much of this work was from a lack of planning; much was from laziness (not doing earlier in the week what I left to do on Sunday); and most was from lack of faith in God to show me the way not to work on Sunday. As I look back, I regret that I was not more faithful in seeking rest on Sunday so that I could honor God, receive his edification for the other six days of work, and, quite simply, enjoy life more fully.

What would have been different in my life if I had rested consistently on Sundays? What would be different in our society if we got off the treadmill for rest each Sunday? Would more of us be like Truett Cathy—happy in our lives and successful in our work because we had the faith to obey God's prescription for rest?

Our culture has changed radically in my lifetime. In the mid-20th century, we had pro sports on Sundays and the paper was available. A few restaurants and service stations were open. But by and large, at least insofar as commercial activity was concerned, we kept the Sabbath holy, or at least free of most work.

Perhaps we are like the frog in the water being heated to a boil—because the changes have been gradual, we simply are unable to see how our honoring of the Sabbath has been corrupted. I have long loved the teaching of Isaiah 58 on the necessity of taking care of the oppressed. This great teaching ends with these words:

"If you keep your feet from breaking the Sabbath

and from doing as you please on my holy day,
if you call the Sabbath a delight
and the LORD's holy day honorable,
and if you honor it by not going your own way
and not doing as you please or speaking idle words,
then you will find your joy in the LORD,
and I will cause you to ride on the heights of the land and to
feast on the inheritance of your father Jacob."
The mouth of the LORD has spoken (Isaiah 58:13–14).

These verses are worth our meditation—or at least *my* meditation. Though Paul says I am to have no worry about the judgment of others on my Sabbath activity, I can ask myself how much happiness and blessing have I lost by not honoring the Sabbath in so often "going [my] own way" and "doing as I please?" Have I no faith in God's promise that "joy in the Lord," "riding on the heights," and a great "feast" await those like Truett Cathy who faithfully honor the Sabbath? Are we not to look at the Fourth Commandment as a promise of blessedness and happiness for those who believe and in faith obey? So seen, it is not a requirement of a stern taskmaster but an invitation to joy, peace, and success.

A Seamless Life

There has been a lot of segmentation in this chapter: core, commission, sharpening the saw, and rest. But the overarching theme of every disciple's life is "Whatever you do, whether in word or in deed, do it all in the name of the Lord Jesus, giving thanks to God the Father through him" (Colossians 3:17). We can segment our lives in analysis to better organize them in obedience to God's calling. But let us conclude this chapter with a thought we stated at the beginning: God is first; God is last; God is all in all. When we get that straight, we can see life as a seamless obedience of faith and much happiness.

We have one last thought to take up. Can our study of obedience and the happiness growing from it help us understand the leadership that produces abundance in life? I think it can.

CHAPTER 25
Obedience and Leadership

IN THIS CONCLUDING chapter, we will continue our discussion of the alignment of wills and happiness, but we will flip the "coin of obedience" and look at the other side; leadership—how wills are aligned in groups and organizations to accomplish noble purposes, produce abundance and generate happiness. Our focus will be on human leadership. The fullness of life and happiness, that which God intended when he created earth and made us in his image, comes only when there is a flourishing of life in society through biblically based leadership and the obedience engendered by it.

Be Fruitful and Multiply

When we open the first few pages of the Bible, we learn immediately that God's initial commission for humankind is to take dominion over the earth, become fruitful and multiply. We are also taught that we are made in the "image of God." And the very first thing we learn about God is that he is creative. "In the beginning God created . . . As we look about and consider the skies above and the earth below teeming with its diverse life that is forever reproducing, it is obvious that he is *very* creative and prolific. We are made in his image to be creative and prolific too.

We can conclude, therefore, that in biblical terms an overarching objective of all organization and enterprise is to be creative and fruitful, to make the most of the resources of this earth, and to equip and empower men and women to be all they can be to the glory of God. That is the ultimate mission of all governments, schools and business organizations, whether they be for profit or not. And under biblical teaching, the role of leadership in all organizations is to craft a worthy mission within God's overarching commission, to align the wills of all to accomplish that mission, and to maximize capability by bringing out the best in every member in their respective roles in pursuing that mission.

Such leadership, we have observed in Chapter 23 can exist in a fast-food restaurant business, and when it does the business thrives, overflowing with customers and profits. Through intensive training and provision of scholarships, making managers potential owners, and a noble purpose, Chick-fil-A brings out the best in each of its employees. And we found it as well in East Lake, Atlanta, where the residents of a whole community were liberated and equipped to more fully reach their potential.

But before any noble mission can be achieved, wills must be aligned; there must be obedience. Everyone needs to be highly motivated to pull together in the same direction in pursuit of the mission. That is a function of leadership.

Aligning Wills—Two Poles

There are two poles between which all leadership seeks to align wills in an organization.

Command and Control

On the one hand, there is the command and control pole where the leader lays down the law and uses necessary power to enforce obedience. Extreme command and control leadership produces a society like that under the Taliban in Afghanistan. The result is a monotonous, fearful life essentially devoid of creativity, productive enterprise and joy. There is always wide-spread poverty.

Russell Kirk, possibly the leading conservative thinker of the

20th century, recounts the dialogue between Septimius Severus, a ruthless emperor in the dying days of the Roman Empire, and his brutal sons who were to succeed him. When Severus was on his deathbed, the sons asked him, "Father, when you are gone, how shall we govern?" The emperor replied, "Pay the soldiers. The rest do not matter."[25] Such is the attitude of dictators who demand obedience through command and control. The only way to keep order is by well-paid soldiers, and no one else matters.

Grant Gilmore, one of the great legal minds of the 20th century, wrote, "The worse the society, the more law there will be. In hell there will be nothing but law and [it] will be meticulously observed."[26] Hell is the ultimate command-and-control society. The declaration of independence from God sends rebels to hell, but once they are there, the autonomy they seek is totally lost. Satan is a control freak, and I imagine with a well-paid army.

Servant Leadership

At the other end of the spectrum is the servant-leadership pole. We could also call it kingdom-of-God leadership. Jesus Christ is its perfect model. The Lord Jesus rejected all governmental power and laid down little law. Whatever commands he left he summed up in the three words inscribed at the church entrance in Le Chambon: "Love one another" (John 15:12).

Jesus' instruction on leadership was a radical departure from all previous thought—and remains brilliant. Paul is right in his insight that in Jesus "were all the treasures of wisdom and knowledge" (Colossians 2:3).

In the last days of his earthly ministry, the mother of his disciples James and John came to Jesus and asked that her two sons be placed at the right and left hands of the heavenly throne. This incensed the other disciples and gave Jesus the opportunity to explain clearly what leadership in the kingdom of God is all about. "Whoever wants to become great among you must become your servant, and whoever wants to be first must be your slave—just as the Son of Man did not come to be served, but to serve, and to give his life as a ransom for many" (Matthew 20:26-27). Leaders in the kingdom of God serve, and do so sacrificially. That is an absolute prerequisite to achieving kingdom greatness, and it is also the only path for generating creative, productive enterprise on earth.

Jesus was not giving pious instruction intended to make Christian leaders morally good but not great as leaders. He was enunciating a principle at the heart of reality. Great production, resourcefulness and enterprise are the result of servant leadership. And interestingly this is the conclusion of Jim Collins' best-selling book on business leadership, *Good to Great*.[27] What Collins describes as Level V leadership, the highest and most productive kind, is servant leadership. Collins synthersized his thesis in a *Harvard Business Review* article that is one of the most popular the *Review* ever ran.[28]

Jesus modeled servant leadership at the Last Supper when he tied a towel around his waist and began to wash his disciples feet, saying,

> "Now that I, your Lord and Teacher, have washed your feet, you also should wash one another's feet. I have set you an example that you should do it as I have done for you" (John 13:14-15).

Leaders who unleash the productive potential of those they lead are *above* in responsibility but *beneath* in service. They exist to bring out the best in all they lead through being servants.

Leadership Producing Fruit

The United States has a secular constitution but our government is indebted to Jesus' model. Our Declaration of Independence deems the "pursuit of happiness" to be an inalienable right, and our Constitution puts strict limits on all command-and-control power, allowing voters to strip officeholders of power when they abuse it. Our government leaders are intended to be servants of the people in whom ultimate sovereignty rests. Though our land is populated by fallen creatures, still there has been within it an abundance of creativity and prolific enterprise that is the marvel of the world. The Communists thought they could outstrip constitutional democracy with a command-and-control government. They failed utterly and created much misery doing it.

Biblical principles of leadership extend to smaller communities, all the way down to the family. I learned it in my own upbringing. My father was a good, caring, and generous man. But he was also a strict disciplinarian with a quick temper. He had many rules, and his children—my two sisters and me—fearfully obeyed them because the consequences of breaking them were scary.

Mother, on the other hand, related to us with sacrificial love. She had few rules other than those such as "brush your teeth," and even these we could bend a little. She expected the best from us, but never said it. We just knew it because she devoted so much of her time and energy to us, giving us help to do our best in whatever we did. She was a servant leader. She subordinated her interests to ours. Whatever striving or productivity there has been in my life, and whatever moral character, has been from my mother's influence and example, not my father's. I obeyed his law to the letter but was not often inspired to move above its minimum requirements. So it is with all command-and-control power.

When General E. Lee retired to his home in Virginia, he turned down more lucrative job offers and became President of Washington College (later Washington and Lee University) in Lexington, Virginia. His leadership there was in the biblical model. One biographer describes it this way:

> General Lee initiated the honor system very soon after he came to Lexington, and made it the basis on which all students were received. Faculty visitation of dormitories and all forms of espionage were abolished. If any breach of discipline occurred or any injury was done to college property, he expected the students who were involved in it to report to him. "We have no printed rules," Lee told a new

matriculate who asked for a copy. "We have but one rule here, and it is that every student must be a gentleman." The first and the final appeal was to a student's sense of honor. "As a general principle," he told a young professor, "you should not force young men to do their duty, but let them do it voluntarily and thereby develop their characters." The code of the college, as Lee developed it, was positive though unprinted.[29]

No rules, no police—Lee's appeal was to an obedience from the heart, in biblical terms, an obedience of faith.

Likewise, the faithful in Le Chambon made enormous sacrifices to shelter the Jewish children, even putting their own safety in jeopardy, but there were no rules and no police to enforce any law. There were no material rewards, no recognition, no ribbons, no headlines. All obedience was anonymous, from the heart, but wills accomplishing a treacherous mission were perfectly aligned.

And what creative productivity there was at Le Chambon, not in terms of manufacture or commerce, but at a higher level, in terms of love! Copious, life-saving love was generated in this community through the inspiration of Jesus; a sacrificial leader (André Trocmé); and strong character.

When Paul writes that "the letter kills but the Spirit gives life" for sure he is talking about our souls and the abundant life within, but he is also stating a principle that has application for all leadership (2 Corinthians 3:6). When the leader resorts to requiring compliance with the "letter" of the law, if his police force is large and well paid, he will get obedience to the letter of the law, but nothing more, and externally there will be no life or happiness in the people, only a grim monotony. On the other hand, where obedience comes from the heart because the vision of the leader and the purpose of the mission is a noble one, flourishing life and productivity will be birthed in the people, and there will be much hope and happiness.

Paul finishes his thought with the comment that, "where the

Spirit of the Lord is, there is freedom" (2 Corinthians 3:16). It is when the wills of those who are led are aligned with the leader's in freedom and love that we have flourishing life and happiness.

In the introduction, we quoted Dallas Willard's insight that "kingdom obedience" is "kingdom abundance." Though Professor Willard was talking about the abundant life within, his principle applies to all abundant productivity that flows from kingdom leadership.

Leadership and Trust

We have examined the marriage of obedience and faith in a spiritual sense. Likewise, obedience must be married to faith (or trust) for the servant-leadership model to function in secular life. If there is to be a minimum of law and police, the leader must be able to trust the people and they likewise must be able to trust him and each other. In fact, we can conclude that trustworthiness and the Christlike character that produces it are keys to all well-functioning groups, nations, companies, teams, and families. For leadership in the secular realm to thrive, there needs to be an obedience of faith.

Edmund Burke, a keen observer of both the French Revolution (including the reign of terror that grew out of it) and England (his native country, whose developing democratic government avoided revolutionary France's horrors), correctly observed that, "society cannot exist unless a controlling power upon will and appetite be placed somewhere, and the less there is within, the more there must be without."[30]

Burke knew that obedience in a society came either from strong character in the people (England) or command and control of these in power (France and the reign of terror). He knew, as all students of democracy are aware, that there can be no freedom or trustworthiness without strong virtue within.

In the United States, our laws are multiplying in the business sector, and much of it flows from corrupt character that has generated fraud and abuse and the disintegration of trust essential for a free market system to function. Many of us are familiar with the Sarbanes-Oxley law, a costly corporate governance measure that was passed in the wake of the accounting scandals of Enron, WorldCom, HealthSouth, and other companies. We are soon to have more laws to control financial institutions, which during the first decade of the 21st century, driven by greed, became recklessly overleveraged. When the crash came, their collapse almost brought the American economy to its knees. As the story of the crisis is told, we are discovering that Wall Street was rife with conflicts of interest that destroy trustworthiness.

These laws will diminish productivity and creativity. They will put thousands of lawyers to work and the enforcement agencies will hire hundreds of police. They will cause American business to obey laws as we move away from trust and freedom and toward command and control; away from virtue within, toward law without.

The Challenge of Servant Leadership

Unfortunately, because we are fallen creatures, servant-leadership societies are very difficult to maintain. They produce success and prosperity and the children of prosperity often have not developed the character of those who produced the success. Cotton Mather once said, "Religion brought forth prosperity and the daughter destroyed the mother."[31]

We see this often in the United States, a society built in large part on immigration. Individuals with courageous characters, yearning for freedom, come to America and in the first generation work sacrificially so their children can have a better life, even a college education. These children, growing up in a household where sacrificial love is modeled for them, and in circumstances where they must find jobs as teenagers to help parents make ends meet, are often productive and successful. The challenge is in the third generation, where character may not be shaped in a home built on servant leadership. The result is a loss of trust and productivity and ultimately the necessity for more law and government.

Maximizing Freedom

In biblical terms, the challenge for every Christian leader, wherever authority may rest, is to move as far toward the servant-leader pole as is possible. Every society or group needs some law and its enforcement, but mature leaders will maximize freedom. A prison warden needs electrically charged fences, prison cells, armed guards and a host of rules and regulations, but the better wardens create honor dorms where the prisoners who obey from within without coercion can be given greater freedom and hopefully grow in their ability to contribute productively on their release. The purpose of military boot camp (command and control) is to develop character that will function well in the free flow of the battlefield even when no commander is looking.

Almost all parents find that different degrees of control and discipline are needed for each unique child. But still the objective for each individually is to develop such character that as each matures there is no need for rules because obedience flows naturally from a character that seeks to honor parents.

A Look at Heaven

In contrast to hell, where there is nothing but law, in heaven there will be perfect freedom (no police), perfect obedience, and perfect delight driven by perfect love for the Leader and total trust in him. We can only dream about all the inspiration, creativity, and excellence that are unleashed in such a society, but surely it is glorious, far more than we can possibly imagine. We can only weep that our sin prevents such creativity—and the joy and happiness that flow from it—from being released fully here on earth. We would know such happiness if our ancestors had not eaten the forbidden fruit and passed their sinful rebellion on to us. And by God's grace, in eternity we will be a part of that creativity and its happiness. That is indeed a blessed hope.

CHAPTER 26
Conclusion

I HOPE OUR discussion has illumined a new way to understand the obedience of faith – to see it as a source of life and energy in our souls as well as fruit in our deeds.

Obedience has both an external function that glorifies God and an internal role in the life and health (and therefore the happiness) of our souls.

We have observed this at every station of the Virtuous Cycle. Obedience and *faith* are inseparably joined as root and branch. Through obedience and faith the chambers of our hearts receive the fullness of the *Holy Spirit*. Through obedience our *love for God* is made complete. The habits of an obedient life shape our *Christ-like character*.

The obedience of faith forms channels through which *life-and-strength-giving grace* flows into every chamber of our inward spiritual life. As Moses tells the Israelites, the commandments are our "life" (Deuteronomy 32:47). And our relationship to Christ in whom alone there is "life" is nurtured and sustained only in the obedience of faith (John 14:15-24).

Take the obedience of faith away and our spiritual life atrophies. There is no spiritual life and energy on the inside; no fruit on the outside. The obedience of faith is, therefore, vital to both the expression of all life that glorifies God and all peace and happiness in our hearts.

* * *

Our discussion has come to its conclusion. I hope at the very least it has helped "rescue the word obedience from the mire" to draw on Oswald Chambers' metaphor again. And I hope we can agree with the great moral that reigns in *Paradise Lost:* "Obedience to the will of God makes men happy and disobedience makes them miserable." For the obedience of faith nurtures our fellowship with God and, as an essential part of a spiritual virtuous cycle, unleashes wisdom and energy in us that, as we grow in Christlike character, frees us to bring glory to God in completing the work he has planned for us to do. It is a key that we need to find and keep safe in our hearts, for it is the hidden key that unlocks the door to happiness.

APPENDIX A
Unmerited, Conditional Grace

I. In *Future Grace, Part VI*, John Piper discusses how grace, always free and unmerited, is often conditional.

> I know that for many people the very term "conditional grace" sounds like a contradiction – like "dry water," or "short skyscraper." This is not entirely bad, because, in fact, not all grace is conditional. And not all grace is conditional in the same way....

> Take, for example, the precious promise of Romans 8:28 that we considered in Chapter Nine. It contains an all-encompassing promise of future grace, namely, that God will work all things together for your good. But this magnificent promise that has carried millions of believers through the darkest times, is doubly conditional. 'We know that God causes all things to work together for good, to those who love God, to those who are called according to his purpose.' The first condition is that we must love God; the second condition is that we must be called according to his purpose.' A vast, eternal panorama of future grace is summed up in the promise that God will work all things for our good. And all this future grace is conditional.

> pp. 231-2.

> It should be plain from this, that fulfilling conditions does not imply earning anything or meriting anything. Grace is still free, even when it is con-

ditional. There is such a thing as unmerited, conditional grace. Do not equate meeting conditions of grace with earning or meriting grace. 'Earning grace' would indeed be a contradiction in terms, like 'hot snow' or 'verdant desert.'

Suppose I say, 'If you are on the plane, you will fly to Chicago." That is a genuine condition that has to be met. But, it does not tell you who will buy your ticket or even if you will be carried, helpless, onto the plane. If someone else buys your ticket, and carries you onto the plane, then you have fulfilled the condition of getting to Chicago, but you have not necessarily earned or merited the ride. It is crucial that we keep this distinction in mind. Not all conditions are means of meriting. In fact, some conditions are means of renouncing merit. That is what I have in mind when I speak for conditional grace.

pp. 234-5.

Piper goes on to discuss how grace may be conditioned on: loving God and his Son; humility; drawing near to God; crying to God for grace; fearing God; delighting in God; hoping in God; taking refuge in God; and waiting for God.

pp. 239-249

* * * * *

II. In *With Christ in the School of Prayer*, Andrew Murray develops the biblical foundation for our obedience in relation to partaking in God's blessings:

Entire consecration to the fulfillment of our calling in the condition of effectual prayer, is the key to the unlimited blessings of Christ's wonderful prayer promises.

There are Christians who fear that such a statement is at variance with the doctrine of free grace. But surely not of free grace rightly understood, nor with so many express statements of God's blessed word. Take the words of St. John (1 John 3.22): 'Let us love in deed and truth; *hereby* shall we assure our heart before Him. And whatsoever we ask, we receive of Him, *because* we keep His commandments, and do the things that are pleasing in His sight.' Or take the oft-quoted words of James: 'The fervent effectual prayer of a *righteous* man availeth much;' that is, of a man of whom, according to the definition of the Holy Spirit, it can be said, 'He that doeth righteousness, is righteous even as He is righteous.' Mark the spirit of so many of the Psalms, with their confident appeal to the integrity and righteousness of the supplicant. In Psalm 18 David says: 'The Lord rewarded me according to my righteousness; according to the cleanness of my hands hath He recompensed me.... I was upright before Him, and I kept myself from mine iniquity: therefore hath the Lord recompensed me according to my righteousness.' (Psalm 18.2—26. See also Psalm 7.3-5, 15.1, 2, 17.3, 6, 26.1-6, 119.121, 153). If we carefully consider such utterances in the light of the New Testament, we shall find them in perfect harmony with the explicit teaching of the Savior's parting words: '*If ye keep* my commandments, ye shall abide in my love;' 'Ye are my friends *if ye do* what I command you.' The word is indeed meant literally: 'I appoint you that ye should go and bear fruit, *that*, then, whatsoever ye shall ask of the Father in my name, He may give it to you.'

Let us seek to enter into the spirit of what the Savior here teaches us. There is a danger in our evangelical religion of looking too much at what it offers from one side, as a certain experience to be obtained in prayer and faith. There is another side which God's word puts very strongly, that of obedience as the only path to blessing. What we need is to realize that in our relationship to the Infinite Being whom we call God who has created and redeemed us, the first sentiment that ought to animate us is that of subjection: the surrender to His supremacy, His glory, His will, His pleasure, ought to be the first and uppermost thought of our life. The question is not, how we are to obtain and enjoy His favour, for in this the main thing may still be self. But what this Being in the very nature of things rightfully claims, and is infinitely and unspeakably worthy of, is that His glory and pleasure should be my one object. Surrender to His perfect and blessed will, a life of service and obedience, is the beauty and the charm of heaven. Service and obedience, these were the thoughts that were uppermost in the mind of the Son, when He dwelt upon earth. Service and obedience, these must become with us the chief objects of desire and aim, more so than rest or light, or joy or strength: in them we shall find the path to all the higher blessedness that awaits us.

With Christ in the School of Prayer, p. 128-129

* * * * *

III. Charles Hodge, the great Reformed theologian, writes in his *Systematic Theology* that though all of God's blessings flow from supernatural grace, still God's grace in sanctification calls for our "unremitting and strenuous exertion."

The effects of grace, or fruits of the Spirit, are above the sphere of the natural. They belong to the supernatural. The mere power of truth, argument, motive, persuasion, or eloquence cannot produce repentance, faith or holiness of heart and life. Nor can these effects be produced by the power of the will, or by all the resources of man, however protracted or skilful in their application. They are the gifts of God, the fruits of the Spirit. Paul may plant and Apollos water, but it is God who gives the increase.

In this latter sense of the word supernatural, the cooperation of second causes is not excluded. When Christ opened the eyes of the blind no second cause interposed between his volition and the effect. But men work out their own salvation, while it is God who worketh in them to will and to do, according to his own good pleasure. In the work of regeneration, the soul is passive. It cannot cooperate in the communication of spiritual life. But in conversion, repentance, faith, and growth in grace, all its powers are called into exercise. As, however, the effects produced transcend the efficiency of our fallen nature, and are due to the agency of the Spirit, sanctification does not cease to be supernatural, or a work of grace, because the soul is active and cooperating in the process....

It has already been shown that although sanctification does not exclude all cooperation on the part of its subjects, but, on the contrary, calls for their unremitting and strenuous exertion, it is nevertheless the work of God....

The work of sanctification is carried on by God's giving constant occasion for the exercise of all the graces of the Spirit. Submission, confidence, self-denial, patience, and meekness, as well as faith, hope, and love, are called forth, or put to the test, more or less effectually every day the believer passes on earth. And by this constant exercise he grows in grace and in the knowledge of our Lord and Savior Jesus Christ. It is, however, principally by calling his people to labour and suffer for the advancement of the Redeemer's kingdom, and for the good of their fellow-men, that this salutary discipline is carried on. The best Christians are in general those who not merely from restless activity of natural disposition, but from love to Christ and zeal for his glory, labour most and suffer most in his service.

pp. 215, 226, 230

* * * * *

IV. Wayne Grudem, in his popular, modern *Systematic Theology*, is in accord with Professor Hodge:

C. God and Man Cooperate in Sanctification

Some (such as John Murray) object to saying that God and man "cooperate" in sanctification, because they want to insist that God's work is primary and our work in sanctification is only a secondary one (see Phil. 2:12-13). However, if we explain the nature of God's role and our role in sanctification clearly, it does not seem inappropriate to say that God and man cooperate in sanctification. God works in our sanctification and we work as well, and we work for the same purpose. We are not saying that we have equal roles in sanctification or that we both work in the same way, but simply that we cooperate with God in ways that are appropriate to our status as God's creatures. And the fact that Scripture emphasizes the role that we play in sanctification (with all the moral commands of the New Testament), makes it appropriate to teach that God calls us to cooperate with him in this activity....

Unfortunately today, this "passive" role in sanctification, this idea of yielding to God and trusting him to work in us "to will and to work for his good pleasure" (Phil. 2:13), is sometimes so strongly emphasized that it is the only thing people are told about the path of sanctification. Sometimes the popular phrase "let go and let God" is given as a summary of how to live the Christian life. But this is a tragic distortion of the doctrine of sanctification, for it only speaks of one half of the part we must play, and, by itself, will lead Christians to become lazy and to neglect the active role that Scripture commands them to play in their own sanctification....

It is important that we continue to grow both in our passive trust in God to sanctify us and in our active striving for holiness and greater obedience in our lives. If we neglect active striving to obey God, we become passive, lazy Christians. If we neglect the passive role of trusting God and yielding to him, we become proud and overly confident in ourselves. In either case, our sanctification will be greatly deficient. We must maintain faith and diligence to obey at the same time.

Wayne Grudem, *Systematic Theology*, 753, 754, 755

APPENDIX B
Paul's Prayers

2 Corinthians 13:14

May the grace of the Lord Jesus Christ, and the love of God, and the fellowship of the Holy Spirit be with you all.

Ephesians 1:15-19

Ever since I heard about your faith in the Lord Jesus and your love for all the saints, I have not stopped giving thanks for you, remembering you in my prayers. I keep asking that the God of our Lord Jesus Christ, the glorious Father, may give you the Spirit of wisdom and revelation, so that you may know him better. I pray also that the eyes of your heart may be enlightened in order that you may know the hope to which he has called you, the riches of his glorious inheritance in the saints, and his incomparably great power for us who believe. That power is like the working of his mighty strength.

Ephesians 3:14-21

I kneel before the Father, from whom his whole family in heaven and on earth derives its name. I pray that out of his glorious riches he may strengthen you with power through his Spirit in your inner being, so that Christ may dwell in your hearts through faith. And I pray that you, being rooted and established in love, may have power, together with all the saints, to grasp how wide and long and high and deep is the love of Christ, and to know this love that surpasses knowledge—that you may be filled to the measure of all the fullness of God. Now to him who is able to do immeasurably more than all we ask or imagine, according to his power that is at work within us, to him be glory in the church and in Christ Jesus throughout all generations, for ever and ever! Amen.

Philippians 1:9

This is my prayer: that your love may abound more and more in knowledge and depth of insight, so that you may be able to discern what is best and may be pure and blameless until the day of Christ, filled with the fruit of righteousness that comes through Jesus Christ—to the glory and praise of God.

Colossians 1:9-14

Since the day we heard about you, we have not stopped praying for you and asking God to fill you with the knowledge of his will through all spiritual wisdom and understanding. And we pray this in order that you may live a life worthy of the Lord and may please him in every way: bearing fruit in every good work, growing in the knowledge of God, being strengthened with all power according to his glorious might so that you may have great endurance and patience, and joyfully giving thanks to the Father, who has qualified you to share in the inheritance of the saints in the kingdom of light. For he has rescued us from the dominion of darkness and brought us into the kingdom of the Son he loves, in whom we have redemption, the forgiveness of sins.

1 Thessalonians 1:3

We continually remember before our God and Father your work produced by faith, your labor prompted by love, and your endurance inspired by hope in our Lord Jesus Christ.

1 Thessalonians 3:12-13

May the Lord make your love increase and overflow for each other and for everyone else, just as ours does for you. May he strengthen your hearts so that you will be blameless and holy in the presence of our God and Father when our Lord Jesus comes with all his holy ones.

1 Thessalonians 5:23-24

May God himself, the God of peace, sanctify you through and through. May your whole spirit, soul and body be kept blameless at the coming of our Lord Jesus Christ. The one who calls you is faithful and he will do it.

2 Thessalonians 1:11-12

We constantly pray for you, that our God may count you worthy of his calling, and that by his power he may fulfill every good purpose of yours and every act prompted by your faith. We pray this so that the name of our Lord Jesus may be glorified in you, and you in him, according to the grace of our God and the Lord Jesus Christ.

Appendix C
Words of the Lord for Daily Living

Leviticus 19:18

Do not seek revenge or bear a grudge against one of your people, but love your neighbor as yourself. I am the Lord.

Numbers 6:22-26

The Lord said to Moses, "Tell Aaron and his sons, 'This is how you are to bless the Israelites. Say to them:

" " "The Lord bless you
and keep you,
the Lord make his face shine upon you
and be gracious to you;
the Lord turn his face toward you
and give you peace." ' "

Deuteronomy 6:5

Love the Lord your God with all your heart and with all your soul and with all your strength.

Deuteronomy 8:18

Remember the Lord your God, for it is he who gives you the ability to produce wealth.

Joshua 1:8-9

Do not let this Book of the Law depart from your mouth; meditate on it day and night, so that you may be careful to do everything written in it. Then you will be prosperous and successful. . . . Be strong and courageous. Do not be terrified; do not be discouraged, for the Lord your God will be with you wherever you go.

2 Chronicles 16:9

> The eyes of the Lord range throughout the earth to strengthen those whose hearts are fully committed to him.

Psalm1:1-3

> Blessed is the man [whose] . . .
> delight is in the law of the LORD,
> and on his law he meditates day and night.
> He is like a tree planted by streams of water,
> which yields its fruit in season
> and whose leaf does not wither.
> Whatever he does prospers.

Psalm 16:2

> I said to the LORD, "You are my Lord;
> apart from you I have no good thing."

Psalm 16:5-6

> LORD, you have assigned me my portion and my cup;
> you have made my lot secure.
> The boundary lines have fallen for me in pleasant places;
> surely I have a delightful inheritance.

Psalm 18:2

> The LORD is my rock, my fortress and my deliverer;
> my God is my rock, in whom I take refuge.
> He is my shield and the horn of my salvation, my stronghold.

Psalm 20:7

> Some trust in chariots and some in horses,
> but we trust in the name of the LORD our God.

Psalm 25:4-5

> Show me your ways, O LORD,
> teach me your paths;
> guide me in your truth and teach me,
> for you are God my Savior,
> and my hope is in you all day long.

Psalm 27:5

> In the day of trouble
> he will keep me safe in his dwelling;
> he will hide me in the shelter of his tabernacle
> and set me high upon a rock.

Psalm 27:14

> Wait for the Lord;
> be strong and take heart
> and wait for the Lord.

Psalm 31:19

> How great is your goodness,
> which you have stored up for those who fear you,
> which you bestow in the sight of men
> on those who take refuge in you.

Psalm 32:8, 10

> I will instruct you and teach you in the way
> you should go;
> I will counsel you and watch over you. . . .
> The Lord's unfailing love
> surrounds the man who trusts in him.

Psalm 33:11, 18-19

> The plans of the Lord stand firm forever,
> the purposes of his heart through all generations. . . .
> The eyes of the Lord are on those who fear him,
> on those whose hope is in his unfailing love,
> to deliver them from death
> and keep them alive in famine.

Psalm 34:7

> The angel of the Lord encamps around those
> who fear him,
> and he delivers them.

Psalm 36:5

> Your love, O Lord, reaches to the heavens,
> your faithfulness to the skies.

Psalm 37:4-6

> Delight yourself in the Lord
> and he will give you the desires of your heart.
> Commit your way to the Lord;
> trust in him and he will do this:
> He will make your righteousness shine like the dawn,
> the justice of your cause like the noonday sun.

Psalm 50:15

> Call upon me in the day of trouble;
> I will deliver you, and you will honor me.

Psalm 55:22

> Cast your cares on the Lord
> and he will sustain you;
> he will never let the righteous fall.

Psalm 62:2

> He alone is my rock and my salvation;
> he is my fortress, I will never be shaken.

Psalm 86:11-12

> Teach me your way, O Lord,
> and I will walk in your truth;
> give me an undivided heart,
> that I may fear your name.
> I will praise you, O Lord my God, with all my heart;
> I will glorify your name forever.

Psalm 90:17

> May the favor of the Lord our God rest upon us;
> establish the work of our hands for us—
> yes, establish the work of our hands.

Psalm 91:9-10

> If you make the Most High your dwelling—
> even the Lord, who is my refuge—
> then no harm will befall you,
> no disaster will come near your tent.

Psalm 103:2-5

> Praise the Lord, O my soul,
> and forget not all his benefits—
> who forgives all your sins
> and heals all your diseases,
> who redeems your life from the pit
> and crowns you with love and compassion,
> who satisfies your desires with good things
> so that your youth is renewed like the eagle's.

Psalm 112:7

> He will have no fear of bad news;
> his heart is steadfast, trusting in the Lord.

Psalm 118:25

> O Lord, save us;
> O Lord, grant us success.

Psalm 119:35-37, 67, 71-72

> Direct me in the path of your commands,
> for there I find delight.
> Turn my heart toward your statutes and
> not toward selfish gain.
> Turn my eyes away from worthless things;
> renew my life according to your word. . . .
> Before I was afflicted I went astray,
> but now I obey your word. . . .
> It was good for me to be afflicted
> so that I might learn your decrees.
> The law from your mouth is more precious to me
> than thousands of pieces of silver and gold.

Psalm 121

> I lift up my eyes to the hills—
> where does my help come from?
> My help comes from the Lord,
> the Maker of heaven and earth.
> He will not let your foot slip—
> he who watches over you will not slumber;
> indeed, he who watches over Israel
> will neither slumber nor sleep.
> The Lord watches over you—
> the Lord is your shade at your right hand;
> the sun will not harm you by day,
> nor the moon by night.

The Lord will keep you from all harm—
he will watch over your life;
the Lord will watch over your coming and going
both now and forevermore.

Psalm 127:1-2

Unless the Lord builds the house,
its builders labor in vain.
Unless the Lord watches over the city,
the watchmen stand guard in vain.
In vain you rise early
and stay up late
toiling for food to eat—
for he grants sleep to those he loves.

Psalm 138:8

The Lord will fulfill his purpose for me;
your love, O Lord, endures forever.

Proverbs 2:6-8; 3:25-26

The Lord gives wisdom,
and from his mouth come knowledge and
understanding.
He holds victory in store for the upright,
he is a shield to those whose walk is blameless,
for he guards the course of the just
and protects the way of his faithful ones. . . .
Have no fear of sudden disaster
or of the ruin that overtakes the wicked,
for the Lord will be your confidence
and will keep your foot from being snared.

Proverbs 3:5-6

Trust in the Lord with all your heart
and lean not on your own understanding;

in all ways acknowledge him,
and he will make your paths straight.

Proverbs 4:23

Above all else, guard your heart
for it is the wellspring of life.

Proverbs 9:10

The fear of the Lord is the beginning of wisdom
and knowledge of the Holy One is understanding.

Proverbs 15:22

Plans fail for lack of counsel,
but with many advisers they succeed.

Proverbs 16:3

Commit to the Lord whatever you do,
and your plans will succeed.

Proverbs 21:31

The horse is made ready for the day of battle,
but victory rests with the Lord.

Isaiah 26:12

Lord, you establish peace for us;
all that we have accomplished you have done for us.

Isaiah 40:28-31

Do you not know?
Have you not heard?
The Lord is the everlasting God,
the Creator of the ends of the earth.
He will not grow tired or weary,
and his understanding no one can fathom.
He gives strength to the weary

and increases the power of the weak. . . .
Those who hope in the Lord
will renew their strength.
They will soar on wings like eagles;
they will run and not grow weary,
they will walk and not be faint.

Isaiah 45:24

In the Lord alone are righteousness and strength.

Jeremiah 6:16

Stand at the crossroads and look;
ask for the ancient paths,
ask where the good way is, and walk in it,
and you will find rest for your souls.

Jeremiah 17:7-8

Blessed is the man who trusts in the Lord,
whose confidence is in him.
He will be like a tree planted by the water
that sends out its roots by the stream.
It does not fear when heat comes;
its leaves are always green.
It has no worries in a year of drought
and never fails to bear fruit.

Lamentations 3:22-23

Because of the Lord's great love we are not consumed,
for his compassions never fail.
They are new every morning;
great is your faithfulness.

Hosea 10:12

Sow for yourselves righteousness,

reap the fruit of unfailing love,
and break up your unplowed ground;
for it is time to seek the Lord,
until he comes
and showers righteousness on you.

Matthew 6:33

Seek first his kingdom and his righteousness, and all these things will be given to you as well.

Matthew23:11

The greatest among you will be your servant.

Mark10:43-44

Whoever wants to become great among you must be your servant, and whoever wants to be first must be slave of all.

Luke 9:23-24

If anyone would come after me, he must deny himself and take up his cross daily and follow me. For whoever wants to save his life will lose it, but whoever loses his life for me will save it.

John 3:21

Whoever lives by the truth comes into the light, so that it may be seen plainly that what he has done has been done through God.

John 4:34

"My food," said Jesus, "is to do the will of him who sent me and to finish his work."

John10:10

I have come that you may have life, and

have it abundantly.

John 12:26

Whoever serves me must follow me; and where I am, my servant also will be. My Father will honor the one who serves me.

John15:5

I am the vine; you are the branches. If a man remains in me and I in him, he will bear much fruit; apart from me you can do nothing.

John 15:16, 8

I chose you to go and bear fruit—fruit that will last. . . . This is to my Father's glory, that you bear much fruit, showing yourselves to be my disciples.

Romans 5:2-5

We rejoice in the hope of the glory of God. Not only so, but we also rejoice in our suffering, because we know that suffering produces perseverance; perseverance, character, and character, hope. And hope does not disappoint us, because God has poured out his love into our hearts by the Holy Spirit, whom he has given us.

Romans 5:17

If, by the trespass of the one man, death reigned through that one man, how much more will those who receive God's abundant provision of grace and of the gift of righteousness reign in life through the one man, Jesus Christ.

Romans 7:6

Serve in the new way of the Spirit, and not in the

old way of the written code.

Romans 8:28

We know that in all things God works for the good of those who love him, who have been called according to his purpose.

Romans 12:1-2

I urge you, brothers, in view of God's mercy, to offer your bodies as living sacrifices, holy and pleasing to God—which is your spiritual worship. Do not conform any longer to the pattern of this world, but be transformed by the renewing of your mind. Then you will be able to test and approve what God's will is—his good, pleasing and perfect will.

Romans 14:17-18

The kingdom of God is not a matter of eating and drinking, but of righteousness, peace and joy in the Holy Spirit, because anyone who serves Christ in this way is pleasing to God and approved by men.

1 Corinthians 3:7

Neither he who plants nor he who waters is anything, but only God, who makes things grow.

1 Corinthians 4:20

The kingdom of God is not a matter of talk but of power.

1 Corinthians 13:13

> These three remain: faith, hope and love. But the greatest of these is love.

2 Corinthians 5:9, 15

> We make it our goal to please him. . . . And he died for all, that those who live should no longer live for themselves but for him who died for them and was raised again.

2 Corinthians 7:1

> Dear friends, let us purify ourselves from everything that contaminates body and spirit, perfecting holiness out of reverence for God.

2 Corinthians 9:8

> God is able to make all grace abound to you, so that in all things at all times, having all that you need, you will abound in every good work.

2 Corinthians 13:3

> He is not weak in dealing with you, but is powerful among you.

2 Corinthians 13:11

> Aim for perfection.

Galatians 5:6

> The only thing that counts is faith expressing itself through love.

Galatians 5:13

> You, my brothers, were called to be free. But do not use your freedom to indulge the sinful nature; rather, serve one another in love.

Galatians 6:2

> Carry each other's burdens, and in this way you
> will fulfill the law of Christ.

Ephesians 1:11-12

> In him we were also chosen, having been predes-
> tined according to the plan of him who works out
> everything in conformity with the purpose of his
> will, in order that we . . . might be for the praise of his glory.

Ephesians 2:10

> We are God's workmanship, created in Christ Jesus
> to do good works, which God prepared in advance
> for us to do.

Ephesians 3:20

> Now to him who is able to do immeasurably more
> than all we ask or imagine, according to
> his power that is at work within us . . .

Ephesians 5:18-21

> Do not get drunk on wine, which leads to debauch-
> ery. Instead, be filled with the Spirit.
> Speak to one another with psalms, hymns and
> spiritual songs. Sing and make music in your heart
> to the Lord, always giving thanks to God the Fa-
> ther for everything, in the name of our Lord Jesus
> Christ.
> Submit to one another out of reverence for Christ.

Ephesians 6:10

> Be strong in the Lord and in his mighty power.

Philippians 2:12-13

> My dear friends, as you have always obeyed—continue to work out your salvation with fear and trembling, for it is God who works in you to will and to act according to his good purpose.

Philippians 3:12

> I press on to take hold of that for which Christ Jesus took hold of me.

Philippians 4:4-8

> Rejoice in the Lord always. l will say it again: Rejoice! Let your gentleness be evident to all.
> The Lord is near. Do not be anxious about anything but in everything, by prayer and petition, with thanksgiving, present your requests to God. And the peace of God, which transcends all understanding, will guard your hearts and your minds in Christ Jesus.
> Finally, brothers, whatever is true, whatever is noble, whatever is right, whatever is pure, whatever is lovely, whatever is admirable—if anything is excellent or praiseworthy—think about such things.

Philippians 4:13

> I can do everything through him who gives me strength.

Philippians 4:19

> My God will meet all your needs according to his glorious riches in Christ Jesus.

Colossians 1:9-11

> Since the day we heard about you, we have not stopped praying for you and asking God to fill you

with the knowledge of his will through all spiritual wisdom and understanding . . . that you may live a life worthy of the Lord and may please him in every way: bearing fruit in every good work, growing in the knowledge of God, being strengthened with all power according to his glorious might so that you may have great endurance and patience.

Colossians 2:10

You have been given fullness in Christ, who is the head over every power and authority.

Colossians 3:12-17

As God's chosen people, holy and dearly loved, clothe yourselves with compassion, kindness, humility, gentleness and patience. Bear with each other and forgive whatever grievances you may have against one another. Forgive as the Lord forgave you. And over all these virtues put on love, which binds them all together in perfect unity.

Let the peace of Christ rule in your hearts, since as members of one body you were called to peace. And be thankful. Let the word of Christ dwell in you richly . . . with gratitude in your hearts to God. And whatever you do, whether in word or deed, do it all in the name of the Lord Jesus, giving thanks to God the Father through him.

Colossians 3:23-24

Whatever you do, work at it with all your heart, as working for the Lord, not for men, since you know that you will receive an inheritance from the Lord as a reward. It is the Lord Christ you are serving.

1 Thessalonians 5:16-18

> Be joyful always; pray continually; give thanks in all circumstances, for this is God's will for you in Christ Jesus.

2 Thessalonians 1:11

> We constantly pray for you, that our God may count you worthy of his calling, and that by his power he may fulfill every good purpose of yours and every act prompted by your faith.

2 Timothy 2:1

> Be strong in the grace that is in Christ Jesus.

Titus 2:11-14

> The grace of God that brings salvation has appeared to all men. It teaches us to say "No" to ungodliness and worldly passions, and to live self-controlled, upright and godly lives in this present age, while we wait for the blessed hope—the glorious appearing of our great God and Savior, Jesus Christ, who gave himself for us to redeem us from all wickedness and to purify for himself a people that are his very own, eager to do what is good.

Hebrews 12:1-2

> Let us throw off everything that hinders and the sin that so easily entangles, and... run with perseverance the race marked out for us, . . . fix[ing] our eyes on Jesus, the author and perfecter of our faith.

Hebrews 13:20-21

> May the God of peace . . . equip you with everything good for doing his will, and may he work in us what is pleasing to him, through Jesus Christ, to

whom be glory for ever and ever. Amen.

1 Peter 2:6

The one who trusts in [the cornerstone] will never be put to shame.

James 1:2-8

Consider it pure joy, my brothers, whenever you face trials of many kinds, because you know that the testing of your faith develops perseverance. Perseverance must finish its work so that you may be mature and complete, not lacking anything. If any of you lacks wisdom, he should ask God, who gives generously to all without finding fault, and it will be given to him. But when he asks he must believe and not doubt, because he who doubts is like a wave of the sea, blown and tossed by the wind. That man should not think he will receive anything from the Lord; he is a double-minded man, unstable in all he does.

James 4:10

Humble yourselves before the Lord, and he will lift you up.

1 Peter 4:10-11

Each one should use whatever gift he has received to serve others, faithfully administering God's grace in its various forms. . . . If any one serves, he should do it with the strength God provides so that in all things God may be praised through Jesus Christ. To Him be the glory and the power for ever and ever.

2 Peter 1:3-4

> His divine power has given us everything we need
> for life and godliness through our knowledge of
> him who called us by his own glory and goodness.
> Through these he has given us his very great and
> precious promises, so that through them you may
> participate in the divine nature and escape the
> corruption in the world caused by evil desires.

1 John 2:3-6

> We know that we have come to know him if we
> obey his commands. . . . If anyone obeys his word,
> God's love is truly made complete in him. This is
> how we know we are in him: Whoever claims to
> live in him must walk as Jesus did.

Notes

FOOTNOTES

Part 1

Introduction

4.   John H. Sammis, "Trust and Obey," 1887.

5.   Dallas Willard, *The Divine Conspiracy* (San Francisco: HarperSanFrancisco, 1998), 312.

6.   Oswald Chambers, *My Utmost for His Highest*, July 19.

Chapter 1, The Hidden Key

7.   C. S. Lewis, *A Preface to Paradise Lost* (Oxford: Oxford University Press, 1942), 68. Lewis is quoting Joseph Addison, but Lewis agrees with Addison totally. "For there can be no serious doubt that Milton meant just what Addison said: neither more, nor less, nor other than that."

8.   For more about this amazing man in his own words, see John Rucyahana, *The Bishop of Rwanda* (Nashville: Nelson, 2008).

9.   In the last year because of its vast size, the Diocese has been divided into two.

Chapter 2, True Happiness

10.   For more information about the school, see Cornerstone Schools of Alabama, http://www.csalabama.org/.

11.   The root of *happiness* is the Middle English word *happ* meaning chance or fortune. *Happiness* derives from the same root as *happenstance, haphazard, hapless* and *perhaps*. See *Happiness, a History* by Darrin M. McMahon (New York: Grove Press, 2006), 11.

12.   Billy Graham, *The Secret of Happiness* (Nashville, TN: W Publishing Group, 2002), 6.

13.   Gregg Easterbrook, *The Progress Paradox: How Life Gets Better While People Feel Worse* (New York: Random House, 2003), 166.

14.   Augustine, *On the Morals of the Catholic Church*, (3, 4).

15.   Blaise Pascal, *Pascal's Pensées* (New York: E.P. Dutton, 1958 translated by W. F. Trotter), 113, #425.

16.   "The sum of that eternal life which Christ purchased is holiness; it is holy happiness. And there is in faith a liking of the happiness that Christ has purchased and offered." Quoted in John Piper, Future Grace (Colorado Springs: Multnomah Books, 1995), 385. The whole of Chapter 21 in Future Grace discusses Edwards' comfort with happiness as a legitimate part of the Christian life.

17.   For a discussion of one phase of this tendency, see Servais Pinckaers, *Morality, the*

Catholic View (St. Augustine's Press, 1991), 32-37.

18. John Piper, *Desiring God* (Sisters, OR: Multnomah, 2003), 28.

19. Servais Pinckaers, *Morality: The Catholic View* (South Bend, IN: St. Augustine's Press, 2001), 8.

20. Aristotle, *Ethics*, (London: Penguin Books, 1955), 68.

21. Jon Gertner, "The Futile Pursuit of Happiness," *New York Times,* September 7, 2003.

22. Stephen R. Covey, *The 7 Habits of Highly Effective People* (New York: Simon & Schuster, 1990), 33.

23. J. C. Ryle, *Holiness* (England: Evangelical Press, 1979), 42.

24. Charles Murray, *In Pursuit of Happiness* (New York: Simon and Schuster, 1988), 44.

25. Dennis Prager, *Happiness is a Serious Problem* (New York, Regan Books, 1998), 101.

26. D. Bonhoeffer, *The Cost of Discipleship* (New York: MacMillan Publishing Co., 1977), 64.

27. Charles Spurgeon, *Grace and Power* (New Kensington, PA: Whitaker House, 2000), 219.

28. Blaise Pascal, *Pensées* (Paris ed.: Ch M des Granges, 1964), no. 3467, 162, emphasis added.

29. C. S. Lewis, *Mere Christianity*, (HarperSanFrancisco, 1952), 39.

30. *Andrew Murray, The Holiest of All,* (Grand Rapids, Michigan: Fleming H. Russell, 1993), 211, emphasis added.

Chapter 3, The Blessings of Obedience, Part 1

31. "Keep Sending Missionaries," *Baptist Press,* March 24, 2004.

32. C. S. Lewis said of MacDonald, "I know hardly any other writer who seems to be closer, or more continually close, to the Spirit of Christ himself."

33. George MacDonald, *Discovering the Character of God,* (Minneapolis, MN: Bethany House, 1999 20.

34. Oswald Chambers, *My Utmost for His Highest,* October 10, November 17.

35. D. Bonhoeffer, *The Cost of Discipleship,* supra, 86.

36. George MacDonald, *Knowing the Heart of God,* (Minneapolis, MN: Bethany House, 1990), 213.

37. Dante, *Paradise,* canto 3, lines 82-87.

Chapter 4, The Blessings of Obedience, Part 2

38. Charles Hodge is a pre-eminent Reformed theologian who taught at Princeton Theological seminary in the 19th Century. His three volume Systemic Theology

is a masterpiece from which I quote here:

"SANCTIFICATION in the Westminster Catechism is said to be 'the work of God's free grace, whereby we are renewed in the whole man after the image of God, and are enabled more and more to die unto sin and live unto righteousness.'

Agreeably to this definition, justification differs from sanctification, (1.) In that the former is a transient act, the latter a progressive work. (2.) Justification is a forensic act, God acting as judge, declaring justice satisfied so far as the believing sinner is concerned, whereas sanctification is an effect due to the divine efficiency. (3.) Justification changes, or declares to be changed, the relation of the sinner to the justice of God; sanctification involves a change of character. (4.) the former, therefore, is objective, the latter subjective. (5.) the former is founded on what Christ has done for us; the latter is the effect of what He does in us. (6.) Justification is complete and the same in all, while sanctification is progressive, and is more complete in some than in others.

Sanctification is declared to be a work of God's free grace. Two things are included in this. First, that the power or influence by which it is carried on is supernatural. Secondly, that granting this influence to any sinner, to one sinner rather than another, and to one more than to another, is a matter of favour. No one has personally, or in himself, on the ground of anything he has done, the right to claim this divine influence as a just recompense, or as a matter of justice." Charles Hodge, *Systematic Theology*, (Grand Rapids, Wm. B. Eerdmans, reprinted 1986) Vol. III, 213.

39. John Piper, *The Pleasures of God*, (Portland: Multnomah, 1991), 253. Emphasis in the original.

40. Charles Spurgeon, *Grace and Power*, (New Kensington, PA: Whitaker House, 2000), 206.

41. Murray, *The Holiest of All, supra, iii.*

42. Two short books recently have done an excellent job of refocusing our attention on the relationship of our works here on earth and our rewards in heaven. The first is by Randy Alcorn, *The Law of Rewards*. The second is by Bruce Wilkinson, *A Life God Rewards*.

43. B. Wilkinson, *A Life God Rewards* (Sisters, Oregon, Multnomah Publishers 2002), 38-9.

Part 2

Chapter 5, Obedience All Around

1. Pascal, the French mathematician and philosopher who died in 1662, said, "Man's sensitivity to small things, and his insensitivity to the most important things, are surely evidences of a strange disorder."
2. "Him who sent me" = the Father.
3. C. S. Lewis, *The Problem of Pain*, (New York, MacMillan Paperbacks Edition, 1962), 90-91.
4. George MacDonald, *Knowing the Heart of God*, (Minneapolis: Bethany House, 1990), 283.

Chapter 6, The Obedience in the Obedience of Faith

5. Bruce Wilkinson, *A Life God Rewards* (Sisters, Oregon: Multnomah Publishers, 2002), 73.
6. Grantland Rice, "Alumnus Football" in *Only the Brave and Other Poems* (New York, A.S. Barnes & Co., 1941) 144.

Chapter 7, The Marriage of Faith and Obedience, Part 1

7. Luther, *Commentary on Romans* (Grand Rapids, Kregel Publications, 1976) xvii. Luther (1483–1546) was a monk, a preacher, and the chief leader of the Protestant Reformation.
8. George MacDonald, *Knowing the Heart of God: Where Obedience Is the One Path to Drawing Intimately Close to Our Father,* ed. Michael R. Phillips (Minneapolis: Bethany House, 1990), 32.
9. Andrew Murray, *With Christ in the School of Prayer*, (Old Tappan, New Jersey, Spire Books, 1979), 129. Murray (1828–1917) was a South African writer, teacher, and pastor.
10. Charles Spurgeon, *Grace & Power*, (New Kensington, PA, Whitaker House, 2000), 205. Spurgeon (1834–92), a British Baptist, was known as "the Prince of Preachers."
11. Quoted in *Sharing Bread, Daily Dining on God's Divine Word*, (Monday, November 30, 2009).
12. Dietrich Bonhoeffer, *The Cost of Discipleship*, (New York, MacMillan Publishing Co. 1977), 69. Bonhoeffer (1906–45) was a German Lutheran theologian and pastor who was executed by the Nazis near the end of World War II.
13. Karl Barth, *Church Dogmatics, Edinburgh, T&T Clark, 1985)*, Vol. IV, 1, p. 620–1. Barth (1886–1968), a Swiss theologian in the Reformed tradition, is known as the founder of Neo-orthodoxy.

14. D. Martyn Lloyd-Jones, *Romans, An Exposition of Chapter 6*, (Grand Rapids, Zondervan Publishing House, 1977), 220. Lloyd-Jones (1899–1981) pastored Westminster Chapel in London.

15. Watchman Nee, *The Spiritual* Man, (New York Fellowship Publications, 1977), Vol. 2, p. 256. Nee (1903–72) helped to found the Local Church movement and spent the last two decades of his life imprisoned by the Chinese Communists.

16. John Paul II, *Veritatis Splendor [The Splendor of Truth]*, 1993. Originally named Karol Wojtyla, John Paul II (1920–2005) was one of the most influential modern pontiffs of the Roman Catholic Church.

17. Charles Colson, *Loving God*, (Grand Rapids, Zondervan Publishing House, 1983), 37. Colson (b. 1931), formerly chief counsel for President Nixon, is the head of Prison Fellowship and a popular author and radio speaker.

18. John Piper, *The Pleasures of God*, (Portland, Oregon, Mulmomah, 1991), 250, 252. Piper (b. 1946) is a Baptist pastor and the head of Desiring God Ministries.

19. Charles Hodge, *Romans* (Edinburgh, The Banner of Truth Trust, Rev. ed., reprinted 1983), 21.

20. Martin Luther, *Commentary on Romans* (Grand Rapids: Kregel Publications, 1976) xvii.

21. Quoted by Daniel Henninger in the *Wall Street Journal*, August 9, 2007 @ www.opinionjournal.com/columnists/dhenninger/?id=110010444.

22. Ben Hogan, *Five Lessons, The Modern Fundamentals of Golf* (New York: A. Fireside Book, 1957).

Chapter 8, The Marriage of Faith and Obedience, Part 2

23. Isaac Watts, "When I Survey the Wondrous Cross," 1707.

24. Andrew Murray, *The Blessings of Obedience* (New Kensington, PA, 1984), 94.

25. John Piper has written an excellent book on this subject to which this discussion is indebted. John Piper, *Future Grace* (Sisters, Oregon: Multnomah Books, 1995).

26. Charles Spurgeon, *Grace and Power*, p. 22

Chapter 9, Law and Grace

27. Brennan Manning, *The Ragamuffin Gospel* (Sisters, OR: Multnomah, 1990), 91–92.

28. A thorough discussion of the unity between the Old and New Testaments to which I am indebted is found in David P. Fuller, *The Unity of the Bible* (Grand Rapids, Zondervan Publishing House 1992) Chapter 21.

Part 3

Chapter 10, The Village that Saved Five Thousand Lives
1.   Hallie is not one we would expect to be the historian of the valiant work of faithful Christians. While professor of ethics in the philosophy department of Wesleyan University in Connecticut, he specialized in the study of institutional cruelty, especially the inhumane treatment of Jewish children by the Nazis during World War II. His work had driven him to severe depression and near suicide. By chance, in the 1970s, he came across a reference to Le Chambon. So taken was he by what he called the "goodness" of those brave people that he spent years studying it and fortunately preserved his research. Trocmé left diaries of his work as pastor there (and earlier) and the work of the Chambonnais, and because, to my knowledge, Hallie is the only one who has read them and written about them in English, we see the courageous work through the eyes of someone who enormously admires the Chambonnais but who does not share their faith.
2.   Philip P. Hallie, *Lest Innocent Blood Be Shed: The Story of the Village of Le Chambon and How Goodness Happened There* (New York: Harper & Row, 1979), 60.
3.   Hallie, *Lest Innocent Blood,* 66.
4.   Ibid., 68–69.
5.   The title of Hallie's book is derived from Deuteronomy 19:10.
6.   Hallie, *Lest Innocent Blood,* 170.
7.   Ibid., 172.
8.   Ibid.
9.   Ibid., 160.
10. Ibid., 161.
11. Philip P. Hallie, *Surprised by Goodness,* (The Trinity Forum Reading, Fall 2002), 26.
12. Ibid., 24–25.
13. Ibid., 28.
14. Ibid., 30.

Chapter 11, Thy Will be Done: The Key to Obedience
15. George MacDonald, Discovering the Character of God (Bethany House) 89.
16. Oswald Chambers, *My Utmost for His Highest,* July 8, June 6.
17. *The International Standard Bible Encyclopedia Vol. 2* (Grand Rapids: William B. Erdmanns, 1982), 651.
18. Sören Kierkegaard, *Purity of Heart is to Will One Thing* (New York: Harper Torch Book, 1938).
19. George MacDonald, *Your Life in Christ: The Nature of God and His Work in Human Hearts* (Minneapolis: Bethany House, 2005), 79–80 (emphasis in original).

20. Andrew Murray, *The Holiest of All*, supra, 212

21. Murray, 212, emphasis added.

22. Jodi Werhanowicz, *Rogue Angel*, (Phoenix, Arizona: Ezekiel Press, 205), 112–13.

23. M. Scott Peek, *Glimpses of the Devil* (New York: Free Press, 2005) xvi.

24. M. Scott Peck, *Glimpses of the Devil, Id.*

25. Abraham Kuyper , Inaugural Address at Dedication of The University of Amsterdam, 1880.

26. "Worldly" elements such as money, sex, and power need not be tools of Satan. Apart from our self or our sinful nature's misusing of them, they have great potential for good and for enjoyment in life.

27. C. S. Lewis, *The Great Divorce* (New York: MacMillan, 1963), 75.

28. George MacDonald, *Your Life in Christ*, ed. Michael Phillips (Minneapolis: Bethany House 2005), 100.

Chapter 12, The Power to Obey: The Holy Spirit

29. St. Thomas Aquinas, Summa Theologica, I-II 106.1, Emphasis added.

30. John Stott, *Romans, God's Good News for the World*, (Downers Grove, IL: InterVarsity Press, 1994), 216.

31. John Stott, Romans (Downers Grace, PA: Intervarsity Press, 1994) 223.

Chapter 13, It's Not About "Me": Self Denial

32. Malcolm Muggeridge, *Jesus: The Man Who Lives* (New York: Harper & Row, 1975), 123.

33. Calvin: *Institutes of the Christian Religion* (Philadelphia, PA: The Westminster Press, 1960), Volume I, 689.

34. M. Scott Peck, *People of the Lie: The Hope for Healing of Human Evil* (New York: Simon & Schuster, 1983).

35. C. S. Lewis, *The Great Divorce, supra*, iii.

36. C. S. Lewis, *Mere Christianity*, (New York: MacMillan, 1963), 166.

37. *Planned Parenthood v. Casey.*

38. Walter Lippman, *A Preface to Morals*, (New York: MacMillan, 1929), 326.

39. Charles Hodge, *Systemic Theology, III*, 225.

40. Douglas Southall Freeman, *R. E. Lee: A Biography* (New York: Scribner's, 1937–40), Vol 4, 505.

41. Dietrich Bonhoeffer, *The Cost of Discipleship* (New York: Touchstone, 1995), 88.

Chapter 14, Love: The Heart of Obedience, Part 1

42. Jonathan Edwards, *Charity and Its Fruits* (Banner of Truth Trust, 1969) 235.

43. John Piper, *The Pleasures of God* (Portland: Multnomah, 1994) 15, quoting Henry Scougal.

44. Jonathan Edwards, *Charity and Its Fruits*, 1 ff.

45. Thomas Watson, *A Business and Its Beliefs*, (New York: McGraw-Hill, 1963), 5..

The "basic beliefs" or "values" at IBM were: (1) have respect for the individual, (2) provide the best customer service of any company in the world, and (3) pursue all tasks with a view toward achieving excellence. The lecture series discussed how IBM lived into these values and was motivated by them in growing into a great company.

Chapter 15, Love: the Heart of Obedience, Part 2

46. C. S. Lewis, *The Four Loves* (New York: Harcourt Brace Jovanovich, Publishers, 1960), 191-2.

47. Keith Green, "Oh, Lord, You're Beautiful."

48. C. S. Lewis, *Letters*, 8 November, 1952.

49. I have used the alternate translation given in the NIV marginal notes, "love for God." The same phrase is translated "God's love" in the primary text.

50. Bernard of Clairvaux, *The Love of God* (Portland, Oregon: Multnomah Press, 1983), 159, emphasis added.

51. Charles Colson, *Loving God*. (Grand Rapids, Zondervan Publishing House, 1983), 137.

52. D. Martin Lloyd-Jones, *Joy Unspeakable*, (Wheaton, Ill.: Harold Shaw Publishers, 1984), 205.

53. C. H. Dodd, *Gospel and Law: The Relation of Faith and Ethics in Early Christianity*, (New York: Columbia university Press, 1951), 42.

54. Billy Graham, *The Journey* (Nashville: W. Publishing Group, 2000), 208.

Chapter 16, The Mind of Obedience

55. Michael Novak, *This Hemisphere of Liberty*.

56. Derived from Isaiah 6:9–10. See also Matthew 11:25 and Acts 28:26–27.

57. Ian Turnbull Ker, *John Henry Newman: Selected Sermons* (New Jersey: Paulist Press, 1994).

58. Oswald Chambers, *My Utmost for His Highest*, August 31.

59. G.K. Chesterton, *What's Wrong with the World* (San Francisco: Ignatius Press, 1994).

Chapter 17, Emotions in the Obedience of Faith

60. C. S. Lewis, *The Weight of Glory*, (Grand Rapids: Eerdmans, 1965), 2.

61. C. S. Lewis, Reflections on the Psalms, (Orlando, FL: Harcourt, Inc., 1986-1958), 63.

62. John Piper, *Desiring God*, supra. 12.

63. C. S. Lewis, *The Problem of Pain*, supra., 95, 97.

64. Id.

65. Malcolm Muggeridge, *Jesus Rediscovered* (New York: Doubleday and Company, 1969), 216.

66. Aleksandr Solzhenitsyn, *The Gulag Archipelago: 1981–1956*, 2:615–7.

67. C. S. Lewis, *The Problem of Pain*, (New York: MacMillan Publishing Co., 1962).

68. See, http://www.quoteworld.org/authors/oswald_chambers

Chapter 18, Obedience Becoming Natural: The Character of Christ, Part 1
69. Aristotle, *Ethics*, (London, Penguin Books, 1976), 91.
70. Quoted in Norman R. Augustine, *Augustine's Travels: A World-Class Leader Looks at Life, Business, and What It Takes to Succeed at Both* (New York: AMACOM, 1998), 45–46, emphasis added.
71. See, http://www.brainyquote.com/quotes/authors/s/saint_augustine_2.html
72. Jonathan Edwards, The Religious Affections, (Edinburgh, The Banner of Truth Trust, 1984), 239.
73. George Washington, first inaugural address, April 30, 1789, http://www.bartleby.com/124/pres13.html.
74. Jim Collins, *Good to Great: Why Some Companies Make the Leap . . . and Others Don't* (New York: HarperBusiness, 2001), 12–13.
75. Quoted in Richard Foster, *Celebration of Discipline*, (New York: Harper and Roe, 1978), 110.
76. John Milton, *Paradise Lost*, Book I, lines 254-263.

Chapter 19, "Speak Lord!" Discerning the Will of God, Part 1
77. Stephen R. Covey, *The 7 Habits of Highly Effective People: Restoring the Character Ethic*, rev. ed. (New York: Free Press, 2004).
78. Leanne Payne, *Listening Prayer: Learning to Hear God's Voice and Keep a Prayer Journal* (Grand Rapids, MI: Baker, 1994).
79. Leo Tolstoy, "Two Old Men" (1885), http://www.online-literature.com/tolstoy/2891/.

Chapter 20, "Speak Lord!" Discerning the Will of God, Part 2
80. The actual words of Colossians 1:10–12 are these: "We pray this in order that you may live a life worthy of the Lord and may please him in every way: bearing fruit in every good work, growing in the knowledge of God, being strengthened with all power according to his glorious might so that you may have great endurance and patience, and joyfully giving thanks to the Father, who has qualified you to share in the inheritance of the saints in the kingdom of light."

Part 4

Chapter 21, Obedience in Our Daily Lives
1. S. Truett Cathy, *Eat Mor Chikn, Inspire More People* (Decatur, GA: Looking Glass Books, 2002), 42.
2. S. Truett Cathy, *How Did You Do It, Truett? A Recipe for Success* (Decatur, GA: Looking Glass Books, 2007), 95.
3. Cathy, Eat Mor Chikn, 70.

4. S. Truett Cathy, *It's Easier to Succeed than to Fail* (Nashville: Oliver Nelson, 1989), 78.

5. Ibid., 69–70.

6. Cathy, *Eat Mor Chikn*, 122.

7. Ibid., 123–124.

8. Cathy, *How Did You Do It*, 52–55.

9. Cathy, *Eat Mor Chikn*, 193–4.

Chapter 22, Obedience in Real Life: Calling

10. Albert Schweitzer, *The Quest of the Historical Jesus*, (Great Britain: A & C Black, Ltd., 1910), 403.

11. Os Guinness, *The Call: Finding and Fulfilling the Central Purpose of Your Life* (Nashville: Thomas Nelson, 2003), 4.

12. Charles Colson, *Loving God*, (Grand Rapids: Zondevan Publishing House, 1983), 126.

13. See *The Memoirs of Charles Finney*, Chapter 17, Revival in Stephentown.

14. Andrew Murray, *The Holiest of All*, supra, 561-2 (emphasis in original).

15. Jonathan Edwards, *The Religious Affections*, (Calisle, PA: The Banner of Truth Press, 1961), 321-1. The exact text reads: "Regeneration, which is that work of God in which grace is infused, has a direct relation to practice; for it is the very end of it, with a view to which the whole work is wrought. All is calculated and framed, in this mighty and manifold change wrought in the soul, so as directly to tend to this end. yea, it is the very end of the redemption of Christ: Tit. ii, 14 KJV, 'Who gave himself for us that he might redeem us from all iniquity, and purify unto himself a peculiar people, zealous of good works.'"

Chapter 23, Obedience in Real Life: Work

16. Linda Clare, *Heart to Heart, Today's Christian Woman*.

17. ESV Study Bible, Matthew 25:15, note 4.

18. Augustine, *Confessions*, New York, Penguin Books (1961), p. 340

19. It is interesting to reflect on how the phrase "good works" permeates the teaching of Paul. He teaches that the ultimate end of Jesus' ministry and death on the cross was to redeem a people "zealous for good works" (Titus 2:14, ESV). He writes that we are God's "workmanship, created in Christ Jesus for good works" (Ephesians 2:10, ESV). In 2 Corinthians, Paul tells us that all grace is to abound in us so that we can "abound in every good work" (9:8, ESV).

20. George Herbert, *The Elixir*.

21. Abraham Lincoln's second inaugural address, March 4, 1865, http://www.bartleby.com/124/pres32.html.

22. Quoted in Alister E. McGrath, *Reformation Thought, An Introduction* (Malden, Mass.: Blackwell Publishers, 1999), 265.

Chapter 24, Obedience in Real Time

23. Stephen R. Covey, *The 7 Habits of Highly Effective People: Restoring the Character Ethic*, rev. ed. (New York: Free Press, 2004).

24. George Bernard Shaw in an address at the Municipal Technical College and School of Art, at Brighton, England, 1907.

Chapter 25, Obedience and Leadership

25. Russell Kirk, *Redeeming the Time*, (Wilmington: ISI, 1996), 13.

26. Grant Gilmore, *The Ages of American Law*, (New Haven: Yale University Press, 1977), 110-111.

27. Jim Collins, *Good to Great*, op. cit.

28. Jim Collins, *Level 5 Leadership, The Triumph of Humility and Fierce Resolve*, Harvard Business Review, July-August, 2005.

29. Douglas Southall Freeman, op. cit. Vol. 4, p. 278.

30. Edmund Burke, *Letter to a Member of the National Assembly*, 791.

31. Cotton Mather, *The Ecclesiastical History of New England*, (1702).

Index

D

David 71, 84, 97, 105, 156, 199, 200, 230, 231, 235, 315
desire xv, 14, 74, 81, 95, 97, 98, 100, 114, 125, 139, 156, 164, 191, 195, 197, 198, 199, 200, 201, 202, 203, 209, 255, 270, 284, 288, 294, 316
discerning God's will 230
Dodd, C. H. 175, 352
Drucker, Peter 123
duty xiii, 11, 12, 59, 60, 62, 80, 104, 213, 220, 256, 287, 306

E

Easterbrook, Gregg 11, 14, 345
Edwards, Johnathan 11, 163, 165, 180, 218, 269, 345, 351, 353, 354
emotions vii, 197
Epicureans 13, 60
Esther 85

F

fear 4, 45, 60, 84, 123, 126, 192, 197, 204, 206, 207, 208, 209, 217, 224, 315, 327, 328, 329, 330, 331, 332, 333, 339
Finney, Charles 267, 268, 354
freedom 4, 35, 61, 87, 152, 153, 154, 161, 193, 194, 203, 221, 291, 307, 308, 309, 337

G

Gajowniczek, Franciszek 179
Garden (of Eden) 3, 25, 189, 275
Gertner, Jon 14, 346
Gilmore, Grant 303, 355
Good to Great 220, 304, 353, 355
gospel 2, 5, 24, 68, 69, 70, 82, 88, 105, 113, 138, 182, 183, 203, 293
grace iii, xiii, xv, xvi, 2, 4, 5, 7, 10, 16, 18, 22, 24, 26, 29, 31, 34, 35, 36, 37, 38, 45, 49, 50, 53, 61, 62, 63, 66, 68, 69, 70, 71, 72, 73, 74, 75, 82, 84, 85, 86, 87, 88, 89, 92, 95, 96, 97, 98, 99, 100, 108, 117, 126, 127, 129, 130, 131, 136, 137, 140, 141, 145, 148, 153, 154, 155, 157, 163, 164, 166, 169, 170, 178, 183, 184, 185, 193, 197, 205, 208, 213, 216, 220, 221, 235, 237, 258, 263, 265, 266, 267, 268, 269, 270, 271, 273, 278, 285, 286, 287, 288, 297, 309, 311, 313, 314, 315, 316, 317, 318, 321, 323, 335, 337, 341, 342, 354
Graham, Billy iii, 10, 34, 174, 175, 345, 352
Great Commission 46, 82, 278, 291, 292, 293
Groundhog Day 15
Grudem, Wayne 318, 319
Guinness, Os 264, 354

L

Lang, Stephen 73

law 3, 4, 5, 12, 17, 24, 30, 32, 44, 45, 46, 53, 54, 56, 57, 68, 83, 89, 91, 92, 93, 94, 95, 96, 97, 98, 99, 100, 129, 134, 136, 138, 139, 153, 162, 178, 182, 194, 200, 203, 208, 212, 231, 236, 244, 269, 277, 280, 281, 283, 287, 289, 296, 302, 303, 305, 306, 307, 308, 309, 326, 330, 338

Leadership iv, viii, 111, 301, 303, 304, 307, 308, 355

Le Chambon 29, 103, 108, 109, 110, 111, 113, 114, 115, 116, 117, 123, 165, 166, 175, 226, 246, 283, 303, 306, 350

Lee, Robert E. 155, 156, 305, 306, 351

legalism 4, 39, 73

Lewis, C.S. 1, 20, 21, 25, 48, 49, 87, 128, 129, 130, 150, 151, 169, 170, 171, 173, 198, 199, 203, 204, 206, 264, 345, 346, 348, 351, 352

Lincoln, President Abraham 155, 282, 354

Lippmann, Walter 152

Lloyd Jones, D. Martyn 67, 174, 349, 352

love vii, 28, 61, 62, 80, 86, 97, 112, 115, 159, 161, 162, 163, 164, 165, 166, 167, 169, 170, 171, 172, 173, 174, 175, 178, 179, 189, 235, 236, 303, 325, 351, 352

Luther, Martin 4, 55, 66, 71, 82, 119, 281, 283, 288, 348, 349

M

MacDonald, George 25, 27, 49, 66, 120, 123, 124, 132, 194, 346, 348, 350, 351

Manning, Brennan 91, 92, 349

Mann, Marjorie 29, 34

Mather, Cotton 308, 355

metanoia 183

Milton, John 1, 345, 353

mind iv, xv, 3, 31, 69, 95, 106, 120, 121, 134, 139, 142, 145, 147, 153, 162, 169, 181, 182, 183, 184, 185, 186, 187, 189, 190, 191, 192, 193, 194, 195, 197, 198, 201, 202, 209, 214, 218, 219, 228, 232, 234, 236, 240, 241, 245, 250, 293, 314, 316, 336

money 14, 28, 29, 33, 38, 79, 84, 94, 123, 130, 145, 159, 161, 164, 181, 191, 202, 204, 229, 233, 242, 258, 275, 351

Moses 25, 31, 32, 55, 71, 83, 84, 94, 99, 100, 182, 190, 213, 222, 224, 239, 266, 311, 325

Mueller, George 70, 71, 72, 227

Muggeridge, Malcolm 147, 204, 351, 352

Murray, Andrew 20, 21, 35, 66, 81, 125, 268, 269, 314, 318, 346, 347, 348, 349, 351, 354

Murray, Bill 15, 16

Murray, Charles 18, 346

N

New Covenant 45, 133
Novak, Michael 182, 352

O

Old Covenant 93, 95
old self 132, 148, 149, 150, 151, 152, 153, 154, 155, 156, 157, 185, 187, 193, 214, 222

P

pain 85, 177, 197, 203, 204, 206
Paradise Lost 1, 45, 224, 312, 345, 353
Pascal, Blaine 11, 20, 21, 44, 345, 346, 348
Paul viii, 9, 18, 28, 30, 34, 37, 55, 57, 60, 65, 67, 68, 69, 70, 71, 72, 80, 82, 85, 86, 88, 96, 97, 98, 99, 106, 126, 132, 134, 135, 136, 138, 139, 143, 153, 155, 162, 163, 165, 166, 177, 182, 183, 186, 193, 198, 202, 212, 214, 217, 218, 219, 221, 224, 232, 233, 234, 235, 239, 241, 242, 261, 265, 266, 270, 275, 276, 277, 282, 283, 289, 297, 299, 303, 306, 317, 349, 354
peace iii, xii, xv, 6, 10, 19, 20, 21, 24, 29, 30, 58, 113, 139, 141, 187, 194, 200, 201, 209, 240, 242, 243, 252, 257, 268, 269, 281, 282, 299, 311, 323, 325, 332, 336, 339, 340, 341
Peter 27, 46, 72, 82, 84, 123, 162, 199, 222, 239, 261, 264, 266, 282, 291, 342, 343
Pharisaic 4, 132
Pharisees 57, 98, 162, 274
Pinckaers, Servais 12, 345, 346
Piper, John 12, 35, 67, 70, 164, 198, 200, 313, 314, 345, 346, 347, 349, 351, 352
pleasure 2, 13, 14, 15, 20, 50, 57, 60, 154, 160, 181, 256, 288, 316, 317, 319
poor (the) 16, 33, 37, 54, 62, 106, 109, 120, 159, 168, 179, 189, 218, 243, 262, 274, 280, 291, 292, 293
Prager, Dennis 11, 19, 346
prayer iv, xiv, 9, 14, 18, 27, 36, 48, 58, 69, 70, 82, 86, 93, 104, 112, 121, 132, 145, 168, 171, 186, 193, 204, 227, 228, 229, 230, 231, 235, 239, 240, 241, 243, 245, 254, 268, 270, 278, 285, 286, 287, 288, 289, 293, 297, 314, 315, 316, 322, 339
purpose xiii, 2, 7, 18, 19, 35, 45, 54, 56, 67, 68, 69, 70, 92, 122, 133, 139, 161, 174, 178, 207, 215, 217, 222, 223, 225, 230, 240, 254, 255, 258, 259, 265, 266, 268, 269, 270, 271, 274, 286, 297, 302, 306, 309, 313, 318, 323, 331, 336, 338, 339, 341

R

Reagan, President Ronald 212, 213
Record, Robert ix, 197

repent (repentance) 126, 163, 183, 184
Rice, Grantland 57, 348
Rickover, Hyman 219
Rockefeller, John 105, 236
Rucyahana, Bishop John 6, 7, 71, 345
Ryle, J. C. 17, 346

S

Saban, Nick 75, 76
Sabbath 37, 98, 252, 267, 295, 297, 298, 299
salvation 34, 35, 114, 127
Satan 3, 72, 128, 129, 130, 131, 148, 150, 154, 182, 187, 190, 191, 202, 208, 224,
      233, 234, 268, 303, 351
Schweitzer, Albert 262, 263, 264, 354
self-denial 146, 147, 152, 154, 155, 156, 157, 221, 240, 318
self-emptying 217, 218, 221, 222, 223, 225, 235, 293
Sevier, Kirby 285
Shaw, George Bernard 296, 352, 355
Shema 93, 94, 95, 96, 97, 116, 190, 213, 257, 287
Solomon 1
Solzhenitsyn, Aleksandr 205, 206, 352
Spurgeon, Charles 20, 21, 35, 66, 88, 346, 347, 348, 349
stewardship 37
Stockdale, James 73
Stoicism (Stoics) 134
Stott, John 137, 139, 351
success 19, 23, 31, 32, 44, 59, 76, 114, 142, 150, 156, 166, 168, 177, 217, 222, 251,
      252, 256, 269, 287, 294, 299, 308, 330
surrender 48, 66, 126, 139, 145, 146, 147, 149, 171, 180, 194, 203, 262, 316

T

Taylor, Hudson 70, 294
Teresa, Mother 265
Thompson, Nita ix, 9, 18, 71
Tolstoy, Leo 229, 353
Trocmé, André 103, 104, 105, 106, 107, 108, 109, 110, 111, 112, 113, 114, 115, 116,
      123, 136, 165, 171, 225, 226, 236, 283, 306, 350
Trocmé, Magda 283
truth iii, xii, 2, 4, 20, 21, 24, 26, 27, 29, 30, 38, 44, 49, 50, 57, 59, 66, 67, 99, 100, 113,
      114, 115, 122, 125, 128, 131, 136, 139, 162, 171, 177, 184, 185, 186, 187,
      189, 191, 194, 198, 202, 205, 212, 219, 228, 229, 240, 263, 264, 269, 277,
      315, 317, 327, 329, 334
Two Old Men 229, 353

V

W